Contract

Law and Social Theory

Series editor PETER FITZPATRICK
Professor of Law and Social Theory, University of Kent at
Canterbury and Colin Perrin, Law School and Department of
Philosophy, University of Kent at Canterbury

CONTRACT
A Critical Commentary

JOHN WIGHTMAN

Pluto **Press**
LONDON • CHICAGO, IL.

First published 1996 by Pluto Press
345 Archway Road, London N6 5AA
and 1436 West Randolph
Chicago, Illinois 60607, USA

British Library Cataloguing in Publication Data
A catalogue record for this book is available from the British Library

ISBN 0 7453 0548 2 hbk

Library of Congress Cataloging in Publication Data are available.

Printing history: 99 98 97 96 5 4 3 2 1

Designed and Produced for Pluto Press by
Chase Production Services, Chipping Norton, OX7 5QR
Typeset from disk by Stanford DTP Services, Milton Keynes
Printed in the EC by T J Press, Padstow, England

For Heather, Isobel and Joe
and in memory of my mother

Contents

Table of Statutes

Table of Statutory Instruments

Table of Cases

Preface

Books on contract law are now so thick on the ground that a newcomer needs to explain itself. This one aims not to describe, but to offer a commentary on the law of contract, together with the books which expound it, the courses which `deliver' it, and theories about it. I have attempted to reflect the widening debate about all these aspects of contract law, and to further the debate by engaging with some of the arguments. The result is a book which questions not just the content of contract law but also the way it is usually written about and taught. In the process it draws on the margins of traditional contract study – history, theories of contractual obligation, the functioning of contract in reality – and emphasises types of contract outside the commercial mainstream.

Any book which deals with this range of ideas about contract law risks looking like an old fashioned jurisprudence textbook, solemnly working through a series of schools of thought with little sense of their intellectual origin, relationship and significance. I have tried to ward this off by providing a continuous narrative which connects the varied perspectives on contract. Rather than refer to every contributor of interest, I have opted to deal at greater length with a smaller number of leading representative thinkers.

What I expected to be a negative book about the prospects for general contract law has turned out rather differently. This is not so much a change of heart, more a change of view about what contract law can encompass. Many have claimed the general law of contract dealt with in the books is moribund, having neither practical relevance nor rational coherence. Despite the strength of these claims, I have come to believe that general, judge-made contract law has important potential for innovatory change. The traditional perception (and some more critical ones) of what contract law is and what it can do is shaped by a commercial model of contract; placing personal contract law at the centre gives a very different picture.

This book owes a great deal to collaborative teaching on courses at Kent, most of all the stimulating experience of teaching the Contract and Tort Two course over many years. It was in discussion with students and colleagues on that course – especially Nick Jackson and Alan Thomson – that the foundations were laid. I have also found collaboration with Paddy Ireland on Obligations One very valuable; I think we agreed about more than either of us realised at the time.

Peter Fitzpatrick originally suggested this project, and I am grateful to him not only for that invitation but also for his abnormal patience and understanding during its prolonged gestation. Joanne Conaghan provided valuable encouragement at an important time. I am especially grateful to colleagues at Kent for reading drafts: Alan Carruth, Joanne Conaghan, Richard De Friend, Peter Fitzpatrick, Paddy Ireland, Nick Jackson, Per Laleng, Robin Mackenzie, Gerry Rubin, Alan Thomson. Alan Ryan and Venous Telford provided valuable research assistance, made possible by the Law School's Research Committee. I am solely responsible for what is left.

John Wightman
Whitstable
January 1996

1
Introduction

The study of the law of contract in the UK is at an interesting juncture. The proliferation of student texts on contract in the 1990s (sixteen at the last count) suggests a subject in good health, and perhaps widespread contentment with the traditional approach to legal study which nearly all of them adopt. This persistence of the traditional approach to contract study is striking when placed beside the flourishing of contract studies in the United States, where a rich and diverse literature has developed. Despite the common early history and modern similarities which create special affinities between American and English contract law, this American work seems to have had muted impact in the UK.

Yet, there is also clear evidence – alongside the proliferation of orthodox texts – of a gathering momentum in the broadening of contract studies in the UK, which draws beyond the materials of the black letter tradition. The recent appearance of Wheeler and Shaw's casebook (1994) introduces a wider selection of approaches (including many American) than any previous British work, and the recent edited collections *Perspectives of Critical Contract Law* (Wilhelmsson, 1993) and *Welfarism in Contract Law* (Brownsword, Howells, and Wilhelmsson, 1994) apply non traditional approaches to contract and contain contributions from European scholars outside the common law tradition.[2] This widening of approaches to the law to some degree reflects movement in the law itself. The growing impact on the law of contract of the law of the European Union, notably in the shape of the Unfair Terms in Consumer Contracts Regulations 1994, creates the conditions for the unfreezing of parts of contract law where the speed of change had seemed glacial. More generally, the bumping together of Civilian and American influences fosters renewal in both the English law of contract and writing about it.

The aim of this book is to provide not yet another description of the law of contract, but a commentary on it which reflects these wider debates about the law. The commentary engages with ideas about contract law, especially about the reasons for making contractual obligation legally enforceable; about the nature of the changes which have produced modern contract law; and about the potential in the modern law for radical change. The general rules of contract are often seen as moribund, on account of their being so heavily modified in many situations, and as having an inbuilt commercial grain – the legacy of the so called classical law – which makes them ill suited to express non commercial relations. Nevertheless, I will argue that the ordinary rules of contract have important developmental potential.

TWO IDEAS OF CONTRACT

The perception of potential in contract law depends to a degree upon the conception which is adopted of the scope and meaning of the idea of contract. It is useful here to distinguish two different senses of contract. Both refer to relations which are consensual in the sense that there was some choice over the creation of the relationship.

The first usage sees the essence of contract as lying in sale. It embodies the liberal ideal of autonomous individuals ordering their own affairs, and implies that the contract relation is free from interference by the state and that the terms of the relationship are created by the parties: freedom of contract is all. Enthusiasts for this ideal tend to see capitalist economies as being based on such relations (De Jasay, 1991). Theorists in the socialist or Marxist traditions deny the reality of such an ideal. The core of this sort of critique is that social relations under capitalism are anything but consensual, and that seeing them as contracts which are the product of consent is a legitimating and therefore powerful illusion. The exploitative nature of relations such as employment is concealed and they appear instead as relations between equals in which individuals are responsible for their own fate (Gabel and Feinman, 1990). Somewhat similar is the critique of some feminists, seeing contract as embodying a gendered conception of human relations, which emphasises an individualism, based on analytical reason, commonly regarded as male (Frug, 1985).

The important point here is that, although the left/feminist critiques are negative, they work with roughly the same meaning of contract. They identify contract above all with the market, and contrast it with the structuring of social relations through status and the redistribution of income, goods and services by the state. It is this understanding of contract which shapes the left's traditional hostility to the further contractualisation of social relations, whether it be the sale of people (surrogacy services, organs for transplant) or the conversion of users of public services into customers. Introducing contract is seen as introducing the market, which is seen as producing an unfair distribution of wealth and being destructive of social solidarity. To a degree, the market has been regarded in an essentialist way – as the key determinant of both the nature of a society and political positions in relation to it. This in turn has been transferred to contract, so that there is a shared view between left and right of the identity of contract and market.

The other meaning of contract is much wider, and potentially includes any relationship which, in either origin or content, is the product – at least in part – of voluntary action. The law of contract itself uses a similarly wide meaning of contract. It recognises non market relations as potentially contractual, for example family arrangements and unincorporated associations such as societies and clubs. And within the rules that do apply to market transactions, there are clear limits on what can be agreed by the parties, most clearly in relation to the protection of consumers, employees and tenants. For the law of contract, the idea of contract is that of a legal shell, within which obligations can be fabricated: these will include but are not limited to those expressly undertaken.

In this book it is this second, wider meaning of contract which is adopted, and I will focus on the potential for innovation in general contract law. Although contract law, understood as all the private law relating to contracts, contains a variety of values and norms within the conceptual shell, the dominant tendency in the general rules which form the subject matter of the contract courses and books is still commercial and market orientated. It is in special rules applying only to certain sorts of contract, often the result of legislation, that the range of contractual norms is most extended. I will argue that, instead of being narrowly based in terms of situations of application and homogeneous in terms of the values it embodies, it is both desirable and possible for the general law of contract to become more pluralistic in terms of the values to which it gives voice.

The scope of contract law already transcends ordinary commercial transactions, and the potential exists for law appropriate to a wide range of relations to be fashioned by the courts from the resources of the general law. This includes just consumer relations and other non commercial relations which affect people in a personal capacity, but also the increasingly contractual form of the delivery of public services and the increasingly important intermediate sector of non profit making voluntary associations.

The idea that the UK state has undergone contractualisation since 1979 is now commonplace, and commentators from left and right have tended to see in these changes a revival of the importance of freedom of contract and the market. But arguing for a wider role for contract *law* need not mean endorsing a wider role also for freedom of contract and the market. On the contrary, I will argue that the wider meaning of contract can interpret changes such as the Citizen's Charter, or increased parental involvement in education, in terms which reflect ideas of empowerment and participation rather than distorting them by treating them as commercial contracts.

An illustration of these generalities may be useful before going further. The nature of the legal relationship between students and their educational institutions is obscure. Candidates for admission may hear talk of a contract made by their acceptance of an offer, with the result that they cannot change or take up a place at another university. But is there a contract here? What is the legal position when a student is ejected by their college; or is subject to questionable procedures in an investigation of plagiarism; or when their degree is withheld because of outstanding debts; or if they claim their degree performance has been affected by substandard teaching? Are the answers to these questions affected by whether the student is an overseas student paying a full fee, or a home student who pays no tuition fees? And what are the implications of the move to see students as consumers?

None of these questions have entirely clear answers. The law applying to students is an amalgam of contract and judicial review, particularly the principles of natural justice, and complicated for many of the old universities (other than the former polytechnics) where students are subject to the jurisdiction of a visitor. In fleshing out the legal nature of the relationship between student and educational institution, the courts continue to draw on legal principles developed in the rather different contexts of commercial contracting and the legal control of governmental power. Out of these borrowings emerges an idea of contract that combines voluntary participation and norms of fair treatment which marks a radical departure from the orthodox model of contractual obligation.

The idea that the general law of contract has potential for progressive development cannot be justified out of thin air; it will be important to ground this perspective on contract in a review of the nature of its modern development. But an important obstacle to establishing such a perspective is the past failure of contract to meet important challenges made of it.

DOCTRINAL FAILURE AND RENEWAL

The recent history of contract law displays problems in adopting a flexible approach to issues outside the mainstream of commercial contract. The most notable example of doctrinal failure is to be found in the story of the judicial treatment of standard form exclusion clauses in consumer contracts. The doctrines of incorporation of written terms into contracts meant that very harsh clauses could readily be incorporated by notice or by signature. The first weapon used by the courts was the *contra proferentem* rule of construction, which meant that any ambiguity (sometimes conjured by creative readings) was construed against those relying on the clauses. The problem with a construction approach as a device for dealing with unfair terms, however, is that it retains the written terms as the ultimate source of obligation. Each case exploiting a weakness in the drafting of a clause taught the lawyers how to do better next time, with the result that standard terms were rapidly evolved that were bullet proof against any construction approach.

The next response was the invention of the doctrine of fundamental breach, and the related notion of breach of a fundamental term. In a string of cases culminating in the 1950s, the Court of Appeal held that exclusion clauses, however drafted, could not exclude liability for very serious breaches of contract. Thus consumers who received defective cars after signing hire purchase agreements containing sweeping exclusion clauses were able to rescind the contract or claim damages. The doctrine did not cohere into a settled form and was put under severe strain by attempts by lawyers to argue for its application to ordinary commercial contracts. The terms in which the doctrine had been expressed made it difficult to confine to consumer contracts and in *Suisse Atlantique Societe d'Armement Maritime SA* v. *Rotterdamsche Kolen Centrale NY* (1967) the House of Lords held that there was no rule of law to the effect that there were some breaches of contract for which it was impossible to exclude liability. Everything depended on the construction of the contract, and all the doctrine of fundamental breach meant was that very clear words indeed were needed to exclude liability for serious breaches. It was said that the principle of freedom of contract was preserved – in that people could still 'agree' to be bound by extremely onerous clauses – but at the expense of consumer protection. Ambiguities in the judgments in the *Suisse Atlantique* case provided sufficient room for the Court of Appeal under Lord Denning to continue to rub the lamp of fundamental breach to useful effect, at least as far as consumers were concerned (*Farnsworth Finance* v. *Attryde* (1970); *Levison* v. *Patent Steam Carpet Cleaning Co* (1978)).

However, this effort was already being overtaken by work on the problem by the Law Commission, and its proposals were put in to legislative form by the Supply of Goods (Implied Terms) Act 1973 and the Unfair Contract Terms Act 1977. The need for the doctrine of fundamental breach had gone and it was laid to rest by the House of Lords in *Photo Productions* v. *Securicor* (1980).

Why was the court's attempt to deal with the problem of exclusion clauses unsuccessful? It was not because the solution was difficult to frame or politically controversial. The solution eventually adopted was straightforward. It treated consumer contracts differently from other sorts, and provided that some implied obligations were unexcludable and that some others could be excluded if it was reasonable to do so. Neither approach was novel as there were precedents for both, and there was enthusiastic academic support for the judicial development of fundamental breach.[3] The principal reason why the doctrine was eventually rejected was that it was seen as an infringement of freedom of contract. But it was in one sense rather odd to depict rejection of fundamental breach in *Suisse Atlantique* as a reassertion of freedom of contract. After all, if there was one thing that was clear about the consumer cases it was that the consumer party never read or understood the exclusion clauses. It was only possible to argue that freedom of contract required that they should be bound because the clauses in question were, by virtue of the rule in *L'Estrange* v. *F Graucob Ltd* (1934), regarded as terms of the contract. It was the courts' inability or unwillingness to prise consumer contracts apart from other kinds that locked them into applying a strict rule about incorporation by signature, that was most appropriate in commercial contracts, to contracts in general.

The result of this doctrinal failure is that no differentiated conception of a consumer contract has emerged from the case law: the special rules applying to consumers are derived from legislation. Why should it matter that the case law was unable to develop such a conception? Because it represents a further narrowing in the available resources of contract law. This is part of a process which starts with a body of general rules covering a wide variety of situations, not all of which are commercial. As special rules are developed for particular kinds of situation, the issue the rules concern is withdrawn from the scope of the general rules. And as the scope of the application of the 'general' rules narrows, so does the variety of situations with which those rules have to engage. Thus, as private tenancies, employment and consumer contracts are substantially withdrawn from the scope of the general rules, the legal and policy dilemmas they raise are withdrawn too. In consequence the general rules come to embody a model of social relations which is homogeneous, and which is essentially commercial in nature. Thus, what may be called the socialisation of contract – the use of contract for the purposes of employee, tenant and consumer protection – has had the paradoxical effect of releasing general contract rules from pressure to accommodate change. And this narrowing gives a further impetus to the process by making it even more difficult in future for the general law to accommodate non commercial issues (Thomson, 1991).

The upshot is that the ability of the general law of contract to renew itself by innovation has been impaired, if not lost completely in non commercial situations. This might not matter if the scope of the general rules was truly confined to commercial law. But, as well as still governing some aspects of the contracts listed above, the general rules still operate as the default rules for situations where no special rules exist.[4]

The inhibiting of renewal has contributed to the gentle speed of change in judge made law of contract over the last thirty years. Continual fine tuning and infilling have taken place, but developments in the scope of contract, or the breaking of new ground, have been sluggish compared with that in, say, tort law or judicial review. I am not suggesting that permanent change is an intrinsically desirable condition but it is striking that the judges have extended the scope of tort liability in areas such as economic loss, liability of public authorities, and nervous shock, while the last thirty years has seen the massive development and extension of judicial review. The dramatic developments in contract on the other hand have come via legislation, most recently the bringing into effect of the European Union directive in the Unfair Terms in Consumer Contracts Regulations 1994.

One result of the narrowed base of the general law being relatively unfriendly to innovatory change means that the texts and courses on contract are rather becalmed: they hardly pulsate with the controversies about the scope of contract, while there *is* controversy in tort and even some particular kinds of contract law, notably employment. Such controversy as there is tends to be about very abstract questions of the basis of the doctrine in promise or acts of reliance and benefits received, or the boundary between contract and restitution. Thus the case which has excited perhaps the most comment in recent years (*Williams* v. *Roffey* (1991)) is notable above all for the startling rupture in the fabric of the orthodox doctrine of consideration: its practical consequences seem likely to be rather smaller. In what follows I hope to show that there are large issues at stake which are deserving of engagement and energetic controversy.

THE PLAN OF THIS BOOK

The argument for pluralism in contract entails not just a claim about its future but a view about its history, its current state, and the perspectives to be employed when addressing the law. The issue of perspective or approach is central, because it profoundly affects the perception of what has happened. In Chapter 2, *Black Letter and Beyond: Broadening the Study of Contract*, I attempt to show how non black letter approaches emerge from taking doctrine seriously. By taking the tricky topic of duress I unfold from the uncertainties within it the problems with agreement and promise based theories of contract, thereby leading on to the search for better rationales and explanations of the rules about duress and contract law in general.

Chapter 3, *The Search for Rationales of Contract*, explores attempts to establish a general, principled basis for contractual obligation, looking especially at promise and reliance based theories. I conclude that none of the available theories are adequate to explain contract law in general as grounded on any master principle, and that it is best to regard the law as inscribed with a variety of principles, some of which conflict.

Another response to inadequacies of the agreement based approach to contract has been to put the law into some context so that the operation of the rules in reality can be observed and their function discerned. In Chapter 4, *Contract Law and Reality*, we see how much of this work – preeminently that of Macaulay and Macneil – damages any claim that the general law of contract is of central practical importance. This perspective, together with the search for better rationales of contract, raises the issue of how it is that contract law has come to occupy such a central place when its claims to ideological coherence and practical importance are dubious. The making of the modern law of contract is the focus of the following three chapters.

In Chapter 5, *The Invention of Classical Contract*, I explore the influential idea of the classical law, and chart how it has been employed to depict a general contract law emerging and becoming the vehicle for the rapid contractualisation of social relations in the late eighteenth and nineteenth centuries, eclipsing other kinds of obligation in the process. In Chapter 6, *Triumph of Contract and the Classical Law*, I argue that there are problems in concluding that, because the rise of capitalism saw the triumph of contract in terms of both dominant ideology and pervasiveness of market relations, the *law* of contract, especially the classical law, was also important. I argue that the classical law, far from being a coherent and influential body of law, in many respects failed. Its dependence on the will of the parties left it without proper means to construct obligation in the absence of agreement and the result was that the most important developments in nineteenth-century commercial law took place outside the classical law, thus ensuring that it was marginal from the outset.

One ramification of this reconsideration of the nature of nineteenth-century contract law is that it begins to question the theories about modern change in contract, notably Collins' theory of a transformation from a law based on exchange justice to one based on what he describes as the justice principles of the social market; this claim is examined further in Chapter 7, *Transformation and Modern Contract*. In Chapter 8, *Divergence and Pluralism in Modern Contract*, I argue that the change which has taken place is one of divergence not transformation, and that while the justice ideal underlying commercial contract law has seen some movement, there has been important change in relation to personal contract law (consumer, employment, residential tenancies, unincorporated associations). Although much of this law is derived from statute, its mark is also visible within the general law, and it provides, alongside the dominance of the commercial model, a source of diversity or pluralism in the values which the general law embodies. The remaining three chapters explore the scope for building on this diversity.

In Chapter 9, *Judicial Review and the Scope of Contract*, I examine one source of pluralism in contract. The principles of rational decision-making developed in the law of judicial review have already been influential in contract, most notably in the application of the principles of natural justice to expulsions from associations. There are signs that the traditional division between private and public law in relation to the control of abuse of power is being blurred, and the scope for carrying this further is explored.

The attempt to build on diversity within existing contract inevitably raises questions about the boundaries of what should be treated as part of the law of contract. In Chapter 10, *The Province of Contract*, I review the boundaries with tort and restitution and argue that, although it is not persuasive to see the categories of the law of obligations as based on distinctive principles, it is possible to regard contract law as concerned with obligation which is consensual and positive, in the sense of an obligation to act for another's benefit. In Chapter 11, *The Potential of Contract*, I explore the potential for the further development of diversity or pluralism within contract by examining the limits on innovation in the law, and speculate about the prospects of the provision of free public services being analysed in contractual terms.

2
Black Letter and Beyond: Broadening the Study of Contract

This chapter is particularly aimed at those readers who may be sceptical about extending the study of contract beyond the traditional approach and materials. Even though the black letter approach has lost some of its former dominance in English law schools, it seems that in some subjects – perhaps especially contract – the adoption of non traditional approaches has to be accounted for. In this chapter I chart the limits of the traditional approach to the law of contract, examining both the range of the material typically included and the method or approach applied to it, commonly called black letter. Then, by unfolding issues from within the traditional material and approach, I attempt to show not only how the range of material and approach can be broadened, but also that this broadening grows out of an engagement with the orthodox materials.

CONTRACT LAW AND CONTRACT BOOKS: THE SCOPE OF THE LAW OF CONTRACT

It is possible to put together a formidable indictment against the subject now commonly taught as the law of contract. Part of it stems from a belief that a black letter approach is not satisfactory on its own. But even from a wholly vocational point of view – a wish to study law which will be relevant in practice – the law of contract is inadequate: it is a successful product but its consumers are getting a bad deal. These frailties result in large part from the peculiar scope of what is traditionally understood as the law of contract.

The scope of the law of contract is both wide and narrow. It is wide in that the books contain principles of very general application, potentially touching an amazing variety of situations from the building of the Channel Tunnel to a bus ride, in fact anything which is the subject matter of a market exchange whether it be a contract for services, sale, hire, employment or virtually any other kind imaginable. And it flows beyond this into non market relations such as certain domestic relations (cohabitation) and unincorporated associations such as clubs and societies.

In another sense the scope of the law of contract as presented in the books is narrow in that it falls far short of describing all the law relating to legally recognised contracts. In the first place, the law of contract is only concerned with private law, that is the law that concerns rights and duties between individuals. It omits the mass of regulation, often backed by criminal sanction, which applies to many kinds of contract. The volume of this is enormous, and where it applies it frequently dwarfs in terms of practical significance the role of private law. For example, the sale of many consumer goods is heavily shaped by specific regulations concerning such things as safety or information to be supplied to consumers, and the conditions of supply are subject to the powers of the Director General of Fair Trading to take action to review anti competitive or unfair trading practices. Other examples of regulatory agencies which affect the rules of contract in operation include the Securities and Investment Board, the Monopolies and Mergers Commission, the Equal Opportunities Commission, the Health and Safety Commission, the trading standards departments of local authorities, and the privatised utility regulators such as Oftel, Ofgas, etc.

Secondly, the contract books do not even contain all the private law relating to contracts. Their focus on general rules means that they leave out vast tracts of contract law that apply only to particular situations. The story of the development of contract law is told later, but a key feature has been the way in which over the last century more and more situation specific rules have developed in such areas as sale of goods, employment, consumer protection, tenancies, contracts for the sale of land, shipping contracts, building contracts and so forth. The position has now been reached so that no major category of contracting activity is entirely free of such special rules: yet hardly any of these special rules appear in the pages of the books on the law of contract. The consequence of this is that the statement of the law found in these books is simply unreliable as a guide to what the law actually is in many situations. Although this may not matter from the point of view of the students who use the books (their exams are set on the law of contract as described in the books) it undermines defences of the traditional accounts of the law of contract on the grounds of their practical utility.

In summary, the scope of the law of contract is limited to the general rules of private law which apply to the enforceability of contracts: the result is a body of law which contains a bit of the law on a lot of situations but the whole of the law – even the law of contract – on rather few.

THE BLACK LETTER APPROACH

The approach adopted by the orthodox texts and courses modelled on them is black letter or expository in that they are concerned to describe the doctrine and transmit understanding of it in its own terms. This includes explaining the meaning of the structure of concepts and using cases both to illustrate their application and (depending on the book) to discuss the difficulties of application in marginal cases. There is a presumption that the rules are determinate and so legal uncertainty tends to be minimised. But where doubt about the state of law is acknowledged it is generally the stopping point rather than the starting point for debate, with either a terse assertion of the author's opinion of the better view, or a shrugging of the shoulders in the direction of 'policy'. Such an approach omits other questions about the law: about its practical relevance, origin, context, values embodied, interests served. This is not to say that the black letter approach is wrong, only insufficient. At its best, especially when combined with detailed analysis of cases, the black letter approach can foster an intellectually challenging questioning of the meaning and implications of the rules. But at its worst, this approach can descend into treating the under-standing of law as little more than memorisation of facts, which demands rather little in terms of analytical sophistication.

The black letter approach can implicitly define the type of under-standing expected of students as passive rather than critical or reflective, thereby squeezing out other questions and issues. Contract seems par-ticularly prone to this tendency: the degree of closure which the use of orthodox black letter texts can exert is greater than with other legal subjects. Courses and even books on subjects such as tort and land law can introduce non black letter perspectives on the law without much difficulty. Evaluative or explanatory questions can only be raised if the law is first put into some context, and there is little difficulty in selecting a context such as accident compensation for tort, or domestic property, even simply land transfer for land law. Contract has a double problem. It is not just that the generality of the rules means that it has no context – it is even wider than market exchange – but even when a particular context is selected, the role of special rules outstrips that of the general ones contained in the orthodox texts. Thus, although contextual issues can be raised about topics such as consumer contracts, employment contracts, or commercial sales, the general rules are not well addressed by such a strategy. It is the same qualified and provisional nature of the law of contract which is responsible for both its limited practical utility and its resistance to non black letter questions.

WHY HAS THE LAW OF CONTRACT SURVIVED AS A SUBJECT OF STUDY?

Why, given the limitations on its scope, has contract survived as a subject? Tradition plays an important part. The traditional conception of the law of contract is passed down like a self justifying dogma, a principal reason for existence being that it exists. Consider the formidable inertial forces protecting its position. It has long been a required subject for the purpose of professional qualification, with the result that law departments must offer a full length course on it. With the broadening appeal of legal education it has become well supplied with texts which all use the same blueprint, finely graded between the comprehensiveness of *Treitel* and the basics of the revision aids. The texts define the courses, and the courses generate the market demand which perpetuates the texts. There does not have to be a very strong substantive argument for the place of the traditional conception of contract in the law curriculum in order for these inertial forces to carry it along. Even so, inertia cannot be a sufficient explanation. Also important is the distinctive structure on which the detail of the law rests. Most legal subjects, at least as reflected in the texts which expound them, consist of loosely connected topics which share either a very general conceptual link (in the case of tort) or focus on a particular subject matter as in the case of land law. Contract is unusual in having an integrated structure which fits all the various topics together as aspects of the same thing. The books, as they move through the canon of formation, contract terms, vitiating factors, remedies, and third party issues, reflect the steps in the making and breaking of an actual contract. This structure based on the chronology of a transaction reflects and is underpinned by a small number of key general principles, most importantly the master concept of agreement and its cognates consent, promise and intention. The idea of agreement transmits its influence to all corners of the law of contract and provides a conceptual framework or skeleton upon which the superstructural detail rests. Although these concepts were all developed incrementally in case law, the interrelated structure they form has reached the point where it has independent existence, detached from the actual cases in which the concepts were developed and refined.

How does this structure make the law of contract more resilient as a subject? It has enabled the law of contract to survive as an object of study because the structure of general contract law remains unaffected by piecemeal change limited to particular contracts. It is the very fact it has become detached from the cases which gave it birth which means that it can continue to live. For example, the case of *L'Estrange* v. *Graucob* (1934) decided that someone who signs a contractual document is bound by the terms in it unless there is fraud, duress or misrepresentation. There are now many situations in which this rule does not apply – mainly because of the Unfair Contract Terms Act 1977 – including the facts of the case itself. Yet the principle in this case continues to structure the account of the incorporation of contract terms contained in the books. The rule in *L'Estrange* v. *Graucob* earned its status as a general rule by applying to nearly all situations: once in place, it can retain its position as long as it applies to *some*. Thus the generality of the rules of the law of contract assists its survival.

The third reason for survival has been the very process of narrowing itself. By casting out the rules only applying to particular kinds of contracts, the shape of the law as applying to contracts in general has been maintained intact. New reported cases on contract are sieved, and those which deal with issues relating only to a particular sort of contract – such as the varieties of commercial contract, employment, consumer or land – are put aside, while those which relate to a general doctrine are stitched into the fabric of the law. Over time this process means that we have moved from a position where the general law of contract applied to virtually all situations to the present where it applies unqualified to few, yet we still give the general law pride of place and allow it structure in our understanding of contractual obligation.

The final reason I would identify for contract's persistence as a subject is that it draws a vicarious importance from the role of the market and contracting in society generally. Surely the law of contract *must* be important in a society based on a market order, especially when contract and market have been celebrated anew by Conservative governments since 1979? Of course contract and market are important, but that is not the same thing as the law of contract; as we will see, its limited scope and insubstantial grasp on the real world cast severe doubt on any claims to practical importance.

TRANSCENDING THE BLACK LETTER APPROACH: UNRAVELLING DURESS

Why should anyone concerned in the study of contract law wish to go beyond the black letter approach? One kind of reason stems from the view about the desirable nature of legal education, scholarship and research which students, teachers, practitioners, scholars, or writers bring to the law; these in turn may have been influenced by the wider methods and goals of the humanities and social sciences. But it is also possible to arrive at non black letter approaches by starting *within* the traditional account of the law. In the rest of this chapter I attempt to unfold the steps by which an engagement with the black letter account of the materials of contract leads into larger questions about the justification for contractual liability and the role of contract law in society.

The example I will use is the doctrine of duress. Duress is usually handled as one of a number of factors, such as mistake or misrepresentation, which if present will vitiate an otherwise valid contract. It concerns the situation where one person enters or modifies a contract as a result of pressure applied by the other party. Legally recognised duress will result in the contract being voidable. The difficult question concerns the *kind* of pressure which will suffice. Until the 1970s English law gave an easy answer to this question: little short of the threat of physical harm would do. Since the mid 1970s the courts have developed a doctrine of economic duress which permits various kinds of economic pressure to count. The courts have made clear, however, that a firm distinction must be drawn between duress and ordinary commercial pressure, which will not affect the validity of a contract. But *defining* the difference between duress and ordinary commercial pressure has proved extraordinarily difficult. A consideration of two cases will illustrate this point: *Pao On* v. *Lau Yiu Long* (1980), and *Atlas* v. *Kafco* (1989). These two cases concern situations in which one party to an existing contract threatens not to perform their obligations under it unless the other agrees to some change in the terms in their favour. The issue in each is whether such a promise is vitiated by duress; we need to examine them in some detail.

Pao On concerned a sale of a building. The plaintiffs were the effective sellers (they held all the shares in the company which owned it) and the defendants were the buyers. The sellers were to receive payment from the buyers in the form of shares in a company called Fu Chip in which the buyers had a majority holding. However, as the buyers were concerned that the price of their retained shares in Fu Chip might be depressed if the sellers offloaded their newly acquired shares in Fu Chip all at once, it was agreed that the sellers would not sell 60 per cent of their Fu Chip shares for a year. The sellers, on the other hand, were concerned that they might lose out if the share price went down during the year, so it was also agreed that the buyers would buy back those shares at the end of the year for $2.50.

Such was the agreement that was finalised for the sale of the building. However, before the transfer of the building was made it dawned on the sellers that the agreement gave the buyers a right to buy back the shares for $2.50 at the end if the year *even if the share price had gone up rather than down*. They therefore refused to go through with the contract unless the buyers cancelled the buy back arrangement. The buyers reluctantly acceded because of the damage which delay and legal action to enforce the original contract might do to confidence in Fu Chip.

The issue which came before the Judicial Committee of the Privy Council for decision was whether the second agreement was vitiated by duress. Lord Scarman found that although the act threatened here was an unlawful one (it was a breach of contract) there was no duress because there was no 'coercion of the will' to vitiate consent.

Atlas v. *Kafco* went the other way. The defendants were a firm importing basketware. They contracted with the plaintiff firm of carriers for the distribution of the basketware to retailers including Woolworths. The agreed price was £1.10 per carton. It later transpired that the carrier's manager had assumed in agreeing the price that a lorry load would take twice as many cartons as was in fact the case. On discovering this, the carrier refused to continue to perform the contract unless the importer promised to double the price. The importer agreed as they could not afford to disrupt their relations with Woolworths, and were unable in the preChristmas stocking up period to obtain a reliable alternative carrier. The carrier sued for the amount owing under the new rate and the importer pleaded duress as a defence. In a short judgment Tucker J cited Lord Scarman in *Pao On* and held that there duress was present because the importer's will had been overborne.

Here we have two cases where the threat of not performing a contract was used to procure a change in the contract terms: in both cases the party insisting on the change considered that they had inadvertently made a bad bargain and attempted to retrieve their position. In *Pao On* the court found that the victim's will was not overborne, whereas in *Atlas* the court found that it was. It is the stuff of the common law to reconcile cases by making distinctions between them which become incorporated in a rule or principle against which the outcomes of the cases are rendered consistent. Uncertainty, in the sense of difficulty in predicting the outcome of the next case, arises when despite casting around the judges do not appear to have alighted on any principle or rule which makes the decisions appear consistent. The doctrine of duress is now in this state of uncertainty.

The core of the problem is that, although all the authorities agree that there is a difference between ordinary commercial pressure and duress, there is no clear test for deciding which is which. There are a number of competing tests in the cases; none are free from serious difficulty and none have emerged as the prime test of duress. The overborne will test (allied with the issue of whether the act was voluntary) is unsatisfactory because, as Lord Diplock pointed out in *The Universe Sentinel* (1983), it is a misdescription of the situation: the party under duress complies with the threat fully intending to do so because the pressure applied renders the alternative less attractive. In any case, as a test it is inoperable because it fails to distinguish true duress from mere commercial pressure which leaves the victim with no realistic alternative.

A slightly different tack is to focus closely on the evidence, carefully weighing such matters as whether the victim protested, whether independent advice was available, or whether there were alternative remedies. This approach lacks any basis in principle and so provides neither consistency nor any rational explanation why some contracts but not others are vitiated by duress.

Another approach has been to regard the lack of effective choice as a threshold requirement with the main focus on whether the pressure applied is illegitimate. One problem with this is that there is no clear understanding of what counts as illegitimate. The threat of a breach of contract appears to qualify, but there is uncertainty about the threat of a lawful act.[1] The larger uncertainty, however, lies with what will count as a threat. The mere communication by one party to another that they will not perform does not necessarily amount to a threat. In *Williams* v. *Roffey* (1991) a carpenter undertaking work on a block of flats got into financial difficulties, and when it became clear that the work would not be finished on time, the main contractor promised more money to finish the work. The issue in the case was whether there was any consideration for the promise, but it was assumed that there was no question of duress here. When will a conditional prediction amount to a threat? Since it is hard to conceive that this will depend on the precise conjunctions used, more is needed to distinguish duress from commercial pressure.

Now, at this point we have reached a ragged edge of the fabric of the common law. The orthodox response of legal scholars to an absence of a satisfactory rationale is to propose an alternative rationale that will make better sense of the cases; which will, in other words, fit the cases together better. We will briefly consider two such alternative rationales of duress.

The first is a general rationale which attempts to explain contract law in terms of the philosophical principles of liberal individualism, and which receives its most persuasive expression in the work of Charles Fried (1981). The foundation of his argument is that it is both morally justified and logically coherent to base contractual obligation on what he calls the 'promise principle'. Thus he argues that contractual obligation should be regarded as the corollary of individual autonomy because it is a necessary condition of individual autonomy to be able to bind oneself by making a promise. Contract law is self-imposed by the parties and is not the product of contingent policy arguments. He clearly recognises the challenge posed by duress: 'it is the make or break challenge to the liberal economic theory of the market' (p 94).

Fried attempts to solve the conundrum of duress by arguing that the test for whether duress is present should turn on whether the person applying the pressure has an independent right to do the thing he threatens. If he does not have such a right then the threat, Fried argues, is of harm to the victim's property, broadly conceived, and therefore illegitimate. Thus a threat to injure, to damage property, or break a contract, would amount to duress and thereby render voidable any promise thereby procured. On the other hand, the threat that you will not rescue someone in an emergency would not amount to duress in the absence of any independent duty to rescue. By this test of duress would have been present in *Pao On* as well as in *Atlas* because all cases of threats to break a contract would be included within the definition. But what about the difficult case of blackmail, where the exposure threatened may be lawful in itself? Here, Fried is forced into arguing that there *ought not* to be an independent right to harm another maliciously, and therefore if the law were to accord with this principle the blackmail situation would be correctly pigeonholed as duress because the threatener would not have the right to threaten such harm.

Fried's own theory of contract was produced in response to the work of many writers, mainly American, who argued that the law of contract could not persuasively be explained as being derived from the ideas of promise or agreement. A common theme is the idea that the rules of contract law are not essentially distinct from tort in that they impose obligation in accordance with prevailing conceptions of fairness or social justice. In the context of duress, this approach can be illustrated by analysing duress in terms of exploitation.

An important feature of Fried's account of duress is that he does not employ any idea of fairness or substantive justice to decide whether duress exists: it is simply a formal question of whether the usual obligation to perform a promise is vitiated because it has been procured by a threat to do something unlawful. Rationalising duress in terms of exploitation, however, involves giving fairness and substantive justice a central place. The gist of the argument runs as follows. A feature of the duress situation is that one party is using the other's difficulties for their own benefit: the judges sometimes speak in duress cases of the victimised party being over a barrel, as when the defendants in *Atlas* had no alternative but to agree to pay double the contract price. The key element is that the victimised party, having made arrangements in reliance on the other party's performance being forthcoming, is now faced with the threatened withholding of that performance in circumstances which make it impossible to make satisfactory alternative arrangements. The exploitation here lies in the other party deliberately using the weak position which reliance on them has brought about for their own gain.[2]

An exploitation theory of duress is based on substantive justice because it is concerned not merely with whether consent was real (Lord Scarman's overborne will test), nor with whether some act formally unlawful has been threatened (the Fried test), but with whether the change brought about by the purported alteration in their contractual relations is fair as between the parties, taking a range of factors into account. Thus a ground of distinction between *Pao On* and *Atlas* could be found in the differing importance of the disputed performances. In *Atlas* the victim was being asked to double the price, the paying of which was his central obligation under the contract, whereas in *Pao On* all that was at stake was the allocation between the parties of the surplus that would arise if the share price of Fu Chip went above $2.50, a price which in any case the plaintiffs regarded as satisfactory. One can speculate whether Tucker J in *Atlas* would have found duress to be present if the price increase had been much smaller, despite the fact the unlawfulness of the threat and absence of an alternative course of action would remain the same. In *Williams* v. *Roffey*, the increase in price was saved from duress because there was no question of the plaintiff carpenter attempting to *exploit* any financial difficulty: the arrangement was clearly in the interest of the defendant as well as the carpenter.

The exploitation theory therefore arguably fills a gap in the development of the law of duress by providing a way of distinguishing between duress and commercial pressure. But the introduction of an alternative rationale such as this poses problems for the rest of the law of contract, for it draws on justifying principles which are not explicitly recognised within the law of contract, and which have the potential to subvert established principles of contract. To see how this potential arises we need to explore why the common law should have had such difficulty in drawing the line.

The fundamental problem lies in expecting the cluster of ideas rooted in consent (which include promise and agreement) to define their own limits. A dominant principle in contract is that of agreement: agreements are freely made but once made are binding. Put another way, it is the voluntary exercise by the parties of their freedom to enter a contract or not which in large part justifies them being held to the agreement when the court enforces it. However, if agreement is only procured after pressure then it rather undermines the idea that the agreement should be enforced as a contract on the ground that it is an expression of the parties' free will. More generally, the persuasiveness of freedom of contract as a political value hinges on there being at least some situations which will not count as contracts because consent, although technically present, should not be treated as real. Thus if consent is to retain its justifying power, the law must be able to distinguish when consent is real. But once the veil is pulled aside and the reality of consent is examined, all kinds of everyday economic pressure or necessity clamour for attention as potentially undermining consent. And since the law of contract has traditionally adopted an objective theory of agreement, where what counts is the appearance of agreement, it is not well equipped to begin to identify real consent. Thus the problem that legal writers face is one of confinement: how to define pressure in a way which will allow the victim to say the consent was not real without thereby undermining doctrines which depend on a much more restrictive conception of consent, the consequence of which would be the unravelling of all manner of contracts which are commonly entered into or modified without any real choice by one party. To draw an analogy with the operation of the human immune system, it is as though the body (contract law) has to defend itself against the threat posed by the infection of duress, but is unable to produce antibodies which can distinguish between the host and the invader. It is therefore not an exaggeration to say that the issue at stake in the future development of duress is whether it can continue to flourish as a developing doctrine without undermining a great deal of what has been taken as settled law.[3]

This problem could be suppressed as long as the law used a very restricted version of duress, but the recognition of economic duress has posed the judges a real problem of confinement. The exploitation theory may well provide part of the answer. But it needs to be grounded on some conception of substantive justice which draws not just on what people have agreed or promised but on the overall weighing of each party's motives and what each gives and receives under the original contract and the modification. Taking duress seriously will therefore arguably lead contract law into a much more explicit recognition of norms of fair dealing and good faith than ever before.

The articulation of alternative rationales, although it begins with the black letter tradition, is itself difficult to confine within that tradition. These rationales are grounded ultimately not in the internal reasoning of the law itself, but in political or moral argument. Moreover, this approach is not limited to justifying legal rules as they happen to be at any time: an advocate of an alternative rationale may claim that it has a better fit with the existing law of contract than any rationale available wholly within the legal sources, but may also go further and argue that, where the law does not fit the rationale, then the law should change so that it does. In this way the search for better rationales crosses the boundary which separates orthodox legal analysis from other forms of argument. We leave behind the traditional emphasis on consistency and investigate the hard questions about ultimate normative justifications. In other words, we are drawn into assessing not only whether arguments are consistent, but also whether they are right.

Dissatisfaction with the coherence of contract doctrine therefore prompts a search for better rationales – ones which offer a better fit for the cases or are normatively superior. It also fosters a greater awareness of change in the law, for debates about rationales of the doctrine can easily become entangled in controversy about fundamental shifts in the law.

THE DURESS DOCTRINE IN CONTEXT

The discussion of rationales has proceeded so far without any reference to how contract law is used in reality. Once we suspect that the wills of the parties are not the only source of contract norms, we may wish to know more about how it is actually applied. What do we know of the context of contract? The only window on reality within the traditional approach to the law of contract is provided by the facts of the reported cases themselves. These isolated, denatured, little narratives mainly function as aids which assist the understanding and explanation of the law. Debate in terms of alternative rationales tends to treat the facts of cases in a similar way, frequently stripping out the court's reasoning and leaving behind only the facts and the final outcome as the raw data to be accommodated within an alternative theory. 'The facts' become the material for thought experiments in which it hardly matters whether the events really took place at all.

Given the resilience of the traditional approach to questions about the context of the doctrine, any understanding of that context must be sought outside the traditional material. In Chapter 4 we will explore some of the work that has attempted to put the law of contract in context and the consequences of so doing for the coherence of traditional accounts of the subject. But it is useful to identify in a preliminary way some of the implications of such an enquiry for an understanding of the doctrine of duress.

The first problem which any attempt to place either the general law of contract or one of its doctrines in context encounters is the selection of a context from the enormously wide and varied range of situations where the rules apply. Duress has no predefined context because duress is simply the name of an abstract legal category which does not correlate with any particular type of contract. A context therefore has to be stipulated. One approach is to consider whether there is any recurrent issue which duress is used to handle. Arguably there is: the modification of existing contractual terms, and empirical investigation would be needed of the practice in this regard in a variety of contexts. Another approach would be to identify duress as being concerned with the general issue of the abuse of economic power, with the result that the context would be defined in terms of the variety of situations in which that abuse could be discerned. With an identified context the question then arises of the relationship between the legal rules and behaviour: do the rules shape behaviour, and if so, how? Understanding this complex issue is an absorbing and important study in its own right, but it leads on to the possibility of identifying both a purpose or function which the law should pursue, and the best rule formulation to produce the desired outcome.

The study of contract law in context gives a further push to analysis of the law in normative (i.e. policy) terms. Within a promise or agreement based rationale, contractual outcomes are seen as a product of the individual choice of the parties and so are less open to political argument. But once the law is seen as an instrument of policy, then the attempt to separate descriptive from normative analysis is more difficult to sustain, because the law is seen as the instrument of public purpose rather than the facilitator of private action. In this way changes in the law not only put into question the coverage of the traditional books (because so many special rules are left out) but also challenge the adequacy of the descriptive or expository approach which they adopt: the sharp line which the black letter tradition draws between the law of contract and other things becomes harder both to discern and to justify. In this light, the preservation of the general scope of the traditional texts by rigorously excluding the special rules not only preserves the agreement based edifice of principle but also maintains the isolation of the descriptive account of the law.

In this chapter I have attempted to unfold from difficulties in the doctrine of duress a series of progressively wider questions. Some may take the view that this takes us beyond what the law of contract is 'really' about. It is true that it goes beyond the subject as it is treated within the black letter tradition, but the point of this chapter has been to show that the fences which guard the integrity of the traditional conception of the law of contract and its appropriate mode of study are in a state of considerable disrepair. In later chapters we will be exploring more of the threats to the integrity of the law of contract as a whole, as well as considering some of the attempts at repair on the boundaries.

3
The Search for Rationales of Contract

How is the imposition of legal obligation to act for another's benefit to be justified? For a body of law cast into its modern form at the time that the philosophy of liberal individualism was taking hold, this is the preeminent question. The classical explanation is in terms of the exchange of promises in an agreement: obligation to act is *self*-imposed. But this understanding of contract has been assailed from a number of directions, and the integrity and viability of contract law as a subject, as well as a ground of obligation, have been put into question. My aim in this chapter is to explore the project of attempting to justify contract law in terms of general principles. First, I will compare the promise theory with its main competitor, that based on the idea of detrimental reliance. I then address two other approaches: the rationale in terms of the goal of allocative efficiency, and the interpretation of contract in terms of conflicting ideals of justice. I will conclude that the aspiration to explain or justify contract rules by reference to a small number of principles is doomed to failure, and that the only viable model is one which recognises a variety of justifying principles.

THE RELIANCE THEORY OF CONTRACT

The reliance theory is American in origin, and was championed by the leading academic Corbin in the negotiations which led to the publication by the American Law Institute of the first Restatement of Contracts in 1932 (Gilmore, 1974, p 61). It is this work that PS Atiyah built on in producing perhaps the most elaborate analysis of reliance in contract, and, as Atiyah's version of the reliance theory is the most familiar to English lawyers, it is the one on which I will focus.

Atiyah's starting point is a fundamental rejection of the idea that the exchange of promises is a necessary or sufficient reason for a contract to be legally enforceable. He has argued that virtually all contract doctrine can be understood as grounding liability on the fact that the plaintiff has relied on the defendant's word or conduct, or that benefits have been received by the defendant.[1]

Reliance is patent as an ingredient of liability in the doctrine of promissory estoppel, where, as the classic decision in *High Trees* (1947) demonstrates, some degree of reliance by the promisee on the promise not to enforce an existing right is an essential part of the doctrine. For Atiyah, the explanatory power of reliance goes much further than this. Developing arguments contained in the article 'The Reliance Interest in Contract Damages' (Fuller and Purdue, 1936), he suggests that reliance can be seen as the basis of most damages awards in contract. Most directly this includes damages for lost expenditure where the plaintiff has spent money in preparing for the contract and the defendant pulls out. But it can also in principle include damages for some loss of profit wherever one can say that by relying on the contract the plaintiff has lost an opportunity to enter another contract which would have generated a similar gain. The idea of compensating loss flowing from a lost opportunity to contract is well illustrated in *East* v. *Maurer* (1991). The plaintiff bought a hairdressing salon from the defendant seller after being assured that the seller would not work at another salon, which he owned, in the same town. In fact he did continue to work, and the first salon lost money through the customers' transferring. Because this was an action for fraudulent misrepresentation and not breach of contract, the plaintiff could not recover damages for the lost expectation, as measured by the profit the plaintiff would have made in the salon if the defendant had not competed. Instead, the damages were assessed as if the defendant had declared his true intent, in which case the plaintiff would have bought a different salon which would have generated profit. Thus the measure of recovery included damages for the plaintiff's loss of the opportunity to make an ordinary profit. Although there was no question in *East* v. *Maurer* of reliance being the explicit basis of recovery, it nevertheless illustrates how damages for lost opportunity may include an element for loss of profit.

Atiyah's other ground of liability in contract is the receipt of a benefit, and his stock illustration of where liability should be understood as benefit based is the action for the price where someone who has tendered goods or a service is claiming payment. In orthodox terms it is said that the buyer is liable because they have agreed to pay, while Atiyah argues that it is more persuasive to regard liability to pay as stemming from the fact that the benefit has been received. It is particularly distorting to regard a promise to repay a loan as creating the obligation to repay: he argues that the promise quantifies an obligation which arises not out of an exchange of promises but out of the fact that a non gratuitous benefit has been conferred.

Atiyah recognises some limits in explaining contract in reliance/benefit terms. He acknowledges that it is difficult to explain the enforcement of a contract which is wholly executory in the sense that no benefit has been conferred and no act of reliance has taken place. It is clear law, for example, that a buyer who changes his mind and withdraws from a contract of sale only seconds after it is made is liable to the seller for damages for loss of any profit incurred, even if there is no act of reliance or benefit received. Atiyah's response to this is in two parts. On the one hand he accepts that there is a good argument for the enforcement of some purely executory contracts, specifically where a contract is used as a deliberate risk allocation device, the most obvious instance of which is a contract of insurance. On the other hand, he claims that the case for enforcing wholly executory contracts which are not deliberate allocations of risk is weak, and that wholly executory contracts are rarely enforced in practice. He considers, for example, that there is little reason for making a consumer liable for a seller's loss of profit, in the absence of reliance, in the situation described above.

RELIANCE, BENEFIT AND PROMISE IN THE LAW OF OBLIGATIONS

An important ramification of the reliance/benefit thesis is the way it dismantles not only the conventional underpinning of contract law, but also the category of contract as a coherent entity. Atiyah argues that ideas of benefit and reliance can be seen to underpin not only the law of contract but also much of tort law and the law of restitution. For example, he argues that much of the law of restitution can be understood as resting on the same principle of liability following the receipt of a benefit which underlies contract: the three categories of the law of obligations do not reflect fundamentally different justifying principles, but reflect instead the accidents of history which saw the precursors of modern tort and restitution doctrine severed from contract as part of the process which gave birth to a separate classical law of contract.

It is the denial of the fundamental distinctiveness of the traditional categories of the law of obligations which has drawn most critical fire, especially from writers on the law of restitution. Andrew Burrows (1983), in the course of arguing for the coherence of restitution as a subject, has defended the traditional justification of contract law as being grounded on promise and agreement. Although in my view his arguments are ultimately not persuasive, his engagement with Atiyah illuminates what is at stake between reliance and promise based theories of contract.

Burrows' basic contention is that the division of the law of obligations into contract, tort and restitution is satisfactory because it separates at least most of the law based on what he calls the three 'cardinal principles': the fulfilment of expectations engendered by promises, the compensation for wrongful harm, and the reversal of unjust enrichment. He sees each of these principles as protecting a different interest, which are: the expectation interest, which is concerned with putting the plaintiff in as good a position as he would have occupied if the defendant had performed his promise; the status quo interest, which is concerned with putting the plaintiff in as good a position as he was before the promise was made or other wrong committed; and the restitution interest, which is concerned with the prevention of gain at the expense of the promisee.[2]

Burrows argues that Atiyah's claim that liability in contract is based on benefit or reliance is flawed. Atiyah's claim that liability becomes reliance based when there is some act of reliance on the contract must mean, according to Burrows, that the plaintiff can only claim protection of his status quo interest. For example, if a seller delivers a piece of machinery for use in a factory, and it proves defective and halts production, what can the buyer claim? According to Burrows, Atiyah must mean that, on a reliance theory, the buyer could only claim expenditure wasted on dealing with the defective machine, but not the loss of profit caused by the lost production. Since it is clear, as a matter of law, that the plaintiff can recover lost profit as the value of his lost expectation (assuming it is not too remote), Burrows concludes that Atiyah's thesis must simply be wrong (p 265).

It is a mistake, however, to assume that a reliance theory of liability can only justify damages for lost expenditure. Fuller and Perdue recognised that protection of the reliance interest could require loss of bargain damages where the opportunity of another contract generating similar profit was lost by relying on the contract that was eventually breached, as already illustrated above by *East* v. *Maurer* (1991). In the example, it is the reliance on the contract with the seller that leads to the buyer not taking steps to obtain a different machine. Burrows, however, does not include the protection of this kind of reliance within the status quo interest, mainly because his conception of it is a static one in which the object is to return the plaintiff to the position he was actually in before the contract was made. This approach takes no account of what the plaintiff might have done if he had not relied on the contract with the plaintiff, that is the opportunities he has lost by relying on a contract with the plaintiff. Burrows, by his method of constructing categories, removes from view an important kind of reliance within the theory of detrimental reliance.[3]

It is important to distinguish two different meanings which the concept of reliance bears in this context. One meaning is as a measure of damages, defined by reference to the plaintiff's position immediately before he entered the contract. This is the meaning used by Burrows. Atiyah, on the other hand, also uses reliance as a *criterion of liability*, that is a reason why someone should be liable. The result is that Burrows attempts to refute a claim by Atiyah about a criterion of liability – that contract is not really promise based – with an argument about the measure of damages. As there is no necessary connection between a criterion of liability and the way in which damages consequent upon that liability should be measured, Burrows' argument does not land a knockout blow on the reliance theory.[4]

THE CONTEST BETWEEN PROMISE AND RELIANCE

Returning to the wider issue, on what basis can one choose between promise and reliance based theories? To answer this question we need to explore further the ways in which general rationales of liability may be tested. There are two different ways in which the justification of an outcome – whether it be a rule or decision in an individual case – by a normative principle may be evaluated. It may be questioned in terms of normative persuasiveness, by arguing that the principle does not justify an outcome because it is morally unconvincing or plain bad. Alternatively, the relationship may be queried not by disagreeing with the normative principle, but by questioning whether, even if it is accepted, it results in the outcome in question. It is possible to identify the plausibility of the fit between a principle and an outcome independently of the normative persuasiveness of the principle. One may agree with a moral principle, but deny that it justifies a particular outcome; conversely, one may disagree with the moral principle, but nevertheless recognise that, if it is accepted, it supports the outcome in question. Before applying these abstractions to promise and reliance as the basis of contract, it is perhaps useful to illustrate them in a different context.

A stark example of the independence between the issues of normative persuasiveness and plausibility of fit can be seen in debates about capital punishment. Suppose that there is strong evidence that capital punishment is an effective deterrent to certain types of murder. I can recognise that this evidence makes deterrence a plausible utilitarian argument for the reintroduction of capital punishment, in the sense that the deterrence argument points towards that outcome. I could at the same time, however, consistently resist the conclusion of the argument on the ground that I find the argument from deterrence (however overwhelming the evidence) normatively disagreeable, for example because I consider it morally repugnant for the state to take human life. Equally, it is possible for me to accept the principle of deterrence – that capital punishment is justified if it deters murderers – but to question whether, on the available evidence, the case is made out. Although the issue of fit here turns on the interpretation of empirical evidence, it illustrates how the normative attractiveness of a principle is separate from the question of whether an outcome can be fitted within it.

How does the Atiyah/Burrows debate appear in the light of this distinction? Most strikingly, the main thrust of each is directed at different aspects. For Atiyah, the main argument against the promise theory is that it is normatively unconvincing: he questions whether the promise theory can provide a morally acceptable explanation of enforceability. Burrows, however, seems more concerned with fit, that it whether the law can be seen as based upon the cardinal principles, which are not themselves subject to any normative analysis. Burrows' conception of fit, however, is of a rather rigid, all or nothing kind. In essence, he makes two claims: that reliance is not the basis of contractual liability, and that promising is. He appears to assume that each of these propositions entails the other, and tends towards a model of the relationship between underlying principles and outcomes which is univocal in both directions: the principle can only be realised by a single outcome, and an outcome can only be justified on the basis of one principle. Arguably, this over estimates the tightness of fit which is possible between general principles and specific outcomes, and it is more useful to conceive of the fit between principle and outcome as much looser. An outcome may be justified by more than one principle, and one principle may support more than one outcome. It is therefore at least conceivable that one could accept Burrows' contention that contract can be seen as based on promise *and* Atiyah's claim that it can be grounded on reliance. In other words, it might be possible to find a plausible fit between most of contract law and both promise and reliance theories.

The assertion that the same outcome may be justified by more that one principle gives little idea of how widespread such overlap of justification may be. Both commentators acknowledge that there are some outcomes reached by the law of contract which are beyond the reach of their principles. Atiyah concedes that the 'pure' executory contract is beyond the reach of his principle for the simple reason that in such a situation there has (definitionally) been no act of reliance nor any benefit conferred. Similarly, Burrows accepts that the doctrine of promissory estoppel – at least as currently understood – is concerned with protecting his status quo interest, and therefore not explicable on a promise based theory. But apart from these cases, each argues that the rest of the law can be brought within their own principle. But while Burrows regards the law of contract as only reconcilable with the promise principle, Atiyah does not wholly deny the plausibility of fit between the promise principle and much of the law of contract. He does claim, however, that there are important parts of contract where it is not even plausible to describe contractual obligations as being based on a promise in any real sense. A stock example is the purchase of a bus ticket, where there are typically few if any promises actually made; the same reasoning applies to the many situations where, because of the use of standard forms, most of the obligations are not agreed by the parties. Burrows, however, claims that this and most other situations where express promises are absent can be brought within the promise principle on the basis that in such cases persons should be counted as making a promise. Burrows calls on the objective theory to qualify his conception of promise, and defines promise as 'a statement or action by which the speaker or actor appears to accept an obligation to do or not do something' (p 244). By using an objective theory of promise he takes the meaning of promise at its widest, recognising as promise based many situations where Atiyah denies there is a promise.

Atiyah also sweeps in many situations within justifying range of his theory. Reliance and benefit are conceptions with very indistinct edges, partly because they are alternative rationales and as such do not appear in a developed form within the law. Atiyah's argument is that they are factual characteristics of situations which are usually an operative condition of contractual liability in that they are the reason for the liability. Even putting on one side problems about identifying the 'real' basis of liability, an important problem with them is that on their own they are over-inclusive. I find little difficulty with Atiyah's claim that one or other is nearly always present where liability is discovered. The difficulty is that they are present even where there is no liability. For example, where limitation and exclusion clauses are given effect they operate despite the person whose claim is denied having relied or provided a benefit: a retail seller denied recourse against a distributor or manufacturer because of a clause limiting liability for defects may well have relied on having redress, and will have provided a benefit in the form of a price. The same is equally true of the distributor or manufacturer: they will have provided value in the form of the goods and may well have relied on the limitation of their liability. As both parties give and receive a benefit here, the fact that a benefit has been conferred does not on its own decide the outcome: it is indeterminate.

Reliance is only retrievable as a criterion of liability by its qualification in terms of *reasonable* reliance. Thus with both benefit and reliance the factual element has to be supplemented with other criteria capable of explaining the actual incidence of liability. There is an important role here, recognised by Atiyah, for promises as one way in which reliance will be reasonable, although promising does not exhaust the possibilities. Conceptions based on substantive fairness, market facilitation, and responsibility for the welfare of others all have a role to play in filling out when reliance is reasonable and which benefits should be paid for. So, even if we accept that reliance and benefit seem to be necessary triggering elements of liability in contract, they are not sufficient criteria of liability on their own: they operate as fairly low threshold requirements beyond which further explanation is needed of why in any case liability is found to exist.

It emerges that some of the differences between Atiyah and Burrows can be traced to the use of different definitions of the chosen governing principles. In the case of promise, Atiyah seeks to restrict its meaning while Burrows applies it much more extensively, and the same is broadly true the other way round in relation to reliance. It is the inherent elasticity of the meaning of such general concepts which enables the stretching practised by the advocate of a principle's explanatory power to be answered by the opponent's minimising of its scope.

In the face of conflicting arguments which purport to connect principles at a relatively high level of generality with detailed rules, it is difficult to be confident that either is demonstrably wrong. Although there are rules which are beyond the outer limits of what such general principles can plausibly justify (the purely executory contract for Atiyah, promissory estoppel for Burrows) one is left with the sense that there is a plausible fit between most of the law of contract and *both* general principles, at least when taken at their widest.

The stretching of the meaning of the promise principle is at great cost to the persuasiveness of the moral argument on which it is based. The argument for the binding force of a promise is strongest where the conduct is a solemn, express promise given freely and with full knowledge of the circumstances and full understanding of the consequences. Such is clearly not the case where, for example, the purchaser of defective consumer goods is held to have 'promised' to forego any claim if they turn out to be defective on the basis of a set of obscure standard terms. Treating the latter situation as in some sense equivalent to the first has the effect of clothing the outcome in the second with some principled justification, albeit one that is barely plausible on the facts. But over time the direction of the flow of legitimation can reverse. Instead of the outcome in the consumer case drawing legitimacy from the strength of the promise principle on its home ground, the profound problems with applying the promise principle in outlying situations comes to discredit the promise principle in general.

To conclude this section on the contest between promise and reliance theories, I would claim that neither the promise nor reliance/benefit principles can be used satisfactorily to ground the law of contract in general. Normative persuasiveness and plausibility of fit pull against each other. Maximising the number of situations which it is plausible to see as within the scope of a principle weakens the normative power of the principle; conversely, a firmer normative principle has less reach in terms of the situations which can plausibly be seen as an application of it. An example of the latter is Fried (1981), who avoids the problems which follow from spreading the promise principle too thinly by using a more confined conception of promising. This approximates more closely to the everyday idea of promising being about explicit undertakings to do things, and he fully recognises that large parts of contract doctrine need to be grounded on principles other than the promise principle, notably where there are gaps in the agreement.

Dissatisfaction with promise and reliance as the basis of contract leads us on: is there some other *general* criterion of liability available? So far the only contender is the rationale in terms of efficiency, sometimes referred to as market failure, and it is this that we now need to examine.

EFFICIENCY AND THE LAW OF CONTRACT

The project of applying economic analysis to legal rules has exerted extraordinary influence on legal studies over the last thirty years, especially in contract, and mainly (but not only) in North America. Although the work of 'law and economics' is by no means homogeneous, the most influential strand has been the evaluation of legal rules according to whether they promote efficiency.

The most commonly cited definition of efficiency in the law and economics literature is that of Posner, who defined it as the maximisation of overall wealth in an economy; although this bristles with difficulties, its gist should be clear enough to allow us to negotiate the next steps in the analysis. The assumption is that efficiency will be reached where the market works: 'if voluntary exchanges are permitted – if, in other words a market is allowed to operate – resources will gravitate toward the most valuable uses' (Kronman and Posner, 1979, p 1). Thus raw materials will find their way to the owner who values them the most highly because he is the one prepared to pay most. If a perfect market existed, then the only law of contract that would be needed to achieve efficiency is a rule that whatever the parties agreed would be enforced.

It is because markets are not perfect, but suffer from kinds of market failure, that the actual rules of contract law matter. Three kinds of market failure are usually identified: monopoly, which theoretically includes all situations where a seller is able, due to size of market share, to push the price above the price a competitive market would produce; imperfect information, which impedes the firm's or consumer's ability to act as a rational maximiser of satisfaction; and transaction costs, which include all the costs of negotiating a contract, including where costs prevent negotiation taking place at all.

According to Posner, the rules of contract should be set to promote efficiency; and, happily, he finds that on the whole they tend to do so. The contract rule should mimic what an agreement in the absence of market distortions would have produced, and where possible provide incentives for parties to bargain around it. Many contract doctrines have been analysed as promoting efficiency; here are a few examples.

Restricting a plaintiff's claim to damages compensating his expectation loss, rather than awarding specific performance or damages based on the defendant's gain, is said to promote efficiency by providing an incentive to break a contract whenever it is efficient to do so, for example because the seller has received a better offer from a buyer than the one with whom he has contracted – the theory of 'efficient breach'(Goetze Scott, 1977). Allowing a change in circumstances after the making of a contract to amount to a discharge under the doctrine of frustration, rather than a breach for which the non performer is liable, is justified as conducive to efficiency unless the non performer is in a better position than the other party either to prevent the risk materialising, or to insure against it the most cheaply. The problem of duress (discussed in Chapter 2) is not seen as one of vitiation of consent, or the overborne will, or wrongful threats, or even exploitation: the key issue is whether there is a situational monopoly. By this is meant a situation in which the victim has no alternative supply of the good or service available with the result that on a micro level the market has ceased to operate (Trebilcock, 1980).

It is a notable feature of the efficiency rationale that it recognises that it is precisely the *absence* of express agreement between the parties to a contract on some matter which creates the need for most contract doctrine, and in so doing locates one of the reasons why so much of contract law is beyond the explanatory reach of a promise based theory of contract – unless, that is, one adopts (like Burrows) a very stretched and therefore normatively weak meaning of promise. One result of this is that efficiency analysis avoids the unsatisfactory vacuities of concepts such as inequality of bargaining power, searching instead for firmer criteria with which to distinguish grounds for not enforcing a contract.

Although efficiency analyses of contract continue to proliferate, powerful arguments have been directed against the viability of the whole project. Following the analysis of promise and reliance above, these criticisms can be divided into two kinds: claims that there is no plausible fit between efficiency and the rules, and claims that, even if there is such a fit, the principle is not normatively persuasive.

In terms of plausibility of fit, the problem is that virtually *any* configuration of the rules can be made to appear conducive to efficiency. The typical method of demonstrating the efficiency of a rule is to show that it produces an efficient outcome by reflecting the transaction costs which inhibit the parties' agreement. But the problem, as Veljanovski has convincingly argued, is that these transaction costs are not established by empirical investigation, but inferred from the law itself:

> [T]he law is rationalised as efficient by assuming a configuration of transaction (and other) costs that makes it so without any attempt

to investigate whether these costs exist in practice. This method of 'testing' the theory often amounts to little more than a restatement of the hypothesis that the common law is efficient by using transaction costs and other costs in a way that makes the whole approach an elaborate tautology. (Veljanovski, 1982, p 96)

This point has added force in relation to general contract law because it is plausible to expect that the transaction cost configuration would vary across the different kinds of contract within the scope of the rules, thus making it especially difficult empirically to ground statements about whether such general rules tend to promote efficiency (Kennedy and Michelman, 1980; Rizzo, 1980; MacNeil, 1981, 1982). Even so, this is not to say that contract is never efficient, only that it might or might not be, depending on a detailed empirical analysis of particular contexts.

The most thorough going critique of efficiency as a rationale has been in terms of its normative persuasiveness: about whether the law *ought* to be based on the goal of efficiency. The most common criticism is that efficiency is unconcerned with distributive justice, that is whether any distribution of resources in society is fair or just. Posner's wealth maximising definition of efficiency is usually treated as broadly equivalent to a concept technically known as the Hicks/Kaldor criterion. This holds that moving from one allocation of resources to another is desirable even if there are losers, as long as the winners gain more than the losers lose. The crucial point is that the Hicks/Kaldor criterion does not require gainers to actually compensate losers, only that potentially they could do so; this is the same principle which is used in the appraisal of public sector projects such as roads in terms of cost benefit analysis. On this basis, it is possible to say that, for Posner, efficiency is wholly separate from the question of how resources are distributed: put simply, efficiency is about maximising the size of the cake irrespective of how its slices are cut and distributed.

The independence of efficiency from distributional concerns has led critics to argue that efficiency is an inadequate normative criterion: even if it is efficient to allow advantage to be taken of the improvident, it is not fair. Taken to an extreme, the efficiency criterion would justify a body of contract law in which distributional fairness plays no role at all. Posner, and most advocates of efficiency, recognise that distributional justice has *some* role, but argue that it should be kept analytically separate from efficiency. This line has been developed furthest by Trebilcock who has argued for an institutional separation of the handling of efficiency and distributional questions: judicial development of the common law of contract should only be concerned with efficiency, while questions of distribution should be settled by a legislature (Trebilcock, 1993). Although this proposal has the possible merit of freeing the courts from deciding how the balance between the different goals should be struck, it remains questionable whether it is in any case coherent to treat efficiency as an independent goal which is capable of being balanced against distributional justice (Dworkin, 1986).

The unsatisfactory handling of distributional questions by no means exhausts the problems with efficiency as a normative concept. Perhaps most fundamentally, it is argued by Dworkin that it shares the defect of all utilitarian theories, which is that it has no place for rights (Dworkin, 1986b). But there is another criticism I want to say more about which falls outside the triangle of efficiency, distribution and rights. It concerns ethical questions which are debated as matters neither of distribution nor rights of individuals. The issue is well illustrated by the debate over commercial surrogacy. This is an instance where the cogency of the efficiency criterion on its own runs out: enforcing the handover of the baby by a reluctant natural mother following a contract with a commissioning couple may be efficient, but maximising wealth does not (I trust) appeal as a sufficient reason for enforcement. Neither is the issue entirely captured by considering what is a fair distribution, for debate will range wider than whether the price was fair, the agreement genuine, the plight of infertile couples, or the welfare of the child. Even a debate in terms of the rights of the individuals in the situation will not fully grasp what is at stake in a debate about whether it is morally right for contracts for the sale of babies or (not necessarily less tendentiously) surrogacy services to be legally enforceable. This is because the issue is about more than the impact on any of the individuals concerned of the decision. It is about how the social relations concerning the birth and rearing of children are constituted, specifically whether they are to be conceived as market transactions. Ultimately this is a question about the kind of society in which we want to live, and there are questions of ethics which affect contract law but which are not encompassed by efficiency, distributive justice, or rights theory.[5]

Given the problems with efficiency, both in terms of the plausibility of its fit with legal rules and as a normative principle, it is striking that it seems to have gained much of its ground with only relatively muted challenge. In some of the literature there is a tendency to slide from (1) the claim that contract rules are efficient, to (2) the claim that efficiency is the goal of the law, culminating in (3) that contract law *ought* to comply with the efficiency criterion (Veljanovski, 1982, p 141). This reasoning would be flawed even if it were possible to establish efficiency as a rationale of the rules; as this (arguably) ultimately fails, the slide to acceptance of the normative claim is doubly wrong.

These problems with the efficiency rationale do not, however, mean that all economic analysis of contract law can be dismissed. One of the key insights has been the focus not on individual instances posed in the cases, but on the general run of such situations beyond litigation, with particular emphasis on the effects brought about by parties negotiating around a legal rule. This aspiration to connect the rationale of the rule with the working of the rule in reality is characteristic of economic approaches to law in general, not just the efficiency analysis, and it is pursued further in Chapter 4.

FROM UNITARY PRINCIPLES TO CONFLICTING TYPES

Although the efficiency rationale departs from the tradition of conceiving of contract as simply promise based, it shares one feature with both promise and reliance based theories: it attempts to explain contractual obligation by reference to general principles applicable to all contracts. This looks to be the last attempt to explain all of contract law by reference to a master principle. The manifest problems in grounding all contract law on a small number of general principles have led to the development of theories of contract which attempt to grasp the normative content of contract law by recognising that it reflects and embodies conflicting and sometimes contradictory principles rather than persistent coherence.

This kind of approach generally involves setting up pairs of types of ideologies (also called rhetorical modes, motives, ideals of justice) against which the rules and outcomes are measured. An early and influential attempt was that of Kennedy (1976), who distinguished individualism and altruism. If we think of the extreme cases of individualism and altruism as the ends of a spectrum, it is possible to analyse cases or rules and position them on the spectrum. A case like *Smith* v. *Hughes* (1871), where the court confirmed the principle of *caveat emptor* by permitting the seller to acquiesce in the 'self deception' of the buyer about the unsuitability of new oats for feeding to horses, is clearly near the individualist pole. Conversely, the consumer exclusion clause cases in which the courts struck down the clauses appear nearer the altruism pole because of the clear limits they impose on the extent one party can pursue their interest at the expense of the other.

The ideal type approach changes the nature of the intellectual operation which is being performed on the raw material of the law. The search for the general principle with the best fit, with its presumption of coherence and determinacy underwriting the straining towards maximum explanatory power, is located securely within the black letter tradition. The analysis of case law in terms of opposed ideal types is refreshingly free from much of the distortion which follows from the need to pull outcomes under the umbrella of an all embracing master principle – diversity and contradiction is expected, not suppressed. It becomes possible to shift attention beyond the issue of fit to identifying and tracing general ideological change in the law, raising the question of whether profound change in the value orientation of the law has taken place in the twentieth century: ideal types are an indispensable part of grasping change in the law at any level other than the doctrinal events themselves.

An important contribution to the debate about new rationales of contract is the transformation theory proposed by Hugh Collins. In *The Law of Contract* (1993a) Collins argues that the justice conceptions underlying contract law have undergone transformation since the nineteenth century. The gist of his argument is that the justice of exchange which underpinned nineteenth-century law has been superseded in a transformed law of contract by the justice ideals of the social market, which he identifies as the fairness of exchange, individual autonomy and cooperation. Collins aims to restate the modern law in terms of these principles and therefore regards them as *describing* the underlying values of the modern law. Collins's transformation thesis is a contribution to a larger debate in the study of contract law: whether the history of contract law – both doctrine and underlying principle – is best characterised as one of continuity or transformation. An evaluation of Collins's thesis therefore needs to engage with the larger issue of transformation in contract. The pursuit of rationales thus compels us to adopt a historical perspective on the law, and this is pursued in Chapters 5 and 6. But first, we turn to another fertile source of problems for black letter approaches to contract: the investigation of the functioning of contract law in reality.

4
Contract Law and Reality

How important is contract law in reality? This question matters because the claim for the central place occupied by the law of contract in legal education turns in part on the notion that contract law is somehow important in the real world. Some law teachers point out the pervasive nature of the practice of contracting by demonstrating to students how many contracts they make unwittingly each day. The thousands of reported cases – which as students soon learn are a fraction of those litigated – provide evidence in the form of situations where contract law has become embroiled. The textbook's confident generalisation of legal principle and how it applies to the facts can result in the impression that those principles are applied in the sort of situations in which they are applied in the books. The tacit understanding (which the text does not discourage) is that a breach of contract will be followed by reparation in the form indicated by the rules, backed by legal threat or actual legal action if necessary. As we will see, this picture is simply wrong.

The study of the general rules, unsullied by much consideration of the use made of them, persists despite the existence of a large body of empirical work which throws into serious doubt the practical significance of what is studied as the law of contract. The insulation of the traditional study of contract from this work may be due partly to the threat it poses to the viability of the traditional emphasis on general rules. This threat is twofold: it not only dethrones the traditional conception of contract around which the books and courses are still structured, but also points the way to a more sophisticated understanding of the role of law in relation to contractual relationships.

In this chapter I explore the implications of a focus on contracting practice for the understanding of contract law, looking principally at the work of Stewart Macaulay and Ian Macneil.

THE USE AND NON USE OF CONTRACT LAW

The simple idea of investigating the use business people actually make of contract law in their dealings was first systematically pursued by Macaulay.[1] His concern was to discover who uses contract law, when and how; and his method was to interview businessmen and lawyers, mainly those involved in manufacturing. He examined two aspects: the rational planning of the transaction with careful planning for future contingencies, and the use of actual or potential legal sanctions for breach of contract.

In relation to the use of contract in planning, he identified four different issues that people might negotiate, each representing a further stage in the thinking through of the implications of a deal. These were: negotiation of the actual performances of each side (the type and quality of goods, delivery arrangements, payment arrangements); negotiation of the effect of various contingencies on these obligations (for example, what is to happen in the event of a strike); negotiation of what is to happen if one side fails to perform; and the negotiation of legally enforceable consequences. He discovered that although most (but not all) negotiated the actual performances, and a majority negotiated the effect of contingencies, about half of his sample did not negotiate the issue of the consequences of non performance and even fewer the issue of a legal sanction.

In his investigation of the second aspect of the use of contract law – the use of actual or potential legal sanctions – he discovered that the adjustment of exchange relationships and the settling of disputes was even less contractual than the creation of exchanges. It was not just that actual litigation (or threat of it) was rare, but that many business people would actively avoid introducing lawyers into a dispute: 'you can settle any dispute if you keep the lawyers and accountants out of it. They do not understand the give and take needed in business' (p 61). Parties to a dispute would frequently disregard the contract or legal sanctions in negotiating a dispute. For example, although the rules of contract clearly provide that a manufacturer can recover any lost profit if the purchaser pulls out of the contract, Macaulay found that cancellations were accepted as long as any major expenditure actually incurred was covered. The picture that Macaulay paints is one where recourse to adversarial dispute resolution through the translation of the dispute in to one about legal rights was not normal, and was often regarded as having undesirable consequences. This picture of the non use of contract law has been confirmed by a number of studies, including some in the UK, most notably that by Beale and Dugdale (1975).

In assessing the wider significance of such studies, however, we need to bear in mind that they each tell us only about one sector or type of contract: they do not provide a sufficient basis for testing hypotheses about the use of contract law in general. Although there do not appear to be any equivalent studies pointing to the systematic *use* of contract law, it is nevertheless clear that some sectors do appear to generate disproportionate amounts of litigation about contract. A notable example is contracts concerning building and construction and it is instructive to probe the role of contract in this area a little further.

At the planning stage it is usual to use one of the industry wide standard forms produced by a body known as the Joint Contracts Tribunal (JCT). The origins of this body date back to 1870 when the Builders Society and the Royal Institute of British Architects produced a standard form contract. It now also includes organisations representing surveyors, engineers, local authorities and property companies. The family of lengthy standard forms produced by the Joint Contracts Tribunal (JCT80, JCT IFC 84, JCT FF 76 etc) effectively constitute a comprehensive legal framework which balances the interests of the usual participants and into which the particulars of most projects can be fitted. In Macaulay's terms, there appears to be a high degree of 'use' of contract at the planning stage, including lengthy provision for allocating responsibility for the myriad risks to which construction work can give rise (Murdoch and Hughes, 1990).

When disputes arise, however, the use of legal sanctions is far from being the first resort. There are a number of procedures, often known as 'ADR' (alternative dispute resolution), which are typically preferred to the travails of either litigation or even arbitration. For example, most large projects will involve the appointment of a contract administrator (often an architect) as the employer's agent and this person may, in addition, be given power to adjudicate on certain disputes. Also, conciliation, where a third party, initially talking to each side separately, attempts to realign the expectations of the parties, is commonly used. These kinds of ADR may actually be provided for in the standard form: one standard form actually contains a clause obliging the parties to attempt to reach an amicable settlement before going to arbitration. Thus even where there is elaborate contractual planning of the construction project it by no means follows that it is inevitable that contract law will be used for dispute resolution in the sense of litigation taking place (Flood and Caiger, 1993).

So far we have addressed the practical importance of contract in terms of the 'use' that is made of it. Discerning such use, however, is not always straightforward. Macaulay, when he refers to the use of the law of contract, speaks of contract law being used in two ways – as a way of planning a transaction, and as a way of dealing with disputes. Yet it is arguable that he is not justified in treating the use of a written agreement providing for eventualities as a use of the *law* of contract at all: it is logically possible to separate the use of contract as a mechanism of planning from the use of contract law (Vincent-Jones, 1989, p 171). Given Macaulay's finding that law is not necessarily important in the enforcement of contracts, it is perfectly possible for people or firms to treat the drawing up of an agreement as simply a clarification and ordering of what they each propose to do. The fact that the law may recognise it as a contract is a separate issue, and in some contexts the parties to an agreement will take deliberate steps to stipulate that it is not to be enforceable, for example in relation to the sale of securities on the Stock Exchange.[2]

On the other hand, it could be claimed that Macaulay may have underestimated the 'use' of contract law in dealing with disputes. Although actual resort to lawyers was uncommon, does this necessarily mean that contract law was not 'used' in cases where lawyers were not called upon? Perhaps the business people concerned made threats about legal action – surely that would be 'using' the law of contract? Maybe it was not necessary even to mention the threat – the possibility was obvious to all concerned and formed the background against which they dealt. And where people told Macaulay that they complied with contracts in difficult circumstances because it was important to honour a deal rather than fear of legal sanction, perhaps the regime of legal enforcement of contract nevertheless underpinned the persistence of such social norms in business, much as the law against theft may be thought (plausibly) to underpin the honesty which most people appear to exhibit most of the time.

The testing of hypotheses such as these bristles with difficulty. However much we may strive to express the indirect role of law in the constitution and maintenance of social practices in metaphor (reflect, shape, imbricate) the brute fact remains that where we have behaviour which correlates roughly with observance of a rule, it can be extremely problematic to ground statements about the relationship between that rule and the behaviour.

One way of clarifying the role of contract law is to investigate the role of non legal sanctions for non performance in situations where there appears to be relatively little use of contract. What are the factors other than fear of ultimate legal action may which shape the parties' behaviour?

NON LEGAL SANCTIONS IN CONTRACTUAL SITUATIONS

Non legal sanctions can be divided into two broad types (Charny, 1990). First, there is the desire not to jeopardise some advantage which the other contracting party has in their power to withhold. The most simple instance is the taking of a deposit as security for performance, as when a deposit of a fraction of the contract price (typically 10 per cent) is required before a booking or reservation for some good or service is taken. The person making the deposit thus has an incentive to take the good or service reserved to avoid losing the deposit with nothing at all in return. The same concern to avoid withholding of an advantage by the other party can be seen in the desire, identified by Macaulay, to maintain good working relations between the firms to ensure the successful conclusion of a contract between them. An obvious point (but one not difficult to forget when focused on doctrine) is that, when it is in a person's interest for an exchange to take place, it is self interest, rather than legal obligation, that motivates performance. A similar argument applies especially to future dealings, the prospect of which can act (as Macaulay found) as a powerful incentive to smooth over potential disputes in order to maintain a valuable working relationship. The concern to maintain a commercial relationship will be an especially potent sanction whenever market conditions are such that a company is reliant on a small number of large organisations for substantial parts of their business, as for example is the case with many suppliers of large retail chain stores.

The second type of non legal sanction is the desire to maintain a general reputation in terms of the service or goods provided, thereby protecting and stimulating future business. This is distinguishable from the first type because the advantage which it seeks to preserve is not one provided by the other party but one which will be obtained from a range of possible future contracting parties. The reputation may be one that merely needs to be preserved among a small specialist group of regular contractors, or (as in the case of consumer goods) may be disseminated very widely indeed. In the consumer situation the threat to reputation is probably one of the most powerful weapons available (especially when backed up by recourse to publicity in the media) and there seems little doubt that this form of non legal sanction has a far greater role to play in the securing of redress for shoddy goods than either the law of contract or the other kind of legal sanction noted above.

Useful though it can be to focus on non legal sanctions, the very idea of understanding contractual behaviour in terms of sanctions is itself limited. The language of sanctions tends to carry an assumption that parties to a contract are constantly on the look out for an opportunistic escape route, and only carry through with their performance for fear of the consequences which the sanction (legal or non legal) will visit upon them. Also important to the relatively smooth settlement (and avoidance) of disputes, however, is the observance of norms of good faith, trust and cooperation. Respondents in Macaulay's study commonly emphasised the importance of honouring a deal once it was struck. Some commentators would count such norms as non legal sanctions, describing the sanction against lying or breaking trust as the loss of a psychic good such as self esteem or a social good such as friendship (Charny, 1990). Thus ostracism, loss of self esteem, or even guilt may be the 'costs' to be avoided by compliance with such norms. This way of describing how such norms work, however, is misconceived because it obscures what is perhaps their most distinctive feature: that they prevail precisely because they are not treated opportunistically, being instead beliefs which underpin social relations which are cooperative rather than constantly antagonistic. This dimension of contracting behaviour has been explored with great sophistication by Macneil, and his work sheds important light on the non use of contract law.

MACNEIL AND RELATIONAL CONTRACT

Macneil contrasts two types of contract – the discrete transaction and the relational contract – which he sees as the two ends of a continuum.[3] The discrete transaction is one where the parties come together for one transaction and then go their separate ways, so that there is no connection between the individuals concerned, nor any coordination of the performances under the contract with the parties' other activities. Macneil's example is the 'cash purchase of gasoline at a station on the New Jersey Turnpike by someone rarely travelling the road' (Macneil, 1978, p 857). This pure discrete transaction is a simultaneous exchange of goods and money, and so lacks the element of futurity which is created by executory obligations in a contract. The contract, by creating in the present obligations to perform an act in the future, 'projects discreteness into the future'. This is achieved by what Macneil calls *presentiation*. By this is meant the process of treating the future as though it were the present. More familiarly, it means the parties to the contract attempting to anticipate every aspect of the contractual performances by providing exhaustively for the consequences, so that what will happen under all eventualities is rendered certain from the outset. In Macneil's terms, presentiation enhances discreteness because it tends to sever the specific activity with which it is concerned from the flow of social relations of which it is a part.

The opposite pole from the discrete transaction is the relational contract. This is the contract which forms a long term relationship between the parties. It includes not just periodic contracts, such as employment contracts and leases, but also relations such as those between manufacturers and suppliers, or construction firms and subcontractors, indeed any contract which is performed over an extended period of time. Relational contracts are less discrete because they exist over a longer period and are therefore likely to be accompanied by a closer integration of the parties' activities. Presentiation is also likely to be less marked because often it may be neither feasible nor sensible to expect to be able to settle every detail of the conduct of the relationship at the outset: flexibility during the relationship will be necessary. The contrast with discrete contracts was put well by Gordon (1985):

> ... parties treat their contracts more like marriages than one night stands. Obligations grow out of commitment that they have made to one another, and the conventions that the trading community established for such commitments; they are not frozen at the initial moment of commitment, but change as circumstances change; the

object of contracting is not primarily to allocate risks, but to signify a commitment to cooperate. In bad times parties are expected to lend one another support, rather than standing on their rights; each will treat the other's insistence on literal performance as wilful obstructionism; if unexpected contingencies occur resulting in severe losses, the parties are to search for ways of dividing the losses; and the sanction for egregiously bad behaviour is always, of course, refusal to deal again. (p 569)

Instead of rules which minimise the parties' obligations to each other, those of relational contracts require norms which foster cooperation, in particular the preservation of the relationship, readjustment in new circumstances, and the harmonious settlement of disputes. Although terms such as trust and cooperation are used here, it is important to see that there is no suggestion that relational contracting is just a mush of altruism, where self interest has disappeared. The issue is not the existence of self interest, but the form of its expression. Take, for example, the relationship between a main contractor and various subcontractors on a major construction project such as a large bridge. It will be in the self interest of all the firms for the project to be completed successfully, but this will not happen if every technical breach is pounced on as an excuse for terminating or claiming damages. During the course of the project all the parties develop investments in special knowledge and working relationships which cannot simply be replaced if one subcontracting firm is got rid of for breach. The project represents a common means of pursuing self interest, one which is best achieved cooperatively rather than with the constant threat of antagonistic opportunism.

Another way of seeing the nature of the relational contract is as a hybrid between the firm and the discrete market transaction. The firm is a way of organising economic activity without using a market. It is typically characterised by a common purpose which is pursued through a hierarchical system of integrating the efforts of directors, managers, and employees. Because it can draw on cooperation, trust and loyalty as well as high degree of managerial direction and coordination, it is able to operate in certain contexts much more effectively than if it were decomposed into units entering discrete transactions. The relational contract partakes of some of these characteristics within a contractual form.

One of Macneil's most important insights is that not just relational contracting but any contracting at all is only possible if there is a community which has shared understandings and conventions about what participation in exchange relations in a particular field means, which in turn is part of a wider culture in which the practice and varieties of exchange are given meaning. He argues that it is the emphasis on the discrete transaction, seeing it as the product of isolated, individual wills, which obscures the social dimension of contracting behaviour:

> Contract without the common needs created only by society is inconceivable; contract between totally isolated, utility maximising individuals is not contract but war; contract without language is impossible; and contract without social structure and stability is – quite literally – rationally unthinkable, just as man outside society is rationally unthinkable. (1980, p 1)

An express promise or agreement is just one source of contractual obligation, which is interpreted against and supplemented by norms drawn from the social context in which the parties contract. From this point of view, the attempt by Burrows to broaden the meaning of promise – 'a statement or action by which the speaker or actor appears to accept an obligation ...' – can be seen as a way of infusing the individualism of the promise with social meaning drawn from its context. And the reliance theory goes a step further by making the meaning and significance of statement or action depend on the action on the part of others which it prompts. Trying to derive contractual obligation solely from the intentions and actions of parties at the inception of the relationship is like trying to understand a plant by focusing only on the seed from which it grew, without any reference to the environment – soil, climate, microorganisms – which are a precondition and determinant of its flourishing and reproduction.

The analysis of contract in terms of efficiency tends to be oblivious to this point. The conception of the perfect market is an abstraction which is used to identify the causes of failure – especially transaction costs – to which contract law should respond. But from Macneil's point of view, transaction costs are not unwanted friction (as dubbed by economists), more the lubricant which makes exchange possible at all. The point is put well by Campbell and Harris (1993):

> The negotiating, information gathering, organising, and so on within which transactions take place are not *only* costs, they are also the social relations which are essentially facilitative of the transaction. All actions, including transactions, can take place only within a constitutive social system. If one really took away *all* the costs of exchanging, the exchange would not take place cost-free. It simply would not take place at all. (p 178)

RELATIONAL CONTRACT, THE CLASSICAL LAW AND THE BLACK LETTER APPROACH

What are the implications for the understanding of contract law of drawing out the relational dimension of contracting behaviour? First, it helps to explain more fully Macaulay's findings of the non use of contract law. Most simply, litigation and recourse to lawyers can be harmful because it may put the continuance of the relationship at risk, and so undermine an important means of pursuing self interest effectively. But litigation is also avoided because the doctrines of contract law have tended not to reflect relational norms. The law of contract is modelled on contracts which are much nearer the discrete transaction end than the relational end of the continuum, and so are not seen as serving well the parties to a relational contract even where external dispute resolution is required.[4]

The skewing of general contract law towards the discrete transaction which is revealed by a focus on relational contracts throws useful light on the conceptual difficulties which the law has had in dealing in a coherent fashion with the more relational aspects of contractual disputes. An example of the problem is modification of the employment contract, where the application of the common law rules geared to discrete transactions has been given renewed relevance by the introduction of statutory remedies for unfair dismissal. One way an issue about unfair dismissal can arise is when an employee leaves the job after being asked to undertake different work. This may count as a constructive dismissal (and thus potentially trigger a decision on its fairness) if the employee was being required to do something she was not obliged to do under the contract of employment. Tribunals and courts have thus faced the problem of identifying terms: typically there is an incomplete definition of the job obligation at the beginning of employment and, over a period, the work the employee actually does is changed, sometimes coupled with statements from the employer about what the employee may be called upon to do. A common source of difficulty is whether an employee can be expected to work in a place other than that where she was originally employed. The tribunal is then faced with the prospect of sifting this evidence for the definitive contract term defining what the scope of the employee's job actually is. Both the Court of Appeal and the Employment Appeal Tribunal have experienced great difficulty in analysing these situations in orthodox terms using the conventional concepts of consideration and offer and acceptance. Some judges have strained to maintain the clear line (which orthodoxy demands) between the definition of the terms in the original contract and their later modification, while others have given up the struggle and run the issues together. The result has been an incoherence in the decisions which continues because, although the courts have balked at a full application of the orthodox concepts, they have not felt able completely to cut free from them. As Davies and Freedland (1984) put it:

[the] contrast between the lawyer's static model of the formation of terms and the evolutionary character of actual practice enables us to understand why the legal requirement of consideration for each variation of contract and the distinction between variation of an existing contract (requiring fresh consideration) and the replacement of an existing contract by a new one (for which the consideration is supplied by the mutual abandonment of the contract) are obscure and would be rather incongruous if widely applied in practice. (p 299)

The relational approach of Macneil and the functional perspective of Macaulay also have profound implications for the method of study of contract. Most directly, work on the use or operation of the law gives a strong impetus to an instrumental or purposive view of the place of the law of contract. Digging around behind the smooth surface of the general rules and principles allows the law and the reality to which it supposedly refers to be placed neatly side by side. One result is that the assumption that the account of the rules reflects all we need to know about the circumstances of their application is revealed as starkly inadequate. More generally, the elaboration of doctrine by appellate courts is decentred as the main focus of study. The traditional accounts are absorbed in the expressions of contract doctrine found in decisions selected for report on account of their deciding points of legal novelty or significance. The reach of an instrumental approach, on the other hand, extends beyond this, not just to the routine and everyday application of rules in courts, but to the less visible role of law in contractual behaviour. The attention which the traditional accounts lavish on difficult doctrinal points is usually irrelevant from an instrumental perspective. The painstaking unravelling of a case such as *Williams* v. *Roffey* flows from the fact that it appears to breach what was regarded as a settled part of the doctrine of consideration, and commentators on contract law focus particularly on the conceptual conundrums which are posed when principle is ruptured. But from an instrumental point of view, the coherence or otherwise of principle is in itself irrelevant; the only issue is whether it would make any difference in the way the rules were used. The traditional academic concern with conceptual housekeeping – promoting coherence and consistency in legal concepts – is therefore marginalised by an instrumental approach.

Once we set off down the road of looking at the working of contract law in reality we find before long that the object of study we started with (general contract law) and the traditional approach to it (exposition of doctrine) are left behind and replaced by both different objects of study and different approaches to them. The instrumental approach, therefore, does not just not generate alternative objects and methods of study, but also directly undermines the coherence of the conception of contract law on which the texts and courses are modelled. The result is that much of the recent and most sophisticated work on contract is in places only tangentially concerned with general contract doctrine.[5]

The contract law which is modelled on discrete rather than relational transactions is commonly referred to as 'classical'.[6] This is part of a generalised use of the term to refer to the body of general law which took shape in the nineteenth century and which still structures the standard texts. The classical law is also seen as the origin of the idea of promise as being at the centre of contractual obligation. It has come to be seen as a conception of contract which was the creation of laissez-faire capitalism and the embodiment of the shortcomings with which contract is charged. Certainly, the idea of classical contract has played an important part in debates on both the rationales of contract and the legal response to relational contract discussed in this chapter. It has become the medium through which debates about contract have gained a historical dimension, and it is to that aspect of contract's story that we now turn.

5
The Invention of Classical Contract

An engagement with history is a necessary part of any critical understanding of contract. Compared with other legal subjects, the traditional study of contract is one of the least touched by historical analysis, yet is in much need of it. In some subjects a short history is indispensable to orientate the modern appearance of the subject, perhaps most clearly in the case of land law where the structure of law and equity can only be understood chronologically. In the case of contract there is no introductory story or origin myth – we just plunge straight in. Why? Partly because the underlying ideas of contract are more immediately available as a matter of common sense. Also, the structure of contract rules and principles is sufficiently abstract, coherent, and self referential (rather like the rules of chess) for it to be able to stand plausibly on its own without reference to the context – both legal and social – out of which it grew. This appearance of autonomy both reinforces the normative appeal of agreement and consent as the foundational principles of liability and deprives the traditional understanding of the law of any perspective which can introduce competing grounds of obligation. In this sense contract law conceals its history and it is one of the tasks of a critical understanding to penetrate that smooth deflecting surface.

Historical understanding can also demystify the apparent solidity and seeming inevitability of the shape of the modern law by displaying it as the product of a process of development. Tracing the emergence of the mature form can help to recover the sense of open endedness with which earlier generations of lawyers encountered the law, and this in itself can act as an antidote to the closure of the possibilities of change which the slow speed of change in general contract doctrine can exert.

History is also indispensable in any appraisal of transformation theories of contract. The modern understanding of the law of contract has been enormously influenced by relatively recent work on the eighteenth- and nineteenth- century history of contract. Until the 1970s, the study of contract was divided between those concerned with the modern law and a relatively small group of scholars interested in the evolution of the early precursors of contract before the industrial revolution. Where contract law of the eighteenth and nineteenth centuries was addressed it was usually ahistorically as a part of the modern law which happened to reach further back.

This changed in the 1970s principally as a result of the work of Horwitz (1974), Simpson (1975a; 1979) and Atiyah (1979). They treated the eighteenth and nineteenth centuries as a period of rapid change rather than as the repository of case law the main function of which was to be fitted where possible into modern expository accounts of the law. The switch from regarding the nineteenth century as present to regarding it as history relaxed the presumption of determinacy embodied in the expository tradition and that period of contract history was looked at afresh. In the process, a kind of received wisdom emerged about the flourishing of a particular conception of contract law – classical contract law – by the middle of the nineteenth century, albeit neighboured by controversy over what preceded it and what followed; some scholars saw transformation more easily than others. Classical contract was therefore invented in two senses: it was the nineteenth-century intellectual product of the judges and treatise writers, but it was only identified as such by the invention of the construct of the 'classical law' in the 1970s. As we shall see, the emergence of the modern construct was a vehicle both for the criticism of the model of contractual obligation it embodied, and for the attribution to it of greater intellectual coherence than before.

The first step in unravelling the history of contract is to look more closely at the idea of classical contract law which has so dominated modern perceptions of the history: we will consider the broad contours of this dominant view before turning to probe the story in more depth.

THE IDEA OF A CLASSICAL LAW OF CONTRACT

A number of modern writers on contract have made the transformation of contract law in the nineteenth century the linchpin of their account. The version of contract dubbed the classical law or classical model is seen as the mature form which emerged out of the less structured pre classical clutter of cases infused by a conception of substantive fairness, and which was followed by fragmentation at the hands of the regulatory state of the twentieth century. Although I will be strongly disputing its meaning and importance, there can be no denying the influence of the classical law in shaping broad perceptions of the development of the law of contract. We will examine the idea of the classical law in more detail by focusing on three dimensions: its content, the values on which it was based, and the type of transactions where its normative appeal was most plausible.

The leading feature which distinguished the classical law from what went before was the generality of the scope of its rules. By the third quarter of the nineteenth century the law of contract was regarded as consisting of rules which were not only general in form but also applied to most actual contracts. Before the emergence of the classical law there was no sense that the multifarious relations which became later analysed as contracts were instances within the general category of contract: rules were more situation specific with little attempt to develop an overall theory of liability.

It was a necessary property of the generality of the rules that they were abstract. They were addressed to individuals in general (offeror, seller, etc) rather than to individuals standing in specific social relationships to others. As Lawrence Friedman (1967) put it:

> Pure contract doctrine is blind to details of subject matter and person. It does not ask who buys and sells, and what is bought and sold ... [c]ontract law is an abstraction – what is left when all particularities of person and subject matter are removed. (p 7)

Generality and abstractness were ushered in by the spread of the governing idea that both the terms of the contract and its quality of being legally binding was grounded in an exercise of the parties' wills – the 'will theory' of contract. Although the subjectivity of the will theory in its pure form was fairly soon attenuated by emphasising the appearance rather than the reality of consent, its legacy endured in the idea that a contract was formed by the agreement of the parties. A bare agreement – conceptualised as an exchange of promises – came to be seen as a sufficient basis of enforceability, without the necessity for any payment, performance or acts in reliance. This model of contract came to be seen as typical, with the result that all manner of situations were standardly analysed as bilateral executory contracts: bilateral because both parties were bound at once, and executory because the obligations arose before anything was done.

The second dimension of the classical law was the broad moral and political values on which it drew for its justification. At the root was the idea that the only legal obligations imposed on individuals were those not to harm others, which chiefly meant, as far as the civil law was concerned, duties not to interfere with another's property or person. Beyond this, legal obligation could only be incurred by the individual's act of will in agreeing or consenting to be bound. Thus the will theory not only provided the content of contract doctrine with a justification but also connected it with prevailing ideological conceptions of relationships between individuals within a society increasingly penetrated by market relations.

A corollary of the individualistic basis of the classical law was freedom of contract, so that parties were free not only to decide whether to incur consensual obligations at all, but also to determine the extent and content of such obligations. The role of the court was that of neutral referee or umpire, responsible only for enforcing the parties' agreement and not imposing duties which were not agreed nor removing those which had been agreed.

Where it was necessary to go beyond the parties' wills and derive the content of obligation from norms of behaviour, then the norms adopted tended to assume a robust attitude to a person's ability to look after their own interests and would permit advantage to be taken of poor business sense. This was particularly evident in relation to the development of the objective theory of agreement which attended to the appearance of agreement where subjective agreement was not total.

The values which underpinned the classical law were at their most persuasive when applied to something like the following idealised picture of the making of a contract:

- the parties are dealing at arm's length (that is, on a commercial basis without any other connection);
- they are of equal bargaining power (that is, they have similar wealth, knowledge and negotiating skill);
- they negotiate each term of the contract so that the terms are all the product of their deliberation;
- the contract terms provide clearly for all eventualities;
- the parties only come together for one contract (there is no continuing relationship).

Although the classical law could be most plausibly applied to these circumstances, its importance lay in the way it reached out beyond these circumstances and became the default body of rules to apply across a wide range of social relations which came to be regarded as more or less contractual.

In Chapter 6 I argue that the conventional wisdom which aligns classical contract with the more general triumph of contract is very overstated, and that the very idea of the classical law has come to act as an obstacle to the understanding of what is distinctive about modern contract. However, although I am sceptical about many of the transformation theorists' claims, neither do I find the traditionalists' denial of significant change plausible: it is a question of how change is best portrayed. The starting point in the pursuit of that general issue is the circumstances of the emergence of the classical law.

THE EMERGENCE OF THE CLASSICAL LAW: EARLY HISTORY

The question of how the classical law developed – in particular what precisely it evolved from – has excited controversy among historians. In part this is because some of the issues at stake – about the role of consent and substantive justice, the potential of transformatory change, and the extent to which the law reflected economic change – still reverberate in modern debates about contract law. Given the very great level of detail at which the historians' arguments are conducted, it is hardly appropriate in the present work to offer a detailed analysis of or argument for or against any particular view. My primary aim is to provide an overview of the key issues to enable their relevance to the story of contract to become plain, although I shall in the process suggest a degree of synthesis between some of the views put forward.

The history of the emergence of a systematic, abstract, general contract doctrine is in part the history of the systematising of the common law upon substantive principle which in the nineteenth century replaced the organisation according to procedural categories based on the old forms of action. The change was therefore not just a change in the content of the law but a change in the form in which the law was expressed.

It is generally reckoned that the origin of modern contract law lay in the rise of the form of action known as assumpsit at the expense of the older medieval forms of action of covenant and debt. Covenant lay for the breach of an agreement under seal, and could only be enforced by specific performance. Debt lay for the breach of an undertaking to pay a specific sum of money. Although these forms of action enabled some consensual obligations to be enforced, both were procedurally cumbersome and it was this feature which created the space for the development of assumpsit out of the action of trespass on the case from the fourteenth century. To begin with, assumpsit was limited to claims for misfeasance (undertakings badly performed). It was extended to cover actions for nonfeasance in the sixteenth century and after *Slade's* case (1602) could be used in place of debt for the recovery of money. It thus became a way in which actions could readily be brought for breach of informal promises.[1]

The doctrine of consideration developed from the sixteenth century as a means of defining when action would lie in assumpsit, that is which promises were enforceable, although consideration at first meant something rather different from what it later came to mean. A great deal of the rest of modern contract doctrine did not emerge until the nineteenth century – especially offer and acceptance, intention to create legal relations, mistake, misrepresentation, incorporation of express and implied terms, rules about damages. But by the eighteenth century there was a substantial body of law about the scope of assumpsit and it is around this that the controversy about the emergence of the classical law centres.

THE HORWITZ/SIMPSON DEBATE

It was Horwitz (1974) who injected controversy into the hitherto underdeveloped study of modern (post 1700) contract history. He argued that a transformation took place in the law of contract around the beginning of the nineteenth century. His key theme was that a preindustrial contract law, based on ideas of substantive fairness, was replaced by a contract law which derived obligation from the meeting of the wills of the parties. He saw the transformation lying in a number of important doctrinal shifts which took place around 1800. These included a fuller recognition of the executory contract, the demise of the requirement that consideration be of equivalent value to the performance received in return, and the protection of the expectation interest by the award of expectation damages. The stripping out of conceptions of substantive fairness and the concomitant basing of obligation on agreement were claimed to make the law a more suitable vehicle for capitalist development by shifting the courts to a passive and supposedly neutral role. Also, as expectations created by the contract came to be protected, contracts could develop beyond their traditional function as a means of transferring title in goods or land to being an important part of an economy where wealth lay in expectations rather than in possessions.

Horwitz also put forward a controversial theory of how this came about. In essence, he claimed that the transformation of contract rules took place as a piece of deliberate judicial law changing intended to favour commercial interests. When the main changes had been achieved by about 1850 this was followed by a period of formalisation in which the transformed law was frozen against unwelcome change.

Simpson (1979) produced a coruscating critique of Horwitz's transformation theory, testing it by careful and remorseless examination of the underlying evidence. The main thrust of Simpson's case is that the doctrines which were said to mark the emergence of the new law can be traced much further back – into the seventeenth century or beyond – and also that the notion of a pre existing equitable conception of contract is not sustained by the evidence. Perhaps most fundamentally, Simpson argues that Horwitz's conception of a transformation of one body of contract law into another is misconceived: what happened was the creation of new doctrine where little existed before. Between the appearance of Horwitz's account and Simpson's critique, Atiyah broadly supported Horwitz's view in *Rise and Fall of the Freedom of Contract* (Atiyah, 1979).[2] We now turn to consider in detail two central aspects of the controversy: the idea that exchanges should be substantively fair, and the recognition of executory contracts.

THE FAIRNESS OF THE EXCHANGE

Horwitz argued that in the eighteenth century there was a general rule that consideration had to be adequate in the sense of proportionate value to the thing given. He talks of a well established doctrine in chancery that specific performance would be refused where consideration was inadequate, and a rule in the common law courts in sale that warranties of fitness were implied even where nothing was said, the so called sound price doctrine. Simpson's response is to demonstrate that there are few cases that come near to establishing this, and those that do are obscure, explicable on other grounds, or have simply been misinterpreted (Simpson, 1979, p 561).

Atiyah's approach, although favouring the general notion of an equitable theory of contract, is less sweeping than that of Horwitz. He argues that in a number of specific situations the courts were concerned with fairness of an exchange and would refuse to enforce contracts which were grossly unfair. Thus infants (not then a statutory exception), expectant heirs, and sailors were all given sympathetic treatment, probably because such individuals were in a position to sign away assets for which they were unused to being responsible. Critics of Atiyah's discussion of substantive fairness have pointed to many instances where eighteenth-century courts were not concerned with fairness in contracts (Barton, 1987; Hamburger, 1989). Such criticism certainly damages the claim that there was a general concern with fairness, but does not interfere with a conclusion that, although there was concern with the adequacy of consideration in some situations, there was no *general* rule stating that adequacy was either necessary or (as was later established) unnecessary. It is arguable that there was a shift from a variety of approaches to a position where a single one, the classical rejection of the relevance of adequacy, dominated.[3]

THE RECOGNITION OF EXECUTORY CONTRACTS

The second matter of detail is the recognition of the existence of a contract when it is still executory, that is before any performance has taken place. As the enforcement of an executory contract can only be traced to what the parties have agreed rather than actually done, its recognition in contract has been seen as one of the hallmarks of the recognition of the will theory. Horwitz argued that the process whereby the executory exchange became enforceable was not complete until about 1800, the process marking the transition from a title theory of exchange, where the contract transfers present values, to one where it creates future values through binding expectations of performances. Simpson argued, however, that executory contracts were recognised as early as 1577. Atiyah (1979) broadly follows Horwitz, but makes the important point that the recognition of executory contracts is not a single event but comprises a number of elements the recognition of which may be spread over time. Thus the case from 1577 cited by Simpson (*West* v. *Stowell*) concerned the enforceability of a bet on the outcome of an archery contest and appears to be the first to contemplate that mutual promises could be consideration for each other.[4] However, the recognition at this time that a promise could be consideration for the enforcement of another promise falls short of any full recognition of executory contracts. As Simpson has pointed out, this did not mean that during the sixteenth and seventeenth centuries a contract so made was seen as binding from the moment of agreement: in fact there is no discussion of the question of *when* the promise or contract becomes binding until the invention of the doctrine of offer and acceptance in the early years of the nineteenth century (Simpson, 1975a). Atiyah argues that the full recognition of the executory contract arrives only when the courts are prepared to award expectation damages for the breach of a contract which was wholly executory in the sense that it had neither been performed (even in part) nor relied upon. Although Simpson is correct to point out that the expectation interest was long recognised in the award of specific performance (Simpson, 1979), the recognition of expectation *damages* takes that recognition an important step further. Where a defendant has been in breach in not delivering goods or conveying land, then specific performance of the transfer of assets will be as good for a buyer as a damages award for additional cost of a replacement performance: in both cases the plaintiff's expectation of gain under the contract is being protected. The two remedies are not equivalent, however, where there is consequential loss, for example a loss occasioned by the unavailability of a profit earning chattel, or a buyer's lost resale in a falling market. Neither of these are remediable by a decree of specific performance because the plaintiff's loss is not extinguished by a replacement performance.

Atiyah argues that the transition to the executory contract lasted at least until the end of the eighteenth century. Thus the dispute between Horwitz and Simpson can be recast as one about where one places the threshold of recognition – that promises could be consideration for each other, when the timing of enforcement becomes an issue, or the award of expectation damages.

This dispute has been a charged one, in part because some have seen it as being about whether contract law is explicable as a reflex of economic change, or even about how the investigation of legal history should be conducted. Those unable to conduct their own research into eighteenth century contract law may feel disabled before a debate so well ballasted with footnotes. Nevertheless, I suggest (with trepidation) that it is possible, without entering the lists on one side or the other, to use the engagement to clarify a number of important issues.

Horwitz's thesis and therefore Simpson's reply (less so Atiyah) seem to concern issues about when some classical doctrine first appears or is first recognised. This is weak ground for Horwitz to defend because for his thesis to be falsified it only needs the odd case to be dug up that is inconsistent. Partly for this reason Simpson's critique of Horwitz's thesis of a transformation of an equitable theory of contract seems persuasive. What Simpson has done is to clear off the table a rather extreme form of the transformation thesis, leaving behind plenty of questions about the precise nature of the eighteenth-century law and practice concerning those relations which came to be labelled contractual by the classical law. Simpson is not proposing a 'no change' model, however, and it is the nature and extent of change that must be pursued. We can, for example, dispense with Horwitz's idea of defining the 'recognition of executory contracts' as a crucial threshold. However if one defines and therefore dates the recognition of the wholly executory contract, it is arguably not so much when a doctrine is first *recognised* which is most important as when it becomes prevalent or dominant in the sense that it is generally followed.[5]

A plausible hypothesis, which fits with the evidence presented by Horwitz, Simpson and Atiyah, is that what preceded the classical law was not just less substantive doctrine, but doctrine that was not homogeneous in terms of the values which it expressed. It is not satisfactory to suggest (as Horwitz does) that an equitable conception prevailed, but neither will it do to suggest that such conceptions had no part to play in the law: they clearly did in the manner of at least some of the examples quoted by Atiyah. It is possible to look at the general rules of the classical law and declare with confidence (for example) that consideration did not have to be adequate in any of the situations covered, say by the time of *Eastwood* v. *Kenyon* (1840). But when we go back behind the formation of such a general rule we find that the situations later covered by it are covered by situation-specific rules which do not necessarily produce similar outcomes. Within eighteenth-century contract law, and indeed earlier, there coexisted elements of substantive fairness which would lead courts to rewrite bargains, and strong consent related elements where courts would leave bargains well alone. The story of the rise of the classical law is in part the story of the homogenising of the law of transactions by its imperialistic tendencies.

Despite the controversy on the issue of the precursors of the classical law of contract, Simpson agrees with Horwitz and Atiyah that the idea of contract based on agreement, seen as a convergence of the parties' wills, only became the dominant conception in the nineteenth century, and that it was the will theory of contract which fostered the development of an abstract body of general rules structured around the idea of agreement.[6] The homogenising process whereby the classical law of contract was first constructed and then came to occupy a dominant role in the legal conceptualisation of social relations can be broken down into two aspects.

FROM PROMISE TO CONTRACT

The first aspect is the shift in lawyers' perceptions from thinking of breach of promise as the gist of assumpsit to thinking in terms of a breach of contract. The development of doctrine about offer and acceptance after *Adams* v. *Lindsell* (1818) is symptomatic of this change. Previously the only sense in which an action in assumpsit was about an expression of individual will was the fact a person chose to make the promise (Simpson, 1975a, p 260). There was no reference in the law to any necessary equivalent consent or agreement from the other party. But the introduction of acceptance as a requirement meant that the obligation was regarded as created by the convergence of two wills, and an important consequence of this was that the resulting obligation was no longer contained in the promise but a *contract*. The importance of this change is that it facilitated the detachment of the content of obligation from actual promises which had been made. The obligations thus came to form a contract which was distinct from the utterances or behaviour of either side because it only had an abstract or conceptual existence. In this way the term 'contract', which had often been applied to a particular physical manifestation (a written contract), was rendered abstract and could be transferred to all manner of situations where there was less formal agreement or no agreement at all.

This process of abstraction is sometimes called the *reification* of contract. This can be seen in the way that contractual analysis came to be organised in terms of the life cycle of an ideal contract which had a moment of formation, a content of obligation created by the parties' agreement, and which came to an end (was discharged) by performance or breach. This reified legal analysis of contract became embedded in the structure of the early texts and became a template for the analysis of particular instances in which the issues of formation, terms, and breach became nodes in the edifice of concepts which was erected on the foundations provided by the idea of agreement. The agreement of the parties became both the source of the content of the obligations and the reason why the parties are bound by these obligations. For example, the content of the obligations were no longer to be found in actual promises but in *terms*. These were well fitted to go beyond the scope of undertakings made expressly by the person to be bound and, where terms were not explicit, obligations could be drafted in by the use of implied terms, grounded in the intentions of the parties or commercial usage. And the incorporation of written terms in a standard form became normal despite the fact that the other party was typically unaware of their frequently Draconian content.

The idea of contract as simply derivable from agreement gradually exerted a gravitational force on the elements of contract doctrine so that they became aligned in a more ordered way along the axis of agreement. This had various consequences. One was that the base of the doctrine was narrowed so that everything was regarded as ultimately resting on the parties' wills, and this became a necessary and (virtually) sufficient condition of enforceability. Contract law severed many of its connections with other sources of norms about how disputes in the situations which came to be regarded as contractual should be resolved. One result was the eclipse of that part of the law of obligations now known as restitution. Thus claims for money paid under mistake of fact, or the recovery of money paid under an ineffective contract, or a claim for reasonable remuneration for the provision of goods or services in the absence of a contract, all came to be regarded as an adjunct of the law of contract. Although in none of these cases could the claim be based on a promise or agreement, they were regarded as resting on an implied contract theory. The consequence of this approach – described by the leading authority on restitution as a 'meaningless, irrelevant and misleading anachronism' (Goff and Jones, 1986, 10) – was that the proper recognition of the basis of such obligation was stifled. And although such claims survived, others were defeated by what now appears a perverse formalism. For example, in *Cowern* v. *Nield* (1912) a plaintiff who paid a minor for goods which he did not receive (they were part undelivered and part lawfully rejected) could not recover the price paid: the minor did not have capacity to enter the contract and therefore, under the Infants' Relief Act 1874, no action could be brought that derived from the contract. The story of the recognition of restitutionary claims provides an instructive counterpoint to the larger story of the development of modern contract, and we will examine it in Chapter 10.

THE GENERALISATION OF CONTRACT

The second aspect of the spread of the classical law was the way it became generalised and therefore applied to a wider and wider range of situations. The model of contractual obligation based on the executory contract came to be used as a kind of template upon which other situations were superimposed. It carried with it not only the structure of concepts but also the primacy of agreement and freedom of contract, tending to squeeze out other norms. The result was a con-tractualisation of relationships which had not hitherto been regarded as contractual but came to be so regarded when the classical law was applied to them. The transition from master and servant to the employment contract is a prominent example, as also are the common callings such as carrier, innkeeper, or farrier. The history of the position of the common carrier provides a good illustration of the process of contractualisation (Adams, 1983; Fletcher, 1932; Kahn-Freund, 1965).

In the middle of the eighteenth century the status of common carrier meant three things: carriers were bound to carry goods of the sort they professed to carry; the maximum rate was fixed, usually by local justices; and the carrier was liable for loss to the goods carried unless caused by act of God or the King's enemies. These rules about the status of the common carrier were not regarded as arising from any contract but from the common law or custom of the realm (*Forward v. Pittard* (1785)).

It became increasingly widespread from the middle of the eighteenth century for carriers to exhibit notices stating they would not be liable for the loss of valuables unless a higher rate for the carriage of them was paid, and the issue arose of whether these notices could modify the carrier's common law duties. These notices were generally given effect by the courts following the decision in *Gibbon v. Paynton* (1769) where the defendant was not liable for the loss of a nail bag containing £100 which had been hidden in hay and not declared. Bills and notices containing the limitation had been posted widely and it was common knowledge that a premium was payable for carrying money. The court held that the defendant was not liable, not for the modern reason that the notice was incorporated as a term of the contract, but because the carrier had not been paid an adequate premium to bear the higher risk: 'the reward ought to be proportionate to the risque' (Lord Mansfield). The courts would reject this argument if it appeared from the facts that the carrier ought to have realised the value of undeclared goods (*Beck v. Evans* (1812)), but they were prepared to enforce such notices on this basis. The possibility of the carrier limiting liability for a defined list of valuables was put into statutory form by the Carriers Act 1830.

However, the courts did not yet give the same treatment to notices which purported to exclude liability for negligence. These eventually gained recognition on the basis of being part of a 'special contract' which took the place of the usual carrier's obligation. This development appears to have occurred in *Wyld v. Pickford* (1841) where Parke B held that the traditional inviolable carrier's liability for negligence only applied where the carrier insisted on the full price set for carriage by the justices. Where the carrier accepted less he was entitled to insist on his own terms which became a special contract and effectively ousted the traditional obligations attaching to the status of carrier. This development was pressed further in *Carr v. Lancashire and Yorkshire Rly* (1852) where a horse was fatally injured in a horse box by negligent shunting on the defendants' railway. The court regarded the notice excluding liability for negligence as 'the foundation of the contract between the parties' (Parke B). The prospect of fixing a railway company with the obligations of a common carrier seemed distant:

> If it had been the intention of the plaintiff to make the defendants liable as common carriers he ought to have tendered them a reasonable sum for the carriage of the chattel, and, upon their refusal to carry, to have brought his action for not carrying. (Parke B)

Martin B was in no doubt about the courts' role in relation to the contract:

> We cannot enter into the question of what was passing in the mind of the owner of the horse when he assented to the terms; we must look only at the notice ... We have nothing to do except to carry out this contract; the parties concerned, and not ourselves, are to judge of the inconvenience. (p 716)

In this way the status of common carrier was replaced by contract as the effective source of obligation. It marks an important stage in the triumph of contract because it is an example of contractual norms actually *displacing* the imposed obligations which had been regarded as incidents of the relationship. For the first time we see a clause in a printed standard form, prepared by one party to protect their interest but with which the other is unfamiliar, being accepted as the manifestation of agreement between the parties.

The decision in *Carr* and similar cases led to claims that the railways were abusing their market power, and the Railway and Canal Traffic Act 1854 provided that exclusion clauses in carriage of goods contracts were only effective if reasonable. As was increasingly to happen, the rules of a general classical contract law were varied in part for a particular kind of contract. But this opt out from the general rules left behind the accumulated doctrine in the notice cases and it was this, although it had been thought unacceptable in relation to the carriage of goods, which developed into the classic reasonable notice test in *Parker* v. *South Eastern Railway* (1877), It was also the basis of what now seems the extraordinary decision in *Thompson* v. *LMS* (1930), where the plaintiff was deprived of compensation for serious injury inflicted by the railway company's negligence.[7]

This example of contractualisation illustrates how the idea of the abstract contract, formed from the wills of parties, became a template on which transactions could be superimposed so giving a ready made way of determining the issue. But it is important to see what this left behind. In the late eighteenth and early nineteenth century in cases such as *Gibbon* v. *Paynton* (1769) the judges developed the old principles of carriers' liability in a way that took account of notices but which remained in contact with a conception of substantive fairness. Agreement became relevant but not determinative. But over the question of liability for negligence in the cases at the time of

Carr (1852) the judges, by embracing the abstract idea of contract embodied in the classical law, effectively gave away any means of arbitrating on the reasonableness or justice on the content of the terms. The specific power to do this was partially handed back to them in the 1854 Act, but the common law doctrines constructed in the process remained to haunt later generations.

Perhaps the most important impetus behind contractualisation came from the fact that the classical law was so abstract that it formed a presumptive or default body of rules to apply to any relationship which it could identify – according to its principles – as contractual. Before the advent of the classical law it was possible, when a case of first impression arose, for the court to use the looser preclassical doctrines to develop principles that were situation specific. But the triumph of the classical law meant that the scope for developing such rules was reduced and that the ready made body of rules generated outcomes which were grounded principally on agreement rather than on any other substantive norms which might otherwise have influenced the outcome. As with the case of the common carrier, situations became assimilated to the general rules of the classical law.

THE ROLE OF THE TREATISE

An important means through which the influence of the classical law was exerted was the treatise. It is this, in relatively unchanged and much cloned form, that continues to structure modern understanding of the law of contract. We have already seen that at the time of Blackstone's *Commentaries* (1765–69) contract was not regarded as a separate legal subject. By the end of the nineteenth century it had become the preeminent example of a systematic body of law, and had stimulated attempts to systematise the remainder of the law of obligations under the rubric of tort. A large part of the responsibility for this intellectual achievement lay with the treatise writers who attempted to state in a much more systematic form than hitherto the general rules of contract. The first treatise to deal with the whole law of contract was Powell (1790) and there was a steady stream of similar works throughout the nineteenth century. These works contributed to the embedding in legal culture of the classical law of contract as *the* law of contract. They helped develop the framework of general concepts out of the decisions the courts supplied, thus rendering the principles more systematic and coherent than they might otherwise have been (Simpson, 1975a; 1981).

The work of the treatise writers was given wider scope by the abolition of the forms of action by the Common Law Procedure Act 1852. Until then the organisation and categorisation of law was still rooted in the procedural forms in which actions had to be framed in the various courts. The result of the abolition of these forms was that the structure of the law could better reflect principles of liability rather than the well worn but arbitrary ruts of the ancient forms of action. By the end of the nineteenth century, contract had emerged as the preeminent part of the law of obligations, with tort containing (albeit with less coherence) the remainder.

The treatise writers were instrumental in the law of contract becoming not just an area of law but a *subject* which became an increasingly important focus of study by trainee lawyers. As study of the substantive law supplemented and then rivalled the study of procedure it became the norm for students to encounter a foundational legal subject such as contract as a coherent whole at a formative stage in their career. Although the experience of the early treatise writers (and other lawyers of their generation) had been one of imposing a system across a mass of loosely ordered and sometimes conflicting cases, for students the experience was the reverse. They came to see (as students still do today) the abstract principles of the classical law as constituting the law of contract, and the cases as the instances which bore them out: in Danzig's striking phrase, the cases were the 'fruits on a conceptual tree' (Danzig, 1975, p 250). The classical conception of the law of contract thus became part of the basic intellectual furniture of lawyers from the late nineteenth century, in the process reinforcing its influence as the dominant model of contractual obligation.

The influence of the classical law, especially through the textbooks, was clarified by the work of the modern legal historians in the 1970s, no doubt in part stimulated by a recognition that the general rules traditionally regarded as comprising the law of contract were becoming increasingly and visibly marginalised by the development of more special rules applying to particular situations. Yet the paradoxical result of the crystallisation of the history of contract in terms of the classical law was that, although it was seen as out of date by the end of the twentieth century, it was only then regarded as having had an intellectual coherence and importance in its nineteenth-century heyday. Moreover, this impression was enhanced by contract law seemingly being connected to both the increasing functional importance of the practice of contracting in a vigorous capitalist economy and the philosophical arguments in favour of the laissez-faire approach to the role of the state in the economy and the primacy of individual responsibility which were said to underpin it.

For these reasons, the classical law is seen as the linchpin in the modern understanding of contract. I argue in the next chapter that there are strong grounds for doubting both the intellectual coherence and the practical significance of classical contract, and that the conception of classical contract law should not therefore dominate our understanding of modern contract law and its origins.

6
The Triumph of Contract and the Classical Law

In this chapter I will argue that the significance of the emergence of the classical law in the nineteenth century has been very overstated. The placing of classical contract at the forefront of our understanding of modern contract, rooted in place by its apparent umbilical connection to both dominant ideology and economic practice, has distorted our understanding of what has been happening. The classical law has been cast as the centre piece in transformation theories of contract: the transformation identified by Horwitz which resulted in classical contract, and the transformation identified by Collins which saw its eclipse. It will be claimed that these transformations have been overstated, and that important threads of continuity and other dimensions of change are obscured by an emphasis on the classical law as the fulcrum of change. We begin with a brief examination of the connections between contract and capitalism which have come to be treated almost as axiomatic.

CONTRACT AND THE DEVELOPMENT OF CAPITALISM

The core of the conventional wisdom is that the development of the law of contract can be seen as clearly related to fundamental changes which took place between the sixteenth and nineteenth centuries in prevailing forms of economic and social organisation. The work of the German social theorist Max Weber has been particularly influential in shaping perceptions of these changes, and the distinction he drew between status and purposive contracts usefully illustrates some of the key points.

For Weber, the general idea of voluntary agreement as the basis of obligation was not new, and could be found in status contracts such as marriage. Although agreement might be a part of bringing the new status into being, once established it carried with it recognised incidents, involved much more than a glancing economic contact and came to define a person's role and relations to others. Purposive contracts, on the other hand, were money contracts entered into with strangers to achieve specific economic ends. For example, the coordination of factory production meant the making of contracts with suppliers, partners, shareholders, bankers, workers and purchasers, each of whom in turn would be connected in a latticework of transactions concerned with such things as the import of raw materials, the wholesaling to retail outlets and so forth, and, in the case of the workers, the purchase of the means of life. Weber saw the purposive contract effectively replacing older forms of social relations in which the status contracts figured, especially those associated with the agrarian household economy. There, neither labour nor consumption were wholly money based, and the assignment of tasks was based on traditional patriarchal patterns and roles. Buying and selling would occur, but be relatively peripheral to the mainly self sufficient household community (Malcolmson, 1981; Fox, 1974).

Although purposive contracts were by no means novel as early as the sixteenth century, it has been argued that the role of such contracts was transformed in the eighteenth century. Atiyah and Horwitz have argued in similar terms that until the eighteenth century the use of contract as an economic instrument was mainly as a device for the transfer of interests in property. Thereafter the role of contract in creating *future* rights became predominant, reflecting the increasingly widespread use of practices such as selling stock, trading in goods in transit or not yet in existence, borrowing, and the creation of various types of negotiable paper. Wealth consisted increasingly of promises of future performance rather than things or land in present possession. The spread of market relations and the increasing dominance of the contract as a form of social relations have been seen as key features in the accounts which many theorists have provided of the emergence of capitalism, to the extent that precapitalist society is frequently described as precontractual society (Fox, 1974).[1]

The conventional wisdom on the role of contract and the emergence of capitalism stretches further than the recognition that contract as a social institution becomes centrally important. In addition, it is commonly claimed that there are both functional and ideological connections between the emergence of capitalism and the law of contract.

The functional connection lies in the role of contract law in providing a reliable system of enforceable exchanges. It can be argued that the existence of the legal sanction for breach enables those engaged in commercial dealings to embark on enterprises in the secure knowledge that they will be paid, receive goods, etc as agreed, or damages in default.

The ideological connection is said to lie in the close association between the development of the will theory of contract (including the spread of rhetoric of freedom of contract) in many nineteenth-century contract cases, and the body of political philosophy (commonly labelled liberal) espousing the same values. Atiyah has argued that the ideas of classical political economy, especially liberal individualism and the importance of unrestricted markets, variously expounded in the works of Hobbes, Locke, Adam Smith and Bentham in particular shaped the minds of some of those lawyers who became senior judges in the middle of the nineteenth century, most notably Baron Bramwell (Atiyah, 1979, p 294). The claim is that these ideas not only shaped many of the key institutional reforms (the new poor law, the movement toward free trade, the relaxation of controls on usury and limited liability), but actually had a hand in the moulding of the law of contract.

The significance of the spread of classical contract law is thus reinforced by being connected with the functional and ideological change associated with capitalism, a connection which tends to confer even greater coherence and purpose on the classical law. Slightly para-doxically, an institution which approaches a closed system of highly abstract doctrine is, when placed into a functional and ideological context, reinforced rather than weakened in terms of its coherence as an intellectual system. Some recent work suggests there are strong grounds for doubting any straightforward correlation between classical contract and capitalism; we will consider in turn the ideological and functional dimensions of this relationship.

LIBERAL INDIVIDUALISM AND THE ORIGINS OF THE WILL THEORY

The connection between liberalism (especially economic liberalism) and the rise of classical contract seems unassailable. Atiyah (1979) claims:

> the fact is that the freedom of contract was at the very heart of classical economics, and there is good ground for thinking that the common lawyers may have taken over the concept from the economists in the early part of the nineteenth century. (p 294)

He goes on to argue that although further research needs to be done, the connection is established beyond doubt by the material in *The Rise and Fall of Freedom of Contract*.

In exploring the nature of the connection Atiyah points out that the arguments put forward by the classical authors in favour of freedom of contract were virtually all directed to demonstrating that free exchange should be *permitted*. They were concerned hardly at all with the problem of why and how contracts should be *enforced*. Thus although arguments were generated against laws forbidding usury, monopolies, and many other ways in which the state regulated trade, little attention was paid to justifying why an abstentionist state should enforce contracts, and what should be counted as contracts suitable for enforcement. It is difficult to find any coherent explanation in the classical authors of why the will of the parties *should* be a sufficient reason for enforcement, and there is no discussion of such central issues as which agreements should be enforced, how agreement is to be recognised, and how the gaps in an agreement are to be filled.

The distinction between justifications for permitting and enforcing contracts is fundamental, and it is suggestive of a wider point which is not fully explored by Atiyah: that it is very problematic to regard the content of the classical law of contract as being derived from the ideology of liberal individualism. The embrace of freedom of contract permitting free exchange was responsible for the stripping away of older conceptions of substantive justice, as illustrated in the previous chapter by reference to the case of the common carrier. But this had a negative impact on the law, in that it removed preexisting sources of obligation. It did not in itself spell out how obligations were to be derived. In one sense it was in the nature of liberal individualism that it did not stipulate the contractual obligations to which the parties were subject: the whole idea which the will theory came to represent was that it was the will of the parties which both provided the content of their obligations and the justification for the enforceability of their contract. Where there is a clear and exhaustive provision for all eventualities in a document which the parties recognise as their contract, then the will theory can be applied without difficulty. But hardly any of the cases which comprise the law of contract concern such paragons of meticulous prudence. The bald fact is that virtually all of the law of contract is concerned with imperfect agreements of various kinds, and it is precisely those circumstances where it is most difficult to derive the doctrine from the body of liberal thought contained in the writings of classical political economy.

It is conceivable that even without any direct guidance from the classical authors, the judges could have extrapolated from their works inventing doctrines to deal with cases of imperfect agreement. This does not seem, however, to be the way it happened at all. It has become clear that many of the concepts in the framework of classical contract law found their way into the law from a quite different source. Simpson has demonstrated how the idea of deriving obligation from the parties agreement – the will theory – and concepts such as offer and acceptance, intention to create legal relations, mistake, and remoteness rules were borrowed whole from the work of the French jurist Pothier (Simpson, 1975a). An English translation of Pothier's *Law of Obligations* (originally published in French in 1761–64) appeared in 1806 and there are sufficient references to it in both treatises and case law to make the fact of his influence clear beyond doubt. Atiyah follows Simpson in making this link, and presents the result of the reception of Civilian ideas via Pothier in an abstract, general law of contract as very much in line with the ideas of freedom of contract and liberal individualism (Atiyah, 1979, p 399). From that point of view, the significance of the borrowing from Pothier is simply to identify the route into the law of doctrines which expressed well its dominant ideological orientation.

There is, however, something a bit odd about tracing the influence of classical political economy on the law via the work of a French jurist which was completed in the first half of the eighteenth century: the work of Smith, Ricardo and Bentham had not then been published. Considerable light is shed on this problem by Gordley in his recent book *The Philosophical Origins of Modern Contract Doctrine*, and in it he advances a striking thesis which questions the links which have hitherto been assumed between liberal philosophy and classical contract (Gordley, 1991).[2]

Gordley traced back the origins of the doctrines expounded by Pothier into the work of a group of scholars during the sixteenth and early seventeenth centuries and known as the late scholastics or Spanish Natural Law School. These scholars were responsible for producing a synthesis between Roman Law and the work of Thomas Aquinas, who gave Christian expression to much of Aristotle's thought. The detail of Gordley's rich and careful argument must be left for interested readers to consult for themselves, but the gist of the argument is as follows. The synthesis of the late scholastics was only based in part on the importance of will in the making of contracts. An indispensable part of their scheme of thought was that obligations not expressly agreed were derived from the type of contract into which the parties had entered. Elaborate schemes of classification were devised (more or less based on the classification in Roman Law) distinguishing loan, sale, barter, pledge, hire and so forth. Attempts were made to explain why the obligations attaching to such contracts were 'natural', and these were expressed in terms of the Aristotelian ideas of essence and virtue. The Thomist idea of equality in exchange was influential, and one manifestation of it was a duty on a seller to disclose certain types of defect (p 102).

The body of learning developed by the late scholastics was taken up by the northern natural law school (including Grotius and Pufendorf) and eventually by Pothier. However, in the process of its reception into the common law the most important part of it was lost. The idea of types of contract carrying their established incidents, and the moral arguments from which obligations were derived, were left out and only the part of the theory concerned with the role of the parties' will, with its structure of concepts based on offer and acceptance as the expression of the parties' agreement, was retained.

Gordley claimed that as a result classical contract doctrine was incomplete: the process of reception left it without both the concepts and underpinning moral arguments necessary to deal with situations where full provision for all eventualities was absent. The response of the judges was to attempt to conjure out of the doctrines they had borrowed responses to problems which in the late scholastic's system had been dealt with by doctrines which were left behind: they 'bent and stretched the doctrines they had borrowed to do the work of those they had not' (p 135).

Furthermore, Gordley suggests – contrary to Atiyah – that there is little direct evidence of those judges and treatise writers responsible for the reception of the will theory in the nineteenth century borrowed directly from philosophers and political theorists.

> Only rarely do we find any sign of a commitment to liberal values of freedom and individualism. We find almost the opposite: an insistence that the jurist can do his job without taking account of economics, philosophy, politics or values such as freedom. (p 215)

The immediate upshot of Gordley's argument for the conventional wisdom about the triumph of contract is that it undermines the argument that the content of classical contract doctrine was drawn from the otherwise influential philosophers and political theorists. At best (if Gordley is right) the prevailing ideological climate was responsible for exclusion of that part of the late scholastics' system which grounded obligations outside the will of the parties. The exclusion of such uncongenial ideas, however, did not remove the problems which they had previously been employed to solve.

The most fundamental implication of Gordley's argument is that classical contract doctrine (whatever its ideological pedigree) was far from being a systematic and coherent body of thought which provided a powerful way of analysing all contracts. It was radically incomplete because it had no coherent way of resolving problems raised by situations involving bargaining defects such as mistake, or situations where express agreement was silent. In such situations the will of the parties simply runs out: it is not present and therefore cannot on its own justify or give content to the imposition or removal of legal obligation. *Some* conception of substantive justice is indispensable to determine the outcome of such cases, yet contract law was impeded from establishing any secure basis of obligation distinct from agreement or consent because of the undercutting of such attempts by the judges' attachment to will related concepts.

An interesting test of Gordley's views is posed by the case of Baron Bramwell. Bramwell was a judge from 1856 until his death in 1892 and was renowned as a supporter of laissez-faire and the ideas of Smith and Ricardo in particular.[3] He opposed virtually every suggested infringement of freedom of contract, often writing pamphlets in support of his views. Atiyah's demonstration of his use of the classic authors in his judgments certainly establishes an exception to Gordley's thesis of the judges being at a distance from philosophy. Curiously, however, some of Bramwell's decisions in contract cases actually tend to lend weight to the argument that contract doctrine as a whole was not a direct reflection of liberal political economy. Bramwell took seriously the idea that obligation flowed from consent or agreement and it was this which contributed to his dissenting from majority decisions relatively frequently. For example, on the question of whether an offeror should be bound by a posted acceptance which never arrived, he remained unrepentantly of the view that he should not be so bound: 'a communication to affect a man must be a communication, ie must reach him'.[4] Bramwell tended to approach cases as a matter of principle where precedent allowed a leeway (as it frequently did) and the result was that he was often less prepared to reach a pragmatic compromise with commercial convenience than were many of his brethren. Perhaps the most striking instance of Bramwell's argument from principle is to be found in the line he took in one of the most protracted and explicitly ideological debates in private law during the nineteenth century: the battle over workmen's compensation.

From 1850 to 1891 workmen claiming against their employer in respect of injury at work were met by two doctrines: common employment, which provided that an employer was not liable to a worker for the negligence of another worker, and *volenti non fit injuria* which provided that workers who consented to undergo risk could not claim compensation when injured. The outline of the story is that the courts first invented these doctrines which barred recovery and then, partly in response to debate within the political arena, watered down their own restrictions (Bartrip and Burman, 1983, p 103). Bramwell was an important participant in the debate, both in and out of the courts, and his argument was striking both in its clarity and (not only to modern eyes) in its inhumanity (Fairfield, 1898). Bramwell's position was that both common employment and the *volenti* doctrine were at heart contractual issues: if a workman chose to work for a wage in conditions he knew to be dangerous, he could not claim damages if the risk occasioned injury. He became particularly expert at framing this argument, putting it for the final time in his dissenting judgment in the House of Lords in *Smith* v. *Baker* (1891):

But drop the maxim [*volenti non fit injuria*]. Treat it as a question of bargain. The plaintiff here thought the pay worth the risk, and did not bargain for a compensation if hurt: in effect, he undertook his work for his wages and no more. He says so. Suppose he had said, 'If I am to run this risk, you must give me 6s a day and not 5s,' and the master agreed, would he in reason have a claim if he got hurt?

Clearly not. What difference is there if the master says, 'No; I will only give the 5s'? None. I am ashamed to argue it. (p 339)

The standard rebuttal of Bramwell's argument, then as now, is that he failed to see that a workman's agreement to expose himself to risk of injury did not entail as a matter of logical necessity that he consented to forego compensation if injury occurred. In other words, agreeing to run a risk was ambiguous: it could mean agreeing to run a risk with or without compensation. The court in *Smith* v. *Baker* clambered out of the unpalatable implications of Bramwell's full blown conception of volenti by holding that the workman did not *really* agree to forego compensation: the majority drew a distinction between sciens (knowing) and volens (consenting). This is sound as far as it goes, but the rebuttal, like Bramwell's own view, is grounded on an agreement-based argument because the reason for rejecting the employer's defence was that there was no consent to injury without compensation. However, an agreement-based argument not only leaves open the door to claims in later cases that there was sufficient consent, but also cannot establish one way or the other whether a workman *should* receive compensation in the absence of agreement on the matter. Bramwell was correct to point out that employers did not agree to be liable, any more than employees agreed that they should not be: in the absence of agreement, an obligation of this kind is only derivable from some conception of substantive justice independent of consent. In this situation, as in so many others, ideas of agreement or consent are simply indeterminate because they do not point one way or the other.[5] Tort law was able to provide a remedy independently of contract in this situation because personal injury fell readily within the scope of established tort claims. The absence of any obligation which could be established by agreement was to be felt more sharply, however, in situations which could not plausibly be brought within the scope of a tort claim, that is where there was no invasion of an existing personal or proprietary interest.

Thus the partial reception of Civilian ideas left the common law with the tools to destroy preexisting obligation – on the grounds that it was not the product of agreement – but without an equivalent moral and legal basis to construct obligation where the will was not expressed. Contract law was thus left with what Gordley described as a hole, which subsequent legal development has struggled to fill. The hole was partially filled by the adoption around the middle of the nineteenth century of the objective theory of agreement. But even this amelioration of the problem left the need for legal solutions to manifold contractual problems that burgeoning commercial activity was throwing up. It is to the response of the law of contract in the face of that challenge that we now turn.

HOW IMPORTANT WAS CONTRACT LAW IN PRACTICE DURING THE NINETEENTH CENTURY?

It has become a commonplace to identify a clear functional link between the development of the law of contract and the emergence of capitalism. The nature of the link can be given different nuances, but it usually entails seeing the enforcement of contracts as a necessary condition of capitalist development:

> The functioning of such an economic system depends on the guarantee of the law that enterprise or speculation, in so far as it implies contracts for labour, goods, shares, will be protected by the award of damages or specific performance. (Friedmann, 1972, p 121)

Such a view is clearly plausible, but how accurate is it as a generalisation about the heyday of the classical law in the nineteenth century? Does the evidence justify pride of place being given to the classical law on account of its practical importance? Sugarman and Rubin (1984) point out that, despite the plentiful supply of similar generalisations, there has been little detailed research into the issue (p 4). We have already seen in Chapter 4 that any simple connection between the law and behaviour – that people perform contracts because they fear the legal consequences of not doing – is fraught with difficulty. The broad picture which emerged there was a very mixed one where the role of contract law depended very much on the sector concerned and the degree to which non legal sanctions or norms of trust could operate. It is therefore plausible – even before attending to such evidence as there is about the functional importance of nineteenth-century contract law – to expect a similarly patchy picture of the use of contract law to emerge.

In principle, one might expect historical investigation to provide a rough answer to the question of whether the enforcement of contracts was a necessary condition of capitalist economic development. However, the impossibility of conducting survey based research used by contemporary empirical studies poses difficulties and perhaps explains the paucity of systematic investigation of the issue. The leading study of the significance of the guarantee which an enforceable contract provided was conducted by Ferguson (1984). He tested the importance of enforceability by examining commercial activities where for one reason or another contracts were legally unenforceable. In the case of the Stock Exchange he found that contracts for stock which had been rendered unenforceable (and criminal) by statute were routinely entered and regarded as entirely secure. The prospect of stigmatisation as a defaulter and loss of the place on the exchange were potent sanctions. The Chairman of the committee of the Stock Exchange told a Parliamentary Committee in 1875:

> There is not a gentlemen on the Stock Exchange who could stand on the boards one day which refused to carry out the contract he has made, even in spite of Sir John Barnard's Act ... he would be obliged to walk out; he would be expelled, simply because it would be dishonourable. (Ferguson, 1984, p 196)

Legal enforceability was irrelevant because of the strong internal organisation of the exchange.

The other context examined by Ferguson was executory contracts for the sale of goods of over £10 in value which were unenforceable because there was no note or memorandum as required by s 17 of the Statute of Frauds 1677. The picture he paints is mixed. In the north of England, especially in Manchester, sale contracts were usually oral and therefore not in compliance with the statute, but no problem seems to have been caused by this. In London, however, signed memoranda were the norm and the evidence tended to point a greater concern to establish legal enforceability.

Ferguson's conclusion is tentative, and he limits himself to pointing out that a business need for legal protection is not something that can be taken for granted. His picture is in line with the variable importance indicated by research on modern contracting. Other historians have also detected little enthusiasm on the part of nineteenth-century business men for legal dispute resolution. Arthurs (1985) for example found not only a common preference for arbitration over legal action but also a persistent attempt by various chambers of commerce and other commercial associations to bring about the introduction of commercial tribunals, staffed by judges who were merchants or traders. This concerted campaign came to nought, but demonstrated vividly that the merits of legal dispute resolution when argued by the lawyers failed to convince those most directly affected by it. Furthermore, it seems that such landmark reforms as the codification of the Sale of Goods Act 1893 and the Bills of Exchange Act 1882 were pushed by lawyers and were not the result of any clamour by those engaged in the activities to which they applied (Ferguson, 1977).

Despite the clear evidence of the partial use of contract for commercial purposes, it is clear from the law reports that a very considerable flow of such cases reached the courts throughout the nineteenth century; even a small fraction of the disputes amounted to plenty to occupy the courts. But even if we accept that there was an important demand for enforceability, it does not follow that this confirms the importance or centrality of classical contract. This is because the general rules of the classical law seem to have been of much less significance than the bodies of specialist commercial contract law which were developed in such areas as agency, insurance, negotiable instruments and international carriage and sales.

An important source of obligation for commercial contract law was the law merchant or *lex mercatoria*. This was a body of customary law developed in medieval Europe in important trading centres. It was applied in special courts in England and from around the middle of the eighteenth century important parts of it became assimilated by the common law, including much of the law on insurance and negotiable instruments (Trakman, 1983). This was largely the work of Lord Mansfield who is generally credited with attempting to align the law with commercial needs. His habit of sitting with special juries consisting of merchants who would typically hear many cases meant that great heed was paid to the customs of commerce as a source of obligation. Mansfield's attempts to limit the role of consideration, so that a written contract or moral obligation would be sufficient on its own to make a promise enforceable, fit with that goal, and the failure of such an attempt suggests that it was not of the first commercial importance precisely what the classical doctrines contained.

Even after Mansfield the tradition of the law merchant and its orientation to reflecting commercial practice was influential, perhaps most noticeably in the recognition during the nineteenth century of contractual terms 'implied in law'. These were terms implied in a contract which stemmed not from what the parties agreed, nor from some hypothetical agreement they might have made if asked, but because they represented commercial usage. In this way much of the law on special types of contract was developed alongside classical contract without being hindered by the emptiness of the will theory.

The separateness of the special rules from the general law was further emphasised by the reforms and codification of commercial law during the second half of the nineteenth century, including the creation of the Commercial Court in 1884 (Veeder, 1994). This is especially visible in the development of the law relating to forms of corporate organisation. It was not until the end of the nineteenth century that the joint stock company, with artificial legal personality and limited liability, became a dominant form of business organisation. The Bubble Act 1720 had removed the possibility of separate legal personality and limited liability and these only became freely available after the Companies Act 1862. Before then firms operated through forms of unincorporated association, usually the partnership, the law of which was still merely a part of the law of contract. The problems with partnership were not confined to the absence of the privilege of limited liability. It was a cumbersome form for holding of assets because these were the personal property of the partners, and did not provide a negotiable interest in the enterprise in the way that the share came to do. Yet, despite the fact that it was recognised to be in an unsatisfactory state (and without any coherent definition of partnership) it remained popular even after the 1862 Act and it was only supplanted around the time that the intricacies of partnership were overhauled in the codification of the Partnership Act 1890. The eventual displacement of the contractual form of partnership by the joint stock company suggests two things about the practical significance of the enforceability of contracts: that commercial activity prospered despite the ramshackle state of the contractual position of partnership, and that even when this was sorted out in 1890 it was swiftly superseded by the non contractual form of the limited company (Sugarman and Rubin, 1984; Ireland, 1983).

The theme of the separation of the special rules is also well illustrated in the reforms to the enforcement process and the related issues of bankruptcy and security. The introduction of a system of local civil courts by the County Courts Act 1846 provided a cheaper and more effective mechanism for the routine enforcement of debts under £20. This was born in part out of controversy over attempts to abolish imprisonment for debt and the Act of 1846 preserved powers to imprison debtors in some circumstances (Rubin, 1984). There was clearly a demand for the speedy and effective enforcement of bad debts, and the introduction of county courts was a notable step forward. It seems inherently improbable, however, that such routine debt recovery on ordinary executed contracts depended on the luxuriant growth of classical doctrine taking place at the summit of the judicial pyramid.

Closely related to debt collection was the issue of bankruptcy. The widening use of both commercial and consumer credit, particularly after most controls were abolished by the Usury Law Repeals Act 1854, created more scope for insolvency. The problem of how to deal with insolvency was shaped by three forces:

> the desire to punish the bankrupt by public censure, the wish to organise an administration of his assessments so that competitors are treated fairly and efficiently, and the hope that the process could absolve the bankrupt of his liabilities and allow him to rehabilitate himself. (Cornish and Clark, 1989, p 231)

Reconciling these forces in a burgeoning economy proved tricky and after a number of attempts at reform it was the Bankruptcy Act 1883 which overhauled insolvency procedures and established an enduring solution: classical contract and agreement theory had little to contribute.

These and other reforms affecting commercial contract law clearly suggest that for some commercial groups there were aspects of the law of contract which were of great functional significance, sufficient for them to exert pressure for reform.[6] What is also clear, however, is that the evidence does not indicate that the general rules of the classical law had the same functional importance. What we see in the commercial reforms of the later nineteenth century is part of the gradual process of provision for different types of contract by specially adapted rules. In some instances the general rules were obstructive: the privity doctrine posed problems in relation to bills of lading and negotiable instruments where the commercial desire for enforceability by third parties in often complex networks could not be captured within the rigidities of the bilateral contract form. More often, the general rules and the agreement focus they fostered were simply inadequate. The codes of commercial law which the reform process produced went beyond providing for the enforcement of the parties' agreement: they provided, often quite extensively, for situations where that agreement was incomplete or absent.[7]

PATCHING THE HOLE: THE COMPROMISE OF THE OBJECTIVE THEORY OF AGREEMENT

The examination of both the practical importance of classical contract and its ideological underpinning suggests that the will theory on which it was based was neither fully suited to commercial needs nor a viable basis for resolving all the problems it was called upon to solve. Although the wholesale importation of terms implied in law partially filled the 'hole' it was not a complete solution. It was here that the objective theory of agreement came to play an important, but ultimately unsatisfactory, role.

Courts in nineteenth-century contract cases coped with uncertainties accompanying a full blown, subjective will theory by attending to the appearance of agreement rather than speculate about the subjective beliefs of the parties. The classic statement of the objective theory was made by Blackburn J in *Smith* v. *Hughes* (1871)

> If, whatever a man's real intention may be, he so conducts himself that a reasonable man would believe that he is assenting to the terms proposed by the other party, and that other party upon that belief enters the contract with him, the man thus conducting himself would be equally bound as if he had intended to agree to the other's terms.

Strictly, the objective theory could not draw on the will theory's justifying power by explaining that a party was bound by a term because they had *agreed* to it: in the typical case where the objective theory made a difference – the standard form contract – the relevant party had not agreed to it at all. The trigger of obligation was not will but conduct – appearing to agree – and on this basis norms were imported into the law which could not be grounded in the parties' wills.

Nevertheless, it provided continuity with earlier doctrine which had more fully embraced the will theory because it remained nominally as being about agreement, and so did not appear to represent any major breach with the will theory.

The objective theory also served to confine the unravelling which adherence to a full blown subjective conception of the will theory would have given rise. Contract law repeatedly had to deal with situations where there was less than full consent on both sides to a single set of terms, and in such circumstances an insistence on subjective agreement would clearly tend to unravel all manner of transactions. The objective theory neutralised this tendency, as is well illustrated by *Smith* v. *Hughes* itself, the locus classicus of the objective theory of agreement and one of the most important – and puzzling – of nineteenth-century contract cases.

The buyer bought oats by sample for feeding to horses. He thought that the oats were old whereas they were new and unsuitable for the horses. When the oats were delivered and the buyer realised they were new he refused delivery; the seller sued for the price. On appeal, the court had to decide whether the trial judge's direction to the jury was correct. He had said that they should find for the buyer if they thought the seller believed the buyer to 'believe, or be under the impression, that he was contracting for the purchase of old oats'.

The problem with the original jury direction in *Smith* v. *Hughes* was that it was open to interpretation that the contract would be void whenever a seller knew the buyer was mistaken about the nature of the goods. This would subvert *caveat emptor* because it would be tantamount to replacing the general rule that there is no duty to disclose information with a rule that disclosure was required whenever the seller realised that the buyer might be mistaken about some aspect of a deal. At a time when profit was routinely made by not disabusing customers of such misunderstandings – and consumer protection was confined to concerns about the adulteration of food – this would have been a radical departure from prevailing commercial mores. Cockburn CJ put it like this:

> The question is whether under such circumstances, the passive acquiescence of the seller in the self deception of the buyer will entitle the latter to avoid the contract ... The oats were what they were sold as, namely, good oats according to sample. The buyer persuaded himself they were old oats, when they were not so; but the seller neither said nor did anything to contribute to his deception. He has himself to blame. The question is not what a man of scrupulous morality and honour would do under such circumstances. (p 605)

The pragmatic accommodation of commercial practice therefore told against the original jury direction. But it was also difficult, given the influence of the will theory, to ignore mistakes completely. However, as we saw in relation to duress, the will theory was not able to define its own boundaries, and did not develop any coherent account of how mistakes would affect a contract. It had the dangerous potential to unravel 'contracts' which would, on grounds of commercial expediency, be better enforced: the will theory did not *entail caveat emptor* as a matter of logical necessity.

The objective approach confirmed in *Smith* v. *Hughes* meant that what mattered was the appearance of agreement, so that a mistake by one party, which a reasonable person in the other's shoes would not be aware of, would be irrelevant. But even this approach is not enough on its own to protect the seller in *Smith* v. *Hughes*, for the judge's direction to the jury was entirely consistent with this approach. The Court of Appeal went an important step further and decided that the direction to the jury was wrong because it did not make clear that it was insufficient if the seller believed that the buyer merely *thought* that the oats he was buying were old: the seller had to believe that the buyer thought that the oats were *warranted* to be old. This has been understood as requiring that, for a mistake to be operative (that is, to make a contract void) when the parties are at cross purposes, it must be a mistake about the terms of the contract, and it is not enough for it to be a mistake about the quality of the subject matter of the contract unless fundamental.

So it was that a major part of the doctrine of mistake came to rest on the distinction in *Smith* v. *Hughes* between mistakes about the terms of the contract and other mistakes. Yet on closer inspection this distinction does not seem robust enough to bear the doctrinal load resting upon it. The distinction turns on a subjective element – whether the buyer actually thought that the oats were warranted as old, or merely thought the oats were old. The difficulty here is that the distinction assumes that parties to a contract habitually differentiate between such notions in their thoughts. This assumption seems inherently implausible, especially where the contract is wholly or mainly oral.[8] If so, why draw the distinction at all? Arguably, because such distinction was essential if the doctrine of *caveat emptor* was to be reconciled with an apparently agreement based theory of contract. In this way the judges were able to perform the trick of paying due respect to a supposedly foundational principle at the same time as severely restricting its scope.

As well as confining the unravelling tendencies of the will theory the objective theory enabled norms other than merely respecting the will of the parties to be introduced into the law. The doctrine of *caveat emptor* preserved in *Smith* v. *Hughes* illustrates well that the norms which the objective theory was employed to import were based on a robust conception of how individuals should behave in a contractual relationship, with low levels of constraint on what could be done in the pursuit of self interest. In fact, it was largely through the objective theory that the classical law became infused with a particular individualistic commercial morality about bargaining which permitted advantages to be taken of the less skilled, or knowledgeable or imprudent bargainers as long as there was no positive misrepresentation. Although such norms were not derivable from the will of the parties, they could shelter under the will theory's plausibility by claiming that if people behaved as if they agreed then they could be treated as if they had.

The objective theory was therefore a vehicle of compromise between commercial convenience and the doctrine ushered in by the borrowing of the will theory from Pothier. The norms imported by the objective theory went some way to repair the hole in contract doctrine which Gordley identified as having been left when substantive principles of justice had been omitted in the process of its reception into the common law.

THE IMPORTANCE OF THE CLASSICAL LAW RECONSIDERED

In the previous chapter I presented an account of the emergence of the classical law which emphasised its coherence and importance. Yet in this chapter both characteristics have been put into question: where does this leave the classical law?

First, although the emergence of a general law of contract was a striking achievement of eighteenth- and nineteenth-century lawyers, it is probably not to be seen as a direct offspring of the same liberal philosophy which was influential in the spheres of economics and politics. Although the general doctrine, by deploying the ideas of promise and agreement, assumed a much more systematic and abstract form than hitherto, it was incomplete because the focus on agreement left the law unable to deal properly with many situations where agreement was incomplete or absent. In such cases the emphasis on promise and agreement in the doctrine drove out attempts to articulate the substantive principles of obligation on which the doctrine rested.

Secondly, the evidence for practical importance of the general law is weak. Enforceability seems to have been important in particular sectors rather than generally, and where it was important it was usually the special rather than the general rules which seem to have mattered most in practice.

The special rules were one of the two main ways in which the incompleteness of the classical law was ameliorated. First, terms implied in law, codification and reform all played their part in establishing bodies of commercial contract law which stood apart from the classical law. Secondly, within the general law the objective theory of agreement was important in making the agreement based ideas of the classical law more amenable to commercial convenience without either dethroning the foundational ideas of agreement and promise or permitting a full application of them to unravel commercially important doctrines.

These limits on the reach of the classical law do not mean, however, that it was insignificant. Its strength was that it remained the presumptive or default body of rules to apply where no special rules were in existence. Somewhat paradoxically, therefore, it was outside the established categories of commercial transaction that the classical law came to exert most influence. Most strikingly, it left the courts virtually supine before the exploitative use of the standard form contract, with the most unsatisfactory results coming in consumer contracts. As the history of the carriers' liability illustrates, classical contract continued to be an effective destroyer of other grounds of obligation, yet sterile as a source of new principles of obligation to replace them.

The unsatisfactory nature of the classical law as a default body of rules was compounded by its relative isolation from the special rules. The emergence of special rules for different kinds of contract contributed to the erosion of the resources which the judges had at their disposal within the ordinary law of contract to solve the problems with which they were confronted. This is well illustrated by the effect of importing terms implied in law; following the tradition of the law merchant, commercial usage received recognition as implied terms of the contract. Although this met the initial need of finding a content for obligation between the parties, it did so without challenging the classical view of the agreement of the parties as the ultimate source of obligation. In essence the classical doctrine *ignored* terms implied in law: they were a particularistic import which could not be reconciled with any version of the will theory, unlike terms implied in fact. The content of the various implied terms, although springing from particular situations, was inevitably based on more generalisable norms about contracting. For example, good faith was a requirement in insurance contracts, agency relationships and partnership, but these were seen as exceptions to a general rule that good faith was not required. It is conceivable that, had the judges become used to elaborating substantive grounds of obligation, good faith, instead of being a marginal, precarious exception, could have developed into a competing principle which would have been of use in handling the abuse of the standard form contract. Instead of an evolving contract law being strengthened by engaging with and being shaped by the transactional norms which underlie the terms implied in law, the classical law remained relatively isolated from the norms of commercial coexistence which many of the terms implied in law embodied: they were seen as specific to the situation in which they arose and not to be blended by reason with the doctrines applying to all contracts. Generality, the primacy of agreement, and the aversion to the explicit recognition of other contracting norms conspired together to block the processes of replenishment and renewal which engaging with the substantive norms underlying many of the special rules would have provided.

This blocking of the evolution of the general law may have been given an added twist by the statutory codification of some of the special rules, especially the Sale of Goods Act 1893. This codification, which was conducted with commercial rather than consumer contracts in mind, had the effect of partially freezing the law on sale in the form it had then reached. For example, because s 14(1) provided that there were no implied terms about quality of the goods other than those contained in that section, judicial development had to take the form of working with statutory definitions of merchantable quality and fitness for purpose, rather than continue the process of the evolution of different kinds of term. Also, s 55 preserved the right to exclude the implied terms 'by agreement or otherwise', and it may be that by the casting of these rules in statutory form contributed to the later difficulties experienced by the courts post 1945 when there was a serious (albeit unsuccessful) attempt to deal with the abuse of standard forms in consumer contracts through the doctrine of fundamental breach.

In summary, although the nineteenth century saw the triumph of contract as an idea – in terms of the spread of market relations, the importance of legal enforceability, and its philosophical grounding in liberal individualism – there are grounds for doubting the role of the general rules of the classical law in that story. Then, as now, the doctrines of the classical law were marginal.

7
Transformation and Modern Contract

The discussion of competing rationales of contract in Chapter 3 reached the conclusion that the project of attempting to ground contract on general principle has been superseded by approaches which recognise rather than conceal the coexistence of different justifying principles in the law. The exploration of the modern history of contract has added an historical dimension to the debate, so that at issue is not just what principles underlie contract law, but what changes can be detected. Given that there has been a steady change in contract doctrine, does this add up to a shift in the underlying ideology or values in the law, or merely amount to the accretion of more law within an enduring moral framework?

The switch from suppressing to recognising different ideologies swirling around in the sources of the law of contract has not produced any more unanimity among commentators, either about the nature of those ideologies or the extent of change in the law. In this chapter I examine some of the attempts to understand the nature of contract and change within it. The gist of the argument I will develop is that there has been not transformation but a broadening of the values and relations which are given expression in the law. This has produced a pluralism in the sources of contract which is in need of more explicit judicial recognition, and which both probes the orthodox boundaries policed by privity and consideration and contains the potential to produce the most significant renewal in contract doctrine since the nineteenth century.

FREEDOM OF CONTRACT AND CHANGE IN CONTRACT LAW

One of the simplest and commonest ways of detecting different approaches within contract law is to use the concept of freedom of contract. Perhaps the most widespread perception about the modern history of contract is that freedom of contract reached its zenith in the nineteenth century (roughly 1870 according to Atiyah), and since then there has been a gradual decline. This generalisation is not a terribly helpful way of identifying change within contract law, and freedom of contract is surprisingly marginal in many of the developments.

Discussion of freedom of contract requires some clarification of what – in legal terms – is meant. Two different aspects are commonly distinguished. First, it means that parties are free to make or not make a contract; this aspect may be contravened either by legal constraints on entering a contract (prohibition on sale of such things as certain drugs or guns) or by a legal requirement to enter a contract (compulsory purchase, the provision of certain monopolised utilities). Secondly, it means having a free choice over the obligations created by the contract; examples of constraints would be the compulsory obligations in consumer contracts relating to the quality of goods, or in employment contracts relating to unfair dismissal and redundancy. The present focus is purely on legal constraints on freedom of contract: whether individuals have the economic or other bargaining power to use the legal freedom is an issue to which we shall return.

Depicting a decline in freedom of contract since the late nineteenth century runs into the problem that the picture was not uniform across all kinds of contract. Although there is ample evidence of limits on freedom brought about by the regulation of sale in many areas, notably affecting consumers, employees and tenants, there is also clear evidence of a continuing increase in freedom of contract in areas touching personal freedom, partly due to changes in the law relating to illegal contracts.

Nineteenth-century courts continued the practice of using public policy as a ground for rendering contracts unenforceable in three broad kinds of situation: contracts in restraint of trade; contracts prejudicial to government or the administration of justice; and contracts tending to promote immorality or undermine the institution of marriage. Agreements to provide for separation, to procure a marriage, not to marry, or to marry someone already married were all unenforceable. Contracts relating to prostitution or provision for a mistress were affected, even if somewhat remote (for example, the hire of the carriage for the purposes of prostitution in the leading case of *Pearce* v. *Brooks* (1866)). Nor did the impulse to uphold morality fade quickly: in what now seems a quaintly eccentric case, the Court of Appeal held in *Upfill* v. *Wright* (1911) that a landlord could not recover rent on a flat used by a man to meet his mistress. Gambling was another object of moral disapproval which public policy made an exception to freedom of contract, and this status was reinforced when it was given statutory form in the Gaming Act 1845.

We see in the use of the doctrine of public policy the courts choosing to uphold moral ideas which were at odds with freedom of contract, and these instances represent an important exception to the supposed dominance of freedom of contract in the late nineteenth century. Moreover, the twentieth century has not seen a retreat from freedom of contract in the area of personal freedom, but the reverse. The last thirty years especially have witnessed not only a change in contract law's approach to sexual morality (*Heglibiston Establishment* v. *Heyman* (1977); Dwyer (1977)) but also the removal of legal constraints on freedom to enter a range of contracts. Changes have included: the loosening of restrictions on gambling, the deregulation of Sunday trading and leisure activities, the loosening of censorship of pornography, film and theatrical performances; the freer availability of abortion.

This widening of freedom of contract in the area of personal freedom is not the whole story, but nor is it entirely at odds with the expansion of regulatory control of contracting in the interests of consumers, employees and tenants. Regulation of this latter kind is protective, in that it stipulates minimum terms and conditions, either directly as contract terms or indirectly as obligations on, for example, an employer to comply with safety regulations in the work place, or for a manufacturer to comply with product specifications. In the case of personal freedom, the infringement of freedom of contract was a paternalistic imposition on parties, both of whom were willing to contract and neither of whom wanted interference. Protective legislation is in the interests of one party, and not a case of the law holding back willing buyers and sellers; the transaction will take place on terms *preferred* by one side. It is arguable that this is not an infringement with freedom of contract in the same sense at all, and that, as a means of furthering personal autonomy, it is entirely consistent with the removal of legal constraints on personal freedom.[1]

But whatever one makes of regulation in terms of freedom of contract, it would appear that the idea itself has been marginal in the development in the general law. This is because most contract doctrine was – and is – concerned with neither the issue of limits on the kinds of contract people could make, nor with the imposition of obligations in the teeth of agreement. It was concerned with working out what would count as a valid contract and the legal consequences that would flow where the parties had failed to specify these for themselves. Thus the rules about such vitiating factors as duress, mistake, or undue influence are not so much a reflection of freedom of contract, but describe when an imperfect agreement will qualify for the purposes of enforceability. Similarly, rules about the incorporation of express terms, implied terms, remedies, and discharge provide content to the obligations where, as is typical, the parties have not made explicit and exhaustive provision. No general conception of freedom of contract is any use in handling these sorts of issues because it can only have any concrete effect in a given situation when it is established that an agreement has been reached on terms which provide for the eventualities which have arisen.

Despite this, there has been a clear tendency to treat the enforcement of written terms which contain onerous clauses as if it were an application of freedom of contract. It is sometimes said, for example, that when the House of Lords rejected the doctrine of fundamental breach – the notion that a fundamental breach of contract prevented a person relying on an exclusion clause – they struck a blow for freedom of contract against an interventionist Court of Appeal.[2] This view assumes that the written provisions of the contract, duly incorporated, constitute the terms and that, if judges are to remain faithful to freedom of contract, they should confine themselves to construction only. This is plausible, but only if we take for granted that the written provisions in question represent an exercise by the parties of their freedom of contract. Although it was settled as a matter of law that the exclusion clauses in the fundamental breach cases were duly incorporated, the doctrines on the incorporation of written terms which produced this result represented only one way in which the interpretation of language and behaviour can generate the terms of a contract.

When equipped with a different understanding of how the exercise of a party's freedom of contract is to be interpreted, it becomes plausible to see the contortions of the Court of Appeal in the fundamental breach cases as closer to the spirit of freedom of contract, at least in the consumer cases, than the House of Lords. In this reasoning the meaning of freedom of contract flips over, and the legal developments which have been treated as evidence of a decline in freedom of contract now do service to support the opposite proposition, so that 'interference' with general rules of the classical law is seen as moving towards rather than away from freedom of contract.

Intriguing though this may be, the lesson to be drawn is that the idea of freedom of contract is of limited use in detecting or measuring many of the important changes in contract law: freedom of contract is indeterminate in most instances (Kennedy, 1982). The way to measure doctrinal change in relation to the law on exclusion clauses is in terms of underlying values. There has been a shift from the individualistic version of the objective theory of agreement – that parties can look after themselves and that mere signature or bare notice amounts to agreement – to a concern with the fairness of the outcome.

None of this, however, is to deny that the idea of freedom of contract has been influential. In one sense, freedom of contract was least important in the most visible part of the law – the exposition of the doctrines of the classical law. Less visible was the routine application of the law, as with debt collection, and here it can fairly be said that it is enforcement of principal obligations (concerning basic price and performance rather than provisions for unlikely eventualities) where freedom of contract has been a reality. As a background value, it has policed the boundary which has kept the courts from imposing terms in the teeth of both parties' plainly expressed agreement, although such imposition was hardly commonplace even before the nineteenth century.

CONTRACT AS EMBODYING COMPETING IDEALS

Change in contract therefore needs to be measured using concepts other than freedom of contract. A number of commentators have argued for understanding the content of contract law in terms of competing ideals (Adams and Brownsword, 1987, 1994; Feinman, 1983; Kennedy, 1976; Unger, 1983). The most developed argument is that of Collins (1993a), and it is this that we will explore.

Collins sees contract law as being potentially based on two ideals of justice – justice in exchange, and the justice of the social market – and uses these to identify a transformation in the law. He characterises nineteenth-century contract law as being based on the justice in exchange which gives way in the modern law to the justice ideal of the social market.

Collins's ideal of the justice of exchange emphasises liberty, equality and fairness in reciprocity. Liberty is embodied by freedom of contract and comprises the legal freedom to choose whether and on what terms to contract. Equality means formal equality and denotes the idea that the law of contract was blind to distinctions of wealth and status: apart from those categories which the law regarded as lacking legal capacity – minors, lunatics, and married women – all parties had equal capacity to make contracts. By 'fairness in reciprocity' is meant the requirement of the doctrine of consideration that contract law was about exchanges in the sense that both parties obtained something. All these elements were relatively minimal in their requirements. Liberty did not include positive liberty, in the sense of an actually available choice to act in different ways, and equality was formal and not substantive. Fairness was not concerned with equivalence or balance in exchange within the contract. More generally, there was little or no concern about the possibility of exploitation arising from conditions of formal equality, nor of substantive unfairness.

The silences in the justice in exchange ideal are given voice in the social market ideal, which has three themes: concern about unjustifiable domination, the equivalence of the exchange, and the need to ensure cooperation. These themes are seen by Collins as growing òut of a new liberal understanding of the market order, rather than any socialist or other thoroughgoing rejection of the market. In particular, he sees the themes of the social market as converging in a concern for personal autonomy, which is grounded on a positive rather than negative conception of liberty.

Is Collins right in depicting contract law as having been transformed in this way? Evaluation boils down to these questions: to what extent was the nineteenth-century law based on justice in exchange? To what extent has this given way to the justice ideal of the social market, or for that matter, any other ideal of justice?[3]

EXCHANGE JUSTICE, THE SOCIAL MARKET, AND TRANSFORMATION IN CONTRACT

It is striking that, although Collins presents a thesis which is historical in character, he provides little elaboration or analysis of the pretransformation state of the law. Perhaps this is because this part of the thesis, chiming as it does with the conventional wisdom about the triumph of contract, is seen as uncontroversial. We have seen how the use of freedom of contract as a measuring stick of change is not without severe drawbacks. More generally, the critique in Chapter 6, of the conventional wisdom about the role of contract law in the nineteenth century suggests that there are important respects in which the generalisation about exchange justice fails to capture the composition of nineteenth-century law.

Despite the overall concern with the law of market transactions, Collins's references to the untransformed law tend to refer to the general rules of contract law. This is understandable because, as we saw, it is precisely in relation to the general law that the conventional wisdom makes most sense. Collins's ideal of exchange justice specifies little by way of actual obligations, and so captures well much of the law which so effectively stifled bases of obligation other than agreement. However, the view that the nineteenth-century law reflected the elements of exchange justice is questionable in two respects. The first relates to the bodies of commercial contract law which matured in the nineteenth century, and the second to the coexistence even within the general rules of other ideals of justice.

The important developments in nineteenth-century commercial law outside the general rules of classical contract are given scant attention. This is a crucial omission because we see in such areas as partnership, agency, negotiable instruments, insurance, or sale evidence of norms which are not included in the components of exchange justice but arguably appear to fit pretty well within some of the components of the ideal of justice of the social market. These special rules embodied commercial norms, including cooperation and trust, which were derived in part from the law merchant as well as through the implication of terms reflecting commercial usage. Thus the relationship of principal and agent, mainly laid down in the nineteenth century, contains norms of cooperation and trust between agent and principal, for example the agent's obligations in relation to disclosure

(*Robb* v. *Green* (1895)) and the avoidance of conflict of interest (*Lees* v. *Nuttall* (1834)). Customs of particular markets, for example imposing liability on an agent for an undisclosed principal in the hop market (*Pike* v. *Ongley* (1887)), were respected. Partners were obliged to show utmost good faith in their dealings with each other, and this extended to negotiations leading to formation (*Fawcett* v. *Whitehouse* (1829)). Similarly, utmost good faith applied to insurance contracts and imposed a duty to disclose facts affecting the risk. In business sales, *caveat emptor* was displaced by the obligation to provide goods which were of merchantable quality and fit for a notified purpose. And in charterparties, the common 'expected ready to load' clause was interpreted not as a definite undertaking but as an assurance in good faith.[4]

These bodies of special rules provided a legal environment within which business people in the area were acquainted and which reflected their practice. They fostered coordination and cooperation and served the same function of defining the law applicable to a sphere of activity as the sector-wide standard forms came to do later, for example the JCT forms in the building industry or the standard conditions of sale used in the sale of land. And like those standard forms, the provisions of the special rules were not one sided but represented a balance between banker and client, principal and agent, issuer and drawer of a bill, carrier and shipper, and the like.[5]

Elements of cooperation and trust therefore existed alongside the precepts of exchange justice identified by Collins. This does not mean, however, that there was any great discontinuity or contradiction in the law between opposing principles. In many respects the default norms of commercial cooperation fit well with the ideas of liberty, equality and reciprocity which Collins describes. The elements of exchange justice concern the express agreement of the parties, which the courts in the later nineteenth century certainly did respect most of time. The special rules are default rules which provide for background matters which are not typically agreed. For the most part such rules could be displaced by contrary agreement, although it seems from the imperfect evidence of reported cases that this was not widespread. It is their very reflection of commercial practice that suggests that the cooperative element in the special rules meshed well with the elements of exchange justice. Moreover, the fact that these bodies of commercial law were mobilised by parties with roughly equal bargaining power meant that, although the rules were not concerned with preventing exploitation of the weak, neither were they typically used for exploitation.

This filling out of the picture of the law of market transactions in the nineteenth century suggests not so much that Collins's identification of exchange justice as underlying the law is wrong, rather it is incomplete: the recognition of formal liberty and equality did not preclude the recognition of some substantive values such as cooperation and trust, especially in the emergent areas of commercial law. In another respect, however, Collins fails to identify elements which directly contradict the exchange justice conception. These are of two kinds: the survival until quite late of some hierarchical and patriarchal elements in the law which contradicted formal liberty and equality, and the emergence of some concern about exploitation and protection of weaker parties which is allied with Collins's social market conception.

Married women and employees were late entrants to the world of formal liberty and equality. Married women did not have any contractual capacity at common law until the Married Women's Property Act 1882 enabled them to own property separate from their husband's, but even then the extension of contractual capacity was limited. A married woman would only be liable up to the extent of her separate property and could not be declared bankrupt unless carrying on trade separately from her husband (*Scott* v. *Morley* (1887); Reiss, 1934; Stetson, 1982). Full contractual capacity on level terms with men was not obtained until the Law Reform (Married Women and Tortfeasors) Act 1935.

Although the law of master and servant was being assimilated during the nineteenth century to the ordinary law of contract, formal equality – much mocked in this context for its distance from substantive equality – was not attained until the Employers and Workmen Act 1875. Until this Act repealed the Master and Servant Acts (the last being the Act of 1867) the remedies which the master had for the workman's breach of contract included imprisonment. The abolition of this legal imbalance in the relationship was an important but quite late removal of a blatant lack of formal equality between employer and employee. Even so, the employment contract has always struggled to be perceived as a contract even between legal equals. This remains an excellent example of the copious use of implied terms in law to fill out the content of the relationship, and in some of these – notably the implied obligation of the employee to obey the employer – the imbalance in power imposed by the law is so clear that the notion of formal equality becomes very brittle.

Concern about the protection of weaker parties was well in evidence by the middle of the nineteenth century, and there was a formidable list of enactments imposing ad hoc controls on particular activities. Well known examples include: the Truck Acts, which gave manual workers the right to be paid in cash, and the Factories Acts of 1833 and 1844 which at least aimed to ameliorate factory conditions by regulating working hours and safety; the Passenger Acts, which regulated the appalling conditions on board passenger ships to the new world, and the Merchant Seamen Act 1844, which protected seamen's rights to receive their pay. It is true that not all of these provisions operated directly to affect contract rights, but they are part of the whole law of market transactions, which are the basis of Collins's generalisations.

It is therefore arguable that the ideal of exchange justice which defines the first stage of Collins's transformation obscures important themes in the law of market transactions of the nineteenth century. But this does not mean that Collins's ideal of exchange justice is not a useful one. It may not describe the totality of nineteenth-century contract law, but it usefully identifies central features of the general law. Something similar is also true of the social market conception: it is useful, but the extent of change is probably overstated; I will illustrate this by reference to the ideal of cooperation.

Collins's main evidence of a transformation whereby the law embodies the ideal of cooperation is found in the law relating to modification of contract and termination for breach. He makes a plausible case for regarding the emergence of new approaches to modification as fostering and reflecting cooperation. The rigid approach of the classical law in insisting on fresh consideration – derived from *Stilk* v. *Myrick* (1809) and *Pinnel's Case* (1602) – is portrayed as giving way to the more responsive doctrine of estoppel, especially after the decision in *High Trees* (1947). This trend is pushed further by the development in *Williams* v. *Roffey* (1991) of allowing factual as well as legal benefit to count as consideration, this in turn being made possible by the emergence of economic duress to weed out modifications which are exploitative. These doctrines may be said to favour giving effect to good faith adjustment of the relations between the parties, thereby thwarting any opportunistic attempt to exploit difficulties of the other party by seizing on technicalities in the doctrine of consideration.

Although this portrayal of the new principles of modification is plausible, there are difficulties in seeing here a transformation in the values on which the law about modification is grounded. Arguably, what we see here is not a simple change in the values underpinning the law but in part a shift to principles which enable existing value content to become more visible on the face of the law. Collins acknowledges that the rigidities of the modification rules in the classical law were ameliorated by the law on waiver and rescission. Thus in *Panoutsos* v. *Raymond Handley Corpn of New York* (1917), sellers who had accepted payment for deliveries of flour by a means not provided for in the contract were held to have waived their right to terminate the contract for non conforming payment. This is cited as an example where a way was found around the classical rules about variation, but it was not so much an exception as an illustration of how the concept of waiver could be employed in sale of goods cases to ensure that informal alterations in arrangements for delivery, payment etc could not be opportunistically withdrawn (*Leather Cloth* v. *Hieronimus* (1875); *Ogle* v. *Vane* (1868); *Hartley* v. *Hymans* (1920)). The result was great complexity in the rules, as well as difficulties in terminology which still bedevil accounts of this topic in the standard texts, but these qualifications of the strict classical rules are to be understood as being grounded on the idea of cooperation. Although waiver was applied to sale of goods, it did not itself grow into a general doctrine which could reach into all types of contract, or at least it did not until the generalisation of promissory estoppel as a result of *High Trees* (1947), which embodied a more explicit explanation in terms of reliance for giving effect to the alteration of arrangements.

There have therefore been two different kinds of shift in relation to the rules about modification. A change in the substantive law has been brought about by the courts widening the circumstances beyond the old waiver rules in which modifications representing a cooperative adjustment will be binding. But there has been another shift in the way this expansion has been achieved. The development of the *general* doctrines of estoppel, economic duress and redefined consideration has ensured that the earlier ideas of cooperation underlying the waiver and rescission rules can receive less distorted expression than in the exceptions and qualifications of the classical law to which they were previously confined. In short, the law is more transparent and so the elements of cooperation are more visible than before. If these two changes are not distinguished, we run the risk of hailing the modern doctrines as being grounded on values which are entirely new to the law, when in fact they recover and bring to the surface values already present, hitherto marginalised and overlooked but nevertheless important in their sphere of operation. Leaving out this dimension of 'new' doctrine not only results in overstating the extent of transformation in value content but also misses the wider point that modern contract law is arguably increasingly characterised by a greater visibility of underlying values than the classical law. Also, it is possible to regard the emergence of a more explicit judicial discussion of the principles underlying issues such as modification as a response to Gordley's 'hole', which stemmed from the classical law's overdependence on agreement as a source of obligation.

Something similar applies to Collins's other main example of cooperation, termination for breach. Here the argument runs that while the classical law dealt with termination according to whether the term breached was a condition or a warranty, with only breaches of condition justifying termination, the modern law prefers an approach which only permits termination if the consequences of the breach have been serious. Cooperation is thus fostered by leaning against the use of technical breaches to escape contracts which have become unattractive for other reasons, the modern approach being traced to the *Hongkong Fir* case (1962) which created the innominate term as a third category of term. The idea of transformation here is attenuated by the fact that the courts, as Collins acknowledges, will still apply clear provisions by the parties even where these permit termination for a trivial breach. And, as with modification, one can find clear evidence of a cooperative spirit filtering through the less congenial concepts in the classical law. Extreme cases like *Re Moore & Co* v. *Landauer* (1921) (where the buyer was able to reject tins of fruit merely because some of the consignment was packed in cases of 24 instead of the 30 contracted for) should not obscure the important point that before the emergence of the innominate term it was normal for courts to decide whether a term was a condition on the basis of its commercial importance (*Behn* v. *Burness* (1863); *Glaholm* v. *Hays* (1841); *Bentsen* v. *Taylor* (1893); Treitel 1995, p 705). And even where the courts were faced with the statutory conditions in the Sale of Goods Act 1893, there was some scope for opportunistic rejection to be thwarted. There could be room for manoeuvre in deciding whether the right to reject had been lost by accepting the goods,[6] or by holding that custom or usage (preserved by Sale of Goods Act 1979, s 14(4)) curtails the right to reject (*Peter Darlington Partners Ltd* v. *Gosho Co Ltd* (1964)).

The history of the rules of modification and termination does not therefore readily bear an interpretation in terms of transformation. It is true that there have been significant changes in the form of the principles in which the law is expressed, but their importance lies as much in permitting reasoned and undistorted application of norms already present in the law as in changing the outcomes of large groups of cases. More generally, it is important to emphasise continuity in the existence of cooperative norms, and that there is no necessary conflict between cooperation and exchange justice.

The second element in the justice ideal of the social market is a concern with substantive fairness. By fairness Collins means the ratio between price and performance that would be established in a competitive market (1993a, p 271). The main examples he cites of the law's explicit concern to establish fairness are the control in the Unfair Contract Terms Act 1977 of exclusion of minimum obligations in consumer contracts, the requirement of manifest disadvantage in undue influence, the control over extortionate credit bargains and the imposition of price controls through regulation where a competitive market does not exist, as with the utility regulators such as Oftel. He also argues that many common law doctrines (mistake, incorporation by reasonable notice, implied terms) contain sufficient leeways for the courts to take account of fairness in reaching decisions. These examples are fair comment as far as they go, but they do not add up to a transformation of the classical position which Collins characterises in terms of a commitment to the subjectivity of value and a concomitant unwillingness to reopen the question of the fairness of the price. It is fair enough for Collins to point out that there are objective bases available to fix alternative prices – deriving from the idea of a going rate or market price – but it does not follow from this that the courts typically use them. Across the whole field of commercial contracts it is rare for the courts, in the absence of a vitiating factor, to reopen the price:performance ratio which has been fixed by the parties. True, where the provisions for this basic ratio are incomplete, leeways can be found, but in the ordinary commercial case the only basis for the interference with an agreed rate will be in the case of a liquidated damages clause which is penal. The evidence for an overall transformation in contract law in terms of fairness is simply not there, although the change in consumer contract law is clearly made out. We will return to this disparity.

The third element in the justice ideal of the social market is the prevention of unjustifiable domination. Important instances of this are compulsory terms which reinforce the position of groups such as employees. Thus in relation to the rights against unfair dismissal contained in the Employment Protection (Consolidation) Act 1978 Collins argues:

> The social purpose behind this legislation is to alter relations of power in an employment relation by curbing managerial discretion to discipline the workforce at will. (p 235)

In this case domination lies in the power to terminate a periodic contract, and here as in tenancies this power is controlled through a regime providing for compulsory continuation in certain circumstances. Collins does not, however, develop the theme of preventing domination as fully as cooperation and fairness (it has no separate chapter), although other examples which fall into this category are the restraint of trade doctrine as it applies to sole trading arrangements, and the doctrines of duress and undue influence. The argument here seems entirely plausible, and I will argue that the idea of abuse of power has more explanatory potential to be tapped.

TRANSFORMATION IN CONTRACT RECONSIDERED

Where does this leave the claim that modern contract law has been transformed? In the first place the starting point – the nineteenth-century law – is less different from the picture he paints of the modern law than is allowed. Despite a professed concern with the whole law of market transactions, the emphasis on the general rules of the classical law results in the ignoring of the elements of cooperation in much of nineteenth-century commercial law being missed; and there were important counter currents flowing within as well as without the general rules which continued to inhibit a full blown reception of exchange justice. Even with this adjustment in starting point, the depiction of the degree of change in modern contract is overstated. This partly stems from treating the emergence of new concepts and principles which more clearly embody the justice ideals of the social market as evidence of the first reception of those ideals into the law. In some cases at least, this is a process of making more explicit what was already present, rather that the recognition of something novel. Most importantly, however, the overstatement arises from Collins's failure to recognise the extent of persistence and continuity in the law, especially in relation to commercial contract law.

Even though the claim of a general transformation is not (in my view) made out, the analysis in terms of the justice ideals is still valuable and important. Although the account of transformation seems overstated, this in itself does not imply there is anything wrong with the concepts which Collins uses to identify change: it could be a matter of overstating the degree rather than misperceiving the nature of change. However, although the component concepts of the social market conception do reveal much about contract, they also blur important differences. The root of this problem lies in treating the social market ideal as a coherent cluster which stands in opposition to exchange justice. Arguably, what we see in the modern history of contract is not a change from one type of justice to another, but a gradual recognition of a variety of principles which are not helpfully seen as forming a coherent cluster, but rather a more pluralistic conception of contract law in which different and sometimes inconsistent values can receive recognition.

What is the evidence for discontinuities between the components of the social market ideal? A good example is afforded by the Sale and Supply of Goods Act 1994. This Act strengthens the position of the buyer in relation to the rejection of goods which are defective by providing that the right to reject is not lost until the buyer has had a reasonable opportunity to examine the goods, and also by giving the buyer the right to reject part of a consignment of goods even after some have been accepted. It is the consumer buyer's position which is most enhanced here, however. Section 4 modifies the absolute right to reject goods for breach of condition by providing that a non consumer buyer has no right to reject where 'the breach is so slight it would be unreasonable to ... reject them'. How does this fit with the components of the social justice ideal? For non consumer buyers, the limit on opportunistic rejection clearly fits well with the idea of cooperation being applied to the termination of contract. But the treatment of consumers is quite different, because their ability to terminate opportunistically is increased. Perhaps this is an instance of substantive fairness, although it goes beyond what is necessary to achieve this by permitting rejection by a consumer for what may be a trivial breach even where the seller offers a cure or compensation. If anything, the best fit is within Collins's notion of preventing domination, although even this seems a forced accommodation.

The root of the difficulty here is that the ideal of cooperation is in tension with many modern contract rules which are concerned to protect so called weaker parties, notably consumers. Measures such as cooling off periods, or non excludable standards for product safety and quality, strengthen the position of consumers compared with the classical law. This does not so much involve fostering cooperation between consumer and supplier, as giving consumers rights which they are free to use entirely in their own interests, without any need to weigh the interest of the other party. In one sense this is a mirror image of the classical law, with the law loading the dice the other way. Where the classical law allowed businesses to use their resources to foist unfair exclusion clauses on consumers, the modern law intervenes and permits consumers to pursue their interests exclusively. In short, consumers are allowed to be more selfish than is consistent with the idea of cooperation.

Seeing cooperation as merely the opposite of the classical idea of minimal limits on the opportunism by the powerful is therefore incomplete, and the tension between protection and cooperation means that it is difficult to regard the values underlying the social market ideal as homogeneous.

If this is a problem with the social market ideal, it is one that stems from the attempt to synthesise the values in modern contract into too few principles. The range of relationships covered by modern contract is so diverse that there must be some doubt whether they can be grounded on three complementary ideals; Adams and Brownsword also experienced problems in finding any coherent thread in their ideology of consumer welfarism.[7]

In summary, I have argued that Collins's depiction of modern contract law as based on the justice ideal of the social market is open to two objections. It is a considerable overstatement of the extent of change, and it does not fully recognise discontinuities in the 'new' law, such as those between the principles of protection and cooperation.

One response to the problem in grasping change across the whole field of contract is to conclude that such a search is bound to be fruitless, and that coherence can be found only at the level of the law of particular kinds of contract. After all, the aspiration to generalise was a product of the systematisers responsible for the classical law of the nineteenth century, and it has long been claimed that there is no longer a law of contract but a law of contracts. As Collins puts it, on this view:

> ... a different law of contract emerges, with the universalistic principles of nineteenth-century contract doctrine superseded by par-

ticularistic principles tied to particular social categories. (Collins, 1993b, p 294)

Despite finding difficulties with some aspects of the social market ideal, I believe Collins is entirely right to engage with contract in general and eschew the fragmentation of taking a 'law of contracts' to its ultimate conclusion. Modern contract is characterised by diversity and value pluralism, but there are important themes within it which are neither wholly general nor confined to particular contract types. In the next chapter I explore these themes.

8
Divergence and Pluralism in Modern Contract

This book has argued that general theories of contract doctrine – whether based on promise, reliance and benefit, efficiency, or the justice of the social market – are ultimately unsatisfactory. Does this mean a resort to a fragmented law of contracts, with each type of relationship being treated in isolation? There is an intermediate position, which is to work with broad kinds of contractual relationship. I will argue that it is useful to differentiate between commercial and personal contracts, and that this distinction is fruitful in discerning contrasting reasons for imposing legal obligation, as well as providing a more satisfactory understanding of change in the modern law than the approaches discussed in Chapter 7. The analysis of contract law in terms of these two broad kinds of contract points to a clear commercial 'grain' in much of the general law. I will explore the potential for the general rules to become more receptive to the different character of personal contracts.

COMMERCIAL AND PERSONAL CONTRACT LAW

The criterion I use to distinguish whether a contract is commercial or personal is whether a party is contracting for purposes of exchange. Where both parties are contracting for purposes of exchange then this amounts to a commercial contract. Where one or both parties contract for other than exchange purposes – typically for personal use – then the contract is personal. Personal contract law therefore includes all consumer contracts, residential tenancies, private sales, and the membership of unincorporated associations such as clubs and societies and trade unions. The distinction between use and exchange is most readily made with reference to the performance which is paid for, that is the receipt of goods, services, or other non monetary benefits. But where such things are sold in a private capacity – that is where the revenue generated is not intended for business purposes – this counts as non commercial too. Thus employment contracts are included as personal because although the employer contracts for exchange purposes the wage or salary is used for private provision.

The reason these categories deserve separate treatment stems from the fundamentally different nature of the interests of the parties. The defining characteristic of these interests concerns how a breach of contract affects the contracting party in question. Typically, but not invariably, the parties to a commercial contract are firms or organisations of some kind. The loss caused by the breach – whether it be non performance or defective performance of the obligation to deliver goods or render services – is ultimately a loss to the profit making and asset holding capacity of the firm. The performance is never wanted for its own sake, but because of its contribution to the economic wellbeing of the firm. It is wholly satisfactory to define the loss in pecuniary terms because it is only a loss of money or monetary value. This measure of loss is clearest in the case of the joint stock company, where legal and accounting practice give the firm a separate identity from any individual, but it is reflected in the economic organisation of other types of firm too.

In a personal contract, the effect of the breach is the loss of use of the good or service, of employment, of home, of membership. All of these are *experiential* losses, in the sense that these losses unavoidably happen to some specific person who may be affected by them in other than economic ways. It is because of this difference that the consequences of a breach of a personal contract may be much more complex and hard to put into money terms. Losses from the breach of personal contracts can run deep. The social relations centred on work, consumption and home generate meaning in people's lives and are fundamental to our identity and sense of membership of the disparate groups and communities which constitute civil society. Experiences such as being threatened with the sack or eviction, or having nightmare experiences with defective cars, holidays, utilities services, pensions or endowment mortgages may vary in the sympathy they evoke but all have the capacity to rupture lives beyond the impact on the pocket.[1]

The distinction in terms of kind of interest is not limited to how a loss is experienced. A related distinction can be drawn in terms of the different abilities of private and commercial parties to spread or escape the loss. Losses flowing from breaches of contract within the system of production and distribution can frequently be passed on or spread. The manufacturer receiving defective raw materials, or a retailer receiving goods for resale which are defective, will typically find it possible to spread losses by making very small adjustments to prices, investment, dividends or wages, especially where – as is probably most usual – the loss as a proportion of turnover is small. In other words, firms suffering losses which are small in terms of the scale of the firm can act as their own insurers, and are in a position to make contracts of insurance where the scale of loss threatens to be too large. The firm's position in a web of exchange relationships provides the means of coping with losses. Conversely, consumers do not typically have this capacity. They are at the end of the line of production and distribution and are the ultimate consumers not only of the benefits of production but also of its mistakes. They do not have the means available to shift or spread the loss by scattering it among many other customers, workers or shareholders: unless shifted by liability it all falls on their shoulders and can be large as a proportion of an individual's 'turnover'.

Although the general distinction between commercial and personal contracts reflects these different ways in which contracting can affect a party's interests, there are cases where diffentiation can be more difficult. Thus the distinctions between employer and independent contractor, and between private savers and stock market speculators, may sometimes be more difficult to cast in personal/commercial terms. Nevertheless, from the basic differences between personal and commercial contracts flow a number of other important differences which surface as particular problems to be tackled in contract doctrine.

REMEDIES IN PERSONAL CONTRACT LAW

Rules about the quantification of damages bear the marks of the distinction clearly. The basic measure of recovery in contract is the expectation loss, and the aim of damages is to award such sum of money as will put the plaintiff in the position they would have been in if the contract had been performed. In all commercial situations a money value for the loss can be arrived at. Damages are awarded for three different kinds of loss in commercial contract: the additional cost of obtaining a substitute performance, as represented by repair costs or higher market prices; the recovery of wasted expenditure; and the recovery of lost profit. In the first case, the availability of a substitute performance means that there is no consequential loss: the contract is 'performed', albeit at the defendant's expense rather than by him, as for example where a seller of goods fails to deliver and the buyer has to go into the market and pay above the contract price. Wasted expenditure or lost profit arise because no substitute was available, or at least not in time: there the plaintiff firm recovers precisely what it has lost, and the only kind of thing it can lose: money.

Damages for breach of personal contracts may similarly cover the cost of a substitute or, occasionally, wasted expenditure. But they will not cover lost profit because such a loss is not available where the contract is for use not exchange. The equivalent consequential loss, where no substitute is immediately available, is lost satisfaction or enjoyment, sometimes called disappointment or mental distress. This was first recognised in English law in *Jarvis* v. *Swan Tours* (1972) when the Court of Appeal awarded double the contract price to a plaintiff whose ski holiday had been a disaster. This is the true non pecuniary loss in contract and is the equivalent of damages in tort for loss of amenity flowing from physical injury. In both cases the damages are in one sense genuinely compensatory because they cannot be used to buy a substitute performance, and nor is the loss a money loss like lost expenditure or profit: the damages take the place of a loss that cannot be made good in its own terms.

Once the category of non pecuniary losses in personal contracts is opened up, there is no obvious reason for limiting recovery to holiday cases: in principle, such losses will arise wherever someone contracts for use and no substitute is available. In the 1970s damages for disappointment were extended to the case of an employee for the upset of being wrongfully dismissed (*Cox* v. *Phillips Industries* (1976)). This saw the law recognise for the first time that loss of employment represented a loss not just of income but of identity and self esteem which could result in depression, and so was a recognition that work could benefit the worker in ways other than the receipt of money. This approach was curtailed by the decision in *Bliss* v. *South East Thames Regional Health Authority* (1987) since when the award of damages has been limited to contracts to provide peace of mind and freedom from distress, which has been narrowly construed (*Watts* v. *Morrow* (1990), see further below p 160). The attenuation of these damages is an example of how the concepts of general contract law can provide an inhospitable environment for the flourishing of the norms of personal contract law, although the decision in *Hayes* v. *Dodd* (1990) that damages for mental distress were not recoverable in a commercial contract is in line with the argument for treating personal contracts differently from commercial ones.

The different character of the interest in personal contracts is submerged whenever the claim is for the cost of a substitute performance; this can generally be handled within the classical principles developed to apply to commercial contracts. Nevertheless, there is oblique recognition of the different nature of the personal interest in some other parts of the law of remedies. For example, in *Vigers* v. *Cook* (1919) an undertaker was unable to recover the fee for carrying out a funeral when it was not possible to hold the funeral service in the presence of the body because of the smell of decomposition caused by his negligence in the construction of the coffin. The Court of Appeal's application of the entire obligation rule to permit the withholding of the whole fee despite the performance being otherwise complete can be seen as a muffled recognition of the peculiarly painful consequences of the breach. Now, damages for mental distress would probably be recoverable to compensate this loss directly, and these could in principle amount to more than the contract price. The protection of the consumer interest can also be seen as lying behind the preservation of the entire obligation rule. Without it, consumers would be liable on a pro rata basis for unfinished work by builders, and giving them the right to withhold payment in the absence of substantial performance increases their bargaining power, as well as reflecting the inconvenience which delay in completing building work may cause.[2]

The distinctiveness of the personal interest is also visible in the approach to the issue of whether damages should be measured by the cost of curing the breach or by the drop in value of the asset compared with its value if the contract had been performed. The sort of situation where these two measures produce different figures is well illustrated by *Ruxley Electronics* v. *Forsyth* (1995). A householder employed a builder to construct a swimming pool. When built it was about eighteen inches shallower at the deep end than the contract specification, although it was still deep enough for diving, and the discrepancy did not affect the value of the property on which it was situated. The only way of rectifying the error was to reconstruct the pool at a cost of £21,560.

The dilemma here for the court is to decide what is meant by 'putting the plaintiff in the position he would have been if the contract had been performed' in a case of this kind. If that position is defined only in terms of the resultant value of assets, then it points to the drop in value measure. If on the other hand it is defined as the cost of actually bringing about the physical state of affairs contracted for, then the measure is based on the cost of cure. Different tests are visible in the case law, but now the House of Lords in *Ruxley* has set out a clear approach which expressly recognises the different nature of the personal as opposed to the commercial interest. The Court of Appeal had held that the householder was entitled to the cost of cure irrespective of whether he intended to spend the money on rebuilding the pool, but the House of Lords held that damages for the cost of cure were subject to a reasonableness test. This was not satisfied here because it was unreasonable to spend over £20,000 to gain inches of depth which made no difference to the usefulness of the pool. However, the householder received compensation of £2,500 for loss of amenity, which was based on the subjective value of the loss. This approach was explained by Lord Mustill:

> In some cases the loss cannot be fairly measured except by reference to the full cost of repairing the deficiency in performance. In others, and particularly those where the contract is designed to fulfil a purely commercial purpose, the loss will very often consist only of the monetary detriment brought about by the breach of contract. But these remedies are not exhaustive, for the law must cater for those occasions where the value of the promise to the promisee exceeds the financial enhancement of his position which full performance

will secure. This excess, often referred to in the literature as the 'consumer surplus' ..., is usually incapable of precise valuation in terms of money, exactly because it represents a personal, subjective and non monetary gain. Nevertheless, where it exists the law ought to recognise it and compensate the promisee if the misperformance takes it away.[3] (p 127)

The distinction between the personal and commercial interests is clearly recognised, and is used as the basis for awarding damages where cost of cure is too high. It was also recognised that, where the cost of cure is a reasonable measure of the subjective loss, it would be the correct measure even if it was more than any financial loss (*Radford* v. *De Froberville* (1977)).

PERSONAL CONTRACTS AND PRIVITY

Personal contracts raise a distinctive privity problem. It is usual in commercial relations for exchanges to be mediated by market transactions, clothed in enforceability by the law of contract. In contrast, many consumer contracts are a means for one person to acquire goods or services for the benefit of others which will be distributed on a non market basis between members of a family or other social group. This is well illustrated by *Jackson* v. *Horizon Holidays* (1975) where the plaintiff sued the holiday firm after his family suffered a disappointing holiday in Ceylon. The Court of Appeal awarded him damages for his own loss and that of the rest of the family, despite the recovery for the family transgressing the orthodox principle that damages are only to compensate the loss of a party to the contract.

Orthodoxy was restored by the House of Lords in the commercial case of *Woodar Investment Development Ltd* v. *Wimpey Construction UK Ltd* (1980) and, although the approach of Lord Denning in *Jackson* was criticised, the sense behind the decision in a holiday case was recognised. The problem here is that the performance – the provision of enjoyment – is unlike the transfer of goods or services for exchange purposes because it cannot be received by one legal person. Enjoyment of such collective activities as holidays or restaurant meals is unavoidably dispersed between different real people. The only way in which these commonplace transactions involving family or friends can be pressed within the framework of contract law is by adopting the commercial forms for coping with privity: either by construing the person paying as acting as agent for each individual, or by creating a series of distribution contracts so that the payer contracts for the whole performance and then resells it to each user (Treitel, 1995, p 536).

Such strategies attempt to deal with the problem by ignoring its fundamental characteristic, which is that the users are not in an arm's length commercial relationship but share ties of family or friendship within which gift is normal and where the notion of individuals having separate property can become very blurred. The policy ground for recovery of damages for disappointment in these cases is strong, yet the basis of a claim remains precarious, in essence because the special character of these losses has not been fully recognised.

The absence of a contractual nexus in the distribution of goods or services creates a privity problem even where there is no issue of damages for mental distress. Thus where one person buys another a present which proves defective, neither the recipient nor the purchaser has any claim at all against anyone. No doubt in practice this is circumvented – at least with a cooperative retailer – by the original purchaser returning the goods as their own. But how poorly contract doctrine can be attuned to non commercial interests is shown by the fact it would be hard work to construct an argument for the recipient to claim even where the goods had been bought from a supplier (like Marks and Spencer) which publicises widely its willingness to give refunds on unused goods given as presents.

THE BASES OF LIABILITY IN PERSONAL AND COMMERCIAL CONTRACT

Personal and commercial contract law can be plausibly seen as being underpinned by different justifications of liability. We saw in Chapter 3 how Atiyah has argued that the most persuasive ground for liability in contract is reliance. This kind of justification of liability seems most suited to explaining the enforceability of commercial contracts. Because these contracts are for exchange purposes, it will be normal for them to be a cog in larger project: goods for resale, raw materials for manufacture, sale or repair of machine tools, provision of expert advice and so forth. It will be normal for each of these contracts to be relied on in coordinating activities such as production, retailing, construction with the result that the failure by one contractor to perform will have knock on effects.

In personal contracts, reliance by the individual consumer seems a weaker ground for explaining liability. Because consumers contract for use not exchange, for them the contract for the receipt of goods or services is less often part of a framework of interdependent transactions: they do not contract because they want to secure a complex project but simply as the means of obtaining the benefit of the good or service in question. This difference is reflected in the clear tendency for consumer contracts not to be wholly executory. Goods and services are typically paid for at the point of acquisition without any previous element of binding agreement, or are partly executory as where credit is given or where there is a delay before delivery. On the other hand, it is much more common with commercial contracts for there to be an interval between contract and performance precisely so that other arrangements can be coordinated on the strength of the contract.

Atiyah's other liability principle – receipt of benefit – seems to explain the basis of liability in personal contracts better. It means that consumers should in essence get what they pay for – value for money. This is evident in implied terms about quality of goods and services which are unexcludable in consumer contracts and which define what is satisfactory quality by reference in part to the price. Similarly, in employment contracts the employees' right to receive wages for work performed is given special protection and is not subject to ordinary rights of set off; the circumstances in which an employer can make deductions before payment are tightly controlled by the Wages Act 1986.

It is also arguable that there is one respect in which the promise theory of contract is stronger in relation to personal contracts than commercial contracts. This is because the expectation of enjoyment created by a promise can provoke anticipation and longing which, when defeated, results in a much sharper sense of loss than can be experienced by the firm whose bare economic expectation is defeated. In fact it is difficult to see how the firm – as distinct from the individuals working in it – can experience any sense of loss at all other than one which registers economically, which – ex hypothesi – the defeat of the bare expectation without any reliance, does not.

The distinctiveness of the personal interest is also apparent when we consider the grounds of liability of the consumer or employee. In what circumstances will the party acting in a private capacity be liable? Obviously consumers and tenants will be liable for the price of what they have received, but in what kinds of case beyond this could the non business party be liable? One possibility is that the consumer who withdraws from a contract would be liable for any loss of profit thereby incurred. In relation to the sale of goods, it is usually said that the buyer who contracts to buy goods and then withdraws will be liable to the seller for the profit that would have been made on that sale if the seller makes one fewer sale overall (*W L Thompson Ltd* v. *Robinson (Gunmakers) Ltd* (1955)). The courts do not appear to have applied this rule to consumers with any enthusiasm, however. In *Lazenby Garages Ltd* v. *Wright* (1976) the Court of Appeal held it did not apply to a second hand BMW on the ground that each car is unique and no one could be sure that the second customer would have bought a different BMW. Atiyah (1989, p 474) finds this reason for finding in favour of the consumer unconvincing, arguing that the consumer should in any case only be liable for the reliance losses (meaning in this context any wasted expenditure). Moreover, reliance losses will typically be minor because there will not usually be the framework of transactions dependent on the individual consumer sale taking place. And the practice of taking deposits from consumers means not just that the firm has a means of protecting itself against such losses but also that, in the absence of a deposit, the consumer could plausibly argue that any consequential loss was not expected and therefore too remote. A similar reluctance to hold consumers liable can be seen in *Oscar Chess Ltd* v. *Williams* (1957) (consumer not liable to dealer for misdescription of the age of a car traded in part exchange), and in the control on obtaining indemnities from consumers in the Unfair Contract Terms Act 1977, s 4. The reported cases where consumers are held liable seem to be extremely rare.

The equivalent liability of employees is also limited. The leading case of *NCB* v. *Galley* (1958) suggests that the courts are very slow to make individual workers liable for sizeable consequential loss caused by withdrawing labour. The defendant (with other supervisors) refused to work Saturday shifts, with the result that all production was lost for the day. The Court of Appeal held he was only liable for the replacement cost of another deputy, although no replacements were available. Similarly, the common law liability of the employee to indemnify the employer who has been sued as vicariously responsible for the employee's tort was acknowledged in *Lister* v. *Romford Ice* (1957), but the decision occasioned so much concern that change in the law was only staved off by the agreement of the employers' insurers not to enforce the right against employees (Rogers, 1994, p 611).

It is also possible to differentiate between commercial and personal contracts in terms of the normative attractiveness of the efficiency rationale of contract. As we saw in Chapter 3, one of the standard objections to efficiency as a normative principle is that it is not concerned with the fairness of any distribution, only with maximising aggregate wealth. This objection to efficiency is strongest in relation to personal contracts. Because personal contracts affect individuals' lives, it seems more appropriate to evaluate the law in terms of fairness of an outcome than where, as with commercial contracts, it is only the asset:liability ratio of an economic unit which is at stake. *If* the functioning of firms is ultimately to be justified in terms of them serving the interests of consumers, then distributional fairness between them may seem unimportant, and the inequality created by protective laws requiring them to have regard to consumers' interest would not be a matter of concern.

PERSONAL AND COMMERCIAL CONTRACT AND IDEALS OF JUSTICE

Some indication of the ideals of justice underlying personal and commercial contracts has already emerged in the discussion; we can now be more explicit. The approach I will pursue is first to construct a simple model – not of the norms which are visible within the law, but of the kinds of question with which such norms may deal. I will then use the alternative normative principles of individualism and altruism to give content to the possible answers to these questions, exploring in particular the differences between personal and commercial contracts.

The model is based on the distinction between procedural and substantive fairness which is commonly used in debates about contract. The orthodox distinction between procedural and substantive fairness is between fairness in the process of contract formation, and fairness in the terms or performance of the contract. Examples of doctrines containing a procedural approach are the vitiating factors such as misrepresentation or duress, which latch on to some feature of the process leading to the contract as the ground for holding the contract voidable. Doctrines which adopt a substantive approach include the implied term of satisfactory quality in sales contracts, or the rule against penal liquidated damages clauses. Some doctrines contain a double test, notably undue influence, which requires the transaction to be 'manifestly disadvantageous' as well as being procured by undue influence (*National Westminster Bank* v. *Morgan* (1985)).[4]

As we saw, substantive fairness is one of the components of Collins's social market ideal. His definition of it is in terms of the price/performance ratio – effectively value for money. This does not, however, exhaust the ways in which the content of a term may be tested for fairness. Many contract terms do not directly concern the price/performance ratio, but are about how one party may treat the other. Examples are terms which define the circumstances in which contracts will be terminated or renewed, or how issues such as the time, place or mode of performance will be fixed. Thus if an employee is dismissed from their job, or if a supplier claims to be entitled to provide a substitute good, or if a buyer of a timeshare decides to cancel the day after entering the contract, the issue is not about value for money but about whether such treatment of one party by the other is legitimate. To distinguish these two types of substantive fairness we can call the first distributional fairness (as it directly concerns the distribution of wealth between the parties) and the second fair treatment. In the case of distributional fairness a market price (and quality) can provide a rough basis for deciding whether the price/performance ratio under a particular contract is distributionally fair, but is much less suited to act as a yardstick for deciding questions of treatment. This means that if the courts are to draw on anything other than the contract itself for deciding questions of treatment, they must reach for norms beyond agreement or market prices.

There is a variety of approaches to questions of treatment. We noted in Chapter 7 the potential tension between the cooperative and protective approaches, stemming from the way in which rules protecting consumers typically compel suppliers to take their interests into account while permitting consumers to withdraw opportunistically. It is possible to formalise the difference between these approaches by using the concepts of individualism and altruism (Kennedy, 1976). Individualistic norms permit parties to a contract to pursue their own interests with minimal concern for others; *caveat emptor*, the maxim that traditionally left the buyer of goods no recourse for defective goods in the absence of misrepresentation, is a clear instance. Altruistic norms require a party to give more weight to the other's interests, as for example under the doctrine of undue influence when a relationship of confidence has been established. Pure forms of individualism and altruism can be thought of as poles between which there are gradations of mix.

Individualism and altruism can shape the obligations of one or both parties to a contract. Where individualism is applied to both, we have something like the classical law of contract, which still applies to many aspects of commercial contracts. The parties are treated equally, and are subject to few obligations to look after the other's interests. I will call this two party individualism.

Where both parties are subject to norms of altruism, they are also treated as equals by the law. Cooperative norms are the product of what we can call two party altruism, examples of which are the application of estoppel and economic duress to modification and the handling of termination of contract through innominate terms. All of these lean against opportunistic withdrawal from a relationship and foster continuance of it through the mutual adaption to changed circumstances.

The third possibility is where one party is subject to norms of altruism and the other is subject to norms of individualism. Here the parties are not treated as equal because one is effectively being compelled in some way to serve the interests of the other. This is where consumer protection fits, and we can call this hybrid protective individualism.

This model of the norms which can shape the rules within the treatment aspect of substantive fairness can also be applied to the procedural issue of contract formation. Two party individualism imposes few constraints on the process of contract formation, entitling each party to withdraw up to the point of acceptance, while two party altruism will require both parties to deal openly, and clothe precontractual negotiations with some degree of enforceability, for example requiring firm offers to be kept open for acceptance. Protective individualism can require one party (but not the other) to place all their cards on the table, for example requiring the sellers of financial products such as life insurance or mortgages to explain fully the consequences and declare the commission they will receive on a sale.[5]

How do personal and commercial contracts fit into this model? The table opposite shows how the personal/commercial distinction maps onto the combinations of individualism and altruism.

	Personal	*Commercial*
II	private sales	most commercial contracts that are not relational
IA	consumer, employee, tenant, investor, protection	? some standard form contracts (under UCTA)
AA	cohabitation, unincorporated associations	some relational commercial contracts

key:
II = two party individualism
IA = protective individualism
AA = two party altruism

Although it is clear that the personal/commercial distinction does not map simply on to the distinction between altruism and individualism, the distribution between the boxes for personal and commercial contracts is very different. Taking commercial contracts first, these are split mainly between two party individualism and two party altruism, with the former predominating. Two party altruism is characterised by the more cooperative norms of relational contracting described by Macneil. Despite the evidence of change in doctrines on modification and termination, these norms still have limited reach outside the special bodies of rules (for example construction) which provide for cheaper and less disruptive dispute settlement than that offered by contract litigation. Also, the altruism here is clearly limited: the enforcement of cooperation is within the confines of the particular project, and it need not entail a broader, more diffused commonality of interest. A small part of commercial contract could be placed within protective individualism, notably the application of the reasonableness test to exclusion clauses under the Unfair Contract Terms Act 1977, ss 2, 3, 6, 7 and 8.

The distribution of personal contracts contrasts markedly. The category with the most content is protective individualism, where contracts with consumers, employees, and residential tenants are to be found. The category of two party individualism is occupied by contracts where both parties are contracting in a personal capacity. The commonest kind of contract here would seem to be private sales, notably of houses, but also of goods such as second hand cars. Here, the parties are if anything permitted to be more individualistic. There is no implied term relating to quality in contracts for the sale of houses although, in the case of new houses sold by builders, protective terms are typically included. The implied terms relating to satisfactory quality and fitness for purpose in a sale by a business do not apply to private sales. These are situations where both individuals contract irregularly, and it may be that here we see the liberal model of isolated individuals with no other economic or social connection most closely approached: the wholly private sale is free even of the customs of trade which structure many areas of commerce. To adapt Macneil's example of the purchase of petrol on the New Jersey turnpike (where one party was acting in a business capacity), the paradigm of the discrete private sale is perhaps the sale of a second hand car radio at a boot fair just off the M25.

Personal contracts falling within two party altruism are of especial interest. The two types of contract I have placed here are unincorporated associations, such as clubs, societies, or trade unions, and cohabitation. Cohabitation can raise contractual questions whether or not a written contract has been drawn up. One aspect of the relationship between cohabitees which has exercised the courts is the enjoyment of property where the owner has promised the other party that she (usually) can continue to live in the house. Since the 1970s the courts have used the concepts of contractual licence, implied trust, and proprietary estoppel in a notably creative way to provide a degree of security for the non owner.[6] These developments have received mixed reactions from feminists, but one powerfully argued view has been that express cohabitation contracts provide an important opportunity for people in non marriage relationships to construct a relationship which is not simply a reflection of marriage (Kingdom, 1988).

The courts have also been active in filling out the relationship between members of unincorporated associations such as clubs or societies. In legal terms these associations are constituted by a contract between the members on the terms of the rules, although the courts have implied terms about the treatment of members which mirror some of the rules of natural justice as developed in the law of judicial review (*Lee* v. *Showmen's Guild of Great Britain* (1952)).

Neither of these relationships is the simple legal expression of market relations because they are not based on money payment as part of an exchange, and nor are they constituted by two different roles which create the routine possibility of one exploiting the other. They are instances of voluntary association and are characterised by a merging of private interests in a collective interest in a shared project. They are relational contracts, but neither party is involved in order to obtain direct commercial gain out of the relationship. The relationships are open ended and impose complex responsibilities on the participants: the terms of an original agreement may shape these, but the law supplements this with norms that do not assume either that the parties' ultimate interests were antagonistic to each other or that one side is expected to serve the interests of the other.

The unincorporated association is of particular interest because it illustrates contract law being applied to a relationship so distant from the paradigmatic two party commercial sale. Here, contract is the legal form of membership. The contract, typically based on the rules, does not only provide what the obligations of the parties are, but also how they will be changed through a structure of collective decision-making. Contract thus comes into direct contact with democracy, and it is through contract that the practices in so many societies in relation to meetings, resolutions, and committee elections are clothed in legal force. The inclusion of the democracy of associations under the umbrella of contract law is a particularly graphic instance of the normative pluralism contained within it.

Mapping the personal/commercial distinction on to the three combinations of individualism and altruism therefore reveals a diverse picture of kinds of contract and the norms underlying them. We will now explore what changes in contract law are revealed by this analysis.

THE PERSONAL/COMMERCIAL DISTINCTION AND DIVERGENCE IN MODERN CONTRACT

The picture of change revealed by applying the general distinction between personal and commercial contracts is not one of general change, reaching across the whole of contract law, but one of a divergence between these broad categories. Although the most dramatic change has been seen in personal contracts, the law of commercial contracts has not been static, and has also witnessed slower, but different, change.

The biggest changes in personal contracts have come in protective contracts. In consumer law there is a variety of ways in which the law provides for consumers' reasonable expectations to be met. For example, compulsory terms in consumer contracts provide minimum entitlements in relation to the quality and fitness of goods, and the quality of services; the strict rights to reject substandard goods have been preserved for consumers despite their attenuation for non consumers by the Sale and Supply of Goods Act 1994; in relation to consumer credit, there are strict limits placed on repossession of goods bought on hire purchase. But even more important than the changes in the private law is the body of regulation affecting consumer contracts. This includes controls on safety, the description of goods, the advertising of bargain offers, and much else. Particularly striking has been the development of what are effectively different rules of contract formation in credit contracts. The contract must be in writing and the consumer must be provided with a written copy of the final version (Consumer Credit Act 1974, s 62). The consumer's signature must be placed in a box in a prescribed form (Consumer Credit (Agreements) Regulations 1983) and agreements concluded off trade premises can be cancelled by the consumer during a cooling off period. The result is a very different conception of the procedural fairness in the making of the contract compared with the ordinary law.

Employee protection is less developed and more compromised by a legislative concern to avoid limits on employers' flexibility. But the trend towards special treatment is unmistakable, most strikingly in the protection against unfair dismissal, now contained in the Employment Protection (Consolidation) Act 1978. The position at common law was that all employees not on fixed term contracts could be dismissed with appropriate notice, however capricious or arbitrary the reason: dismissal on overt racist grounds, for example, was permitted at common law. Now, employees who qualify by virtue of two years' work have a degree of protection against unfair dismissal.

The emergence of anti discrimination legislation over the last twenty-five years has itself made significant alterations to the law of contract. Under these provisions – principally the Sex Discrimination Act 1975 and the Race Relations Act 1976 – discrimination on grounds of race or sex is unlawful in the following fields: employment, education, provision of goods and services, selling or letting of real property, and the membership of bodies related to occupations, and in the case of race, the membership of clubs. An action for loss caused by such discrimination is available (Sex Discrimination Act 1975, s 66; Race Relations Act 1976, s 6). The cogent criticism of the inadequacy of some of these provisions, their interpretation by the courts, and indeed the limitations of any anti discrimination law should not obscure the radical departure from the conception of justice contained in the classical law: the retailer (or employer) given the absolute freedom to accept or reject someone's offer (or themselves to make an offer or not) by the rules of offer and acceptance finds itself liable for loss caused by a rejection based on the grounds of sex or race. Attempts have been made to add disability and sexual orientation to the list of unlawful grounds of discrimination, although the rapid spread of equal opportunities policies among large (especially public sector) employers means that in many instances employers are already going further than required by law in attempting to eradicate discrimination.[7]

The clearest examples of the different treatment of personal contracts are therefore to be found in the rules deriving from statute but, as the examples used in the differentiation of personal and commercial contract make clear, the marks are to be found in the general law too, albeit in a more concealed form.

Within commercial contract law, perhaps the main change has been the greater recognition of cooperative norms already noticed. However, it is also clear that there is considerable persistence of more orthodox principles which are less concerned with restraining the individualistic pursuit of self interest. For example, in *Walford* v. *Miles* (1992) the plaintiffs were in negotiation with defendants for the purchase of a business, and it was agreed by the defendant sellers that they would not negotiate with another party. After the sellers broke off the negotiations the buyer claimed that there had been a collateral contract to negotiate in good faith. The House of Lords declined to find a collateral contract existed, mainly on the ground of uncertainty. Lord Ackner rejected the argument that the defendants were bound to negotiate in good faith:

> [T]he concept of a duty to carry on negotiations in good faith is inherently repugnant to the adversarial position of the parties when involved in negotiations. Each party to the negotiations is entitled to pursue his (or her) own interest, so long as he avoids making misrepresentations. To advance that interest he must be entitled, if he thinks it appropriate, to threaten to withdraw from further negotiations or to withdraw in fact in the hope that the opposite party may seek to reopen the negotiations by offering him improved terms. (p 138)

Cooperative norms do not therefore hold sway over commercial contract, although they have found a significant foothold and adjusted some of the law in a relational direction advocated by Macneil.

One consequence of the differentiation of personal contract from commercial contract is that, by freeing some rules of general contract from expressing conflicting policies, it permits those rules to resume a more coherent and commercially orientated form. The leading example of this is the decision of the House of Lords in *Photo Productions* v. *Securicor* (1980). The development by the courts from the 1950s of the doctrine of fundamental breach as a means of combating unfair exclusion clauses in consumer contracts created great uncertainty about the effect of such clauses in commercial contracts. The problem for the courts was how to confine to consumer cases a doctrine that addressed exclusion clauses in general. The result was a line of commercial cases in which the courts produced great – and ultimately unretrievable – obscurity in the attempt to reconcile striking down clauses in consumer contracts with permitting them as legitimate devices of risk allocation in commercial contracts (see *Harbutt's 'Plasticine' Ltd* v. *Wayne Tank and Pump Co Ltd* (1970) and *Kenyon Son & Craven* v. *Baxter Hoare* (1971)). The incoherence in the doctrine was remedied by the Unfair Contract Terms Act 1977 which clearly separated consumer from non consumer contracts for the purpose of the control of offending clauses. In *Photo Productions Ltd* v. *Securicor Transport Ltd* (1980) the House of Lords took the opportunity to lay the doctrine of fundamental breach finally to rest:

> After this Act, in commercial matters generally, when the parties are not of unequal bargaining power, and when risks are normally borne by insurance, not only is the case for judicial intervention undemonstrated, but there is everything to be said, and this seems to have been Parliament's intention, for leaving the parties free to apportion the risks as they think fit and for respecting their decisions. (Lord Wilberforce at 843)

Thus the differentiation of consumer and commercial law on exclusion clauses removed the tension which flowed from using one set of rules to discharge contradictory functions, in the process revitalising the law's ability to facilitate commercial exchange. But in some situations, this differentiation is not possible because the situation exhibits both personal and commercial aspects: the development of the doctrine of undue influence illustrates this well. The typical situation in the cases consists of one party, usually the husband, needing to provide a bank or other lender with security to obtain desperately needed finance for a business. The security provided is the home which is jointly owned by the wife, who therefore has to sign the document giving the lender the charge over the property. When the bank needs to realise the security by having the home sold it takes legal action to bring about a sale.

The simple response in these cases would be for the courts to hold the wife bound by what she has signed. That they have not routinely done this is because of the doctrine of undue influence. This was in origin a doctrine of equity which provided that gifts or contracts between parties to certain relationships would be presumed to be the product of undue influence (and therefore liable to be set aside) unless evidence rebutting the presumption could be adduced. The reasoning behind this was that in relationships such as doctor/patient, solicitor/client, or religious adviser/disciple there was a degree of trust placed in one party which could be abused. Undue influence was presumed on the basis that the relationship was inconsistent with the pursuit of commercial self interest by the party in whom trust was placed: showing that the party received independent advice would typically rebut the presumption. A similar approach was also applied to situations where a relationship of confidence could be established on the facts, and since the decision in *Lloyds Bank* v. *Bundy* (1975) the doctrine has been applied increasingly to impugn the validity of charges over property.

In the kind of case described above the wife has two basic arguments. One is the claim that there was a relationship of confidence between her and the bank within which she relied on the bank to protect her interests, and that, as a result, a presumption of undue influence is raised. The other is the claim that the bank knew (or ought to have realised) that the husband had procured her signature on the charge by undue influence or misrepresentation and therefore ought not to be allowed to enforce it. Although the distinction between these two possibilities is important analytically, they both reflect the tension between different justifying principles which surfaces within this triangular conflict of interest.

If it were simply a case of a debtor – typically the husband – securing a business debt on property owned solely by him, there would be little difficulty. It would be an arm's length commercial relationship where the parties would be treated as capable of looking after their own interests. It is the introduction of the third party – typically the wife – as co-owner but not directly associated with the business which brings in the concern with substantive fairness which is more characteristic of personal contract law.

The important features of this triangle are as follows. First, the relationship between husband and wife means that the wife will not simply be pursuing her own interests: she might have signed because of a genuine desire to help her husband, or because of domination (including being misled) arising out of the exploitation of intimacy. Secondly, the bank will often be in a much better position to assess the commercial sense of the business proposal supported by the loan, in particular whether it will be throwing good money after bad. Thirdly, the bank may therefore be aware (or ought to realise) that the wife is acting against her own best interests.

With two sides of the triangle the nature of the relationship is clear: there is an arm's length commercial relationship between the debtor and bank, and non commercial relationship of intimacy between debtor and co-owner. It is the content of the relationship on the third side which is crucial, and here we see the pull between the two different ways of conceiving of contractual relations. The approach developed in the recent case law is a compromise between the two. Broadly, the position now reached is that in these triangular situations the onus is on the bank to see that the charge, and the consequences of its enforcement, are explained to the co-owner, and that she is advised to seek independent advice. In other words, the law is only prepared to regard agreement as effective to bind the co-owner if it is given with full understanding of the content of the contract and its possible consequences. Although what is required from the bank still turns on the analytical distinction between wrongful act by the husband and by the bank, it seems that the practical result of decisions by the House of Lords in 1993 is that lenders now have a general practice of providing full explanations and recommend independent advice to cosignatories of charges on property.[8]

The broad picture of change revealed through a general distinction between personal and commercial contract law is therefore one of divergence, in which the change from the classical law in personal contracts can truly be called a transformation, while change in commercial contract law is much more muted. The result is a marked pluralism in the values which contract law expresses.

PERSONAL CONTRACT LAW AND THE WELFARE STATE

Much of the development of the protective law of personal contracts is due to the activity of Parliament, which can be seen as part of the wider emergence of instrumentalism in the modern law which has been noted by many commentators.[9] It also raises the issue of how far change in contract law can be linked to larger political change. Atiyah, for example, argued in 1979 that the decline of freedom of contract he discerned was connected to the expansion of the role of the state in the twentieth century, and has since suggested that there has been some revival of freedom of contract (Atiyah, 1979; 1986). There have also been attempts to link change in contract law with ideology of the welfare state, or 'welfarism'.

The attempt to connect changes in contract law with the emergence of welfare states in most western countries is understandable, especially in the UK where the pace of doctrinal change – both common law and legislation – has seemed to quicken since 1945. Brownsword has attempted to use a concept of welfarism to discern change in contract law, and has demonstrated that the connections are not simply stated. He defines the welfarist thesis as the argument that the law of contract 'embodies precisely those values which are taken to underpin the modern welfare state' (1994, p 2). To see the extent of the reception of welfarism he elaborates four different conceptions of what those values could be and the concomitant implications for the law of contract. These constitute a spectrum from Contract I, which is in essence the classical law, through II and III which are successively more protective of weaker parties, to IV which is not about protection but about cooperation.

Brownsword recognises that the diversity of sometimes conflicting ideologies underlying the welfare state means that it is sensible to eschew an attempt to distil any essence of welfarism. On the other hand, the problem with this degree of analytical separation is that it tends to undermine the whole idea of tracing the values of the welfare state in contract law. Without some claim about core values of the welfare state, much of the point of tracing them in the law is lost. Brownsword voices the view that the 'new interventionism' lacks any overall coherence (p 58). Welfarism does, in my view, have significant explanatory potential, but his analysis of welfarism does not fully draw this out. One problem is the virtual exclusion of consumer contracts from the idea of welfarism: he appears to argue that consumerism is a separate ideal.[10] Arguably, this is central to any linkage between contract law and the welfare state.

It is easy to point out the manifest obstacles in aligning contract doctrine with welfarist ideas. The main one is that, while contract law concerns market transactions, the motivating spirit of welfare states has been the perception of inadequacies of the market which has led to an attempt to improve the lot of the people by direct state provision which circumvents the market. The original strands of the British welfare state – guaranteed income for those unable to participate in work, old age pensions, free health care and education, and improved housing – were all provided by non market mechanisms. Tracing an ideology which manifested itself in state activity into the law about market transactions clearly poses problems.[11]

Despite the plurality of norms underlying both personal contract law and the welfare state, it is possible to make a link between them through a single shared feature. This is a concern about the *outcome* as it affects ordinary people. If we strip away the differing content of particular welfare state ideologies, what we are left with is a general orientation to the needs and aspirations of ordinary people, which includes the notion that what happens to such people matters. Thus it is not consistent with any justification of the welfare state to argue that the poor should be left to rot, or that the disabled should be left to beg in the streets. Such a concern is nowhere near a basis for any particular welfare state ideology, and is uncontroversially shared by all. Where this weak criterion does bite, however, is in differentiating personal from commercial contract law. Personal contract law which is protective is concerned with outcomes in precisely the same way, which commercial contract law is generally not. The individualism/ altruism mix of protective individualism places responsibility on one party to serve the interests of the other in a way that is remarkably reminiscent of the welfare state. Moreover, the concern about outcome which runs across from the welfare state to protective contract law fits with the ideal of the social democratic tradition that society should guarantee certain basic conditions of human flourishing for its citizens, and in which the role of the state is complemented by a similar responsibility of large corporations.

CONTRACT, CONSUMERS, AND CITIZENS

The developments in the role of the state and private law on which I have founded the general connection between personal contract and the welfare state were almost entirely complete by the 1970s. Since then, the British state has been subject to a series of reforms which, although probably more haphazard than hindsight suggests, have sprung from a basic concern on the part of Conservative Governments to bring market disciplines to bear on state activity. The pillars of this change have been the privatisation of nationalised industries, the use of compulsory competitive tendering in the procurement of goods and services, the introduction of the internal market in the National Health Service, and the conversion of parts of the Civil Service into arm's length 'Next Steps' agencies, such as the Prison Service.

How has this resurgence of market and contract ideas affected the divergence between personal and commercial contracts which had emerged by the 1970s? The first point is that these initiatives do not directly relate to the relationship between the user and the public service in question: they concern instead the internal organisation of service 'delivery', and so if these relations are contractual, they are commercial rather than personal contracts. Nevertheless, many of these reforms have ridden on the rhetoric of seeing the users of public services as consumers or customers in the private sector. Although much of this rhetoric is directed at manipulating the culture of those working in the services,[12] it also surfaces in the relationship between users and public services embodied in the Citizens' Charter Programme (1991). The aim was to raise standards of service and increase responsiveness to users in areas of the public service where the ordinary forces of competition do not operate; it spawned charters for particular services such as the Patient's Charter and the Parents' Charter in which minimum service levels were spelled out and placed alongside existing rights and targets and aspirations for improvement.

It is arguable that we see here the making of a different kind of relationship between contract and the welfare state. The direction of the flow of influence has reversed, and instead of the law of private sector transactions being influenced by the policies of the welfare state, the activity of the welfare state has increasingly been influenced by contractual norms. Thus it has been argued that the Citizens' Charter represents a redefinition of the citizen as economic actor, at the expense of a fuller conception of citizenship which embodies both rights to education and health and rights to democratic participation in decision-making. Barron and Scott (1992) see the relationship between state and citizen in the provision of services becoming a contractual one:

> ... [the services'] *raison d'etre* is to satisfy the wants/preferences of the citizen *as if* the latter were a consumer in the market place, and in this way to discharge a *contractual* obligation to the citizen. The link between state and citizen is implicitly conceptualised in the Citizens' Charter Programme in terms of a contractual nexus; services are provided by the state as a *quid pro quo* for the taxes paid by the citizen ... (text at fn 89)

The idea that the Citizens' Charter Programme represents a resurgence of contractual ideas echoes more general criticism of the Conservative reforms from the left, on the grounds that they introduce a commercialism which corrodes the public service values and ethos on which many services such as health and education have depended. It is a plausible reading of the changes that they signal a revival of classical contract ideas with renewed impetus behind a commercial model of social relations at the expense of the more welfarist norms of personal contract law; but this is not the only reading.

The Citizens' Charter contains a fundamental ambiguity stemming from the fact that the idea of empowerment on which such initiatives draw taps into socialist and social democratic traditions as well as the thinking of the new right. Many on the left of politics have recognised the problems of bureaucratisation and the consequent alienation of users to which public services may be prone. Where the right has expressed the solution in terms of market, the left has tended to use the language of accountability, participation and democracy. The tendency to cast the new into familiar categories was challenged from the late 1980s by the flourishing of a debate on citizenship which has seen attempts to revive the idea of citizenship as membership of society and its communities which is not reducible either to market relations or to state planning by experts. These debates have proved ideologically disorientating because the streams of three political traditions have converged: from liberalism has come the concern with legal rights and the constitutional form in which citizenship is expressed; from socialism the dimension of collective action and concern with substantive equality; and from conservatism, the focus on responsibility, and the importance to community of Burke's 'little platoons' (Andrews, 1991).

In this context, the Citizens' Charter appears as an attempt to recast the relation between public services and their users in a situation which is fluid and in which the basis of that relation remains contested. The danger of pressing the contractual/consumerist analogy is that, by obscuring important counter currents in the Citizens' Charter which create the potential for the expression of a non market vision, one grants it a greater ideological coherence than it deserves. There are three key features which distinguish at least some of the public services covered by the Citizens' Charter from commercial contractual relations: the primacy of consumer interests; the equality of access which results from the separation of paying and using; and the scope for a deeper relationship, involving participation and responsibility. All of these disrupt the analogy with traditional understandings of contract, and therefore pose the question whether contract law is capable of becoming the legal form in which such relationships receive expression. We will consider each of these aspects in turn.

First, the equation between contract and consumerism ignores the important differences between commercial contract and consumer contract discussed above. Most importantly, it obscures the central point that the Citizens' Charter, by making consumers' interests paramount, contains a purer form of consumerism than exists even in the private sector. The lack of inhibition on the part of Conservative Governments in attacking perceived vested producer interests in public services has meant that the language of balancing the interests of consumers against producers – usually that of shareholders – is absent. The idea is propagated that organisations must constantly demonstrate their total commitment to the consumer interest by improving service even when not prodded into doing so by the self-interested response to competition. Private sector firms pursue consumer interests contingently, as a means of their own gain; they will pocket windfall gains, exploit commercial secrets, suppress embarrassing information where possible: in short, the corporate discretion allowed firms by the normal market imperfections will be exercised in the interest of the firm, not consumers. But for public service organisations providing education or health services, better service provision is their *only* substantive goal. In the private sector, the commercial model of a transaction shaped by competitive self interest is attenuated by consumer protection which requires suppliers to take some responsibility for the interests of consumers; in the public sector, the Citizens' Charter contains a virtual abnegation of the supplier's interest.

The second feature which distinguishes most public services from real market transactions is that use is not conditional on payment. Because access is not governed by ability to pay it is based on a principle of equality. This in itself is not new, but the move towards at least some choice of provider, for example in relation to schools, introduces the need for explicit statements of the rules of access which were unnecessary where one simply attended the nearest hospital or school. Thus school admission policies create expectations, some of which are enforceable by judicial review if not contract. From this emerges the language of entitlements, which is some distance from the orthodoxy of the classical law supplier's veto on entering a relationship.

The third difference between at least some public services and commercial contracts is the richer nature of the relationship created. Education is the preeminent example. The process of education, whether at school or university, differs in several fundamental respects from the ordinary commercial or consumer sale. It is here that the commercial jargon of 'product' and 'delivery' jars most. One reason for this is that education is a process in which the pupil or student participates, rather than a preformed product which is acquired. The process takes place within, and is vitally shaped by, an institution of which the pupil or student is a member, and which is constituted by shared traditions, values, aspirations and in which personal relationships based on trust, respect and care play a central part. In the case of schools, this sense of membership may be further reinforced by the involvement of parents as governors, in fund raising by parent–teacher associations, or as classroom assistants.

What are the implications for the law of contract that the public services are resistant to being assimilated by the commercial contract model? Barron and Scott reject the contractualisation of public services which they see as implicit in the Citizen's Charter. But this is to assume that any relationship which takes on or approaches the legal form of a contract is inevitably to be identified with a commercial conception of contract, at odds with public service values which form part of a fuller conception of citizenship than that contained in conceiving of citizens only as commercial buyers and sellers. There is another possibility. This is that contract law accommodates such citizenship relations not by inflicting upon them the clearly inappropriate and distorting commercial model of contract, but by using the resources already present in the law of personal contracts to apply norms which reflect the nature of such relationships. As we have seen, the idea of membership has already found a place within contract law in the rules applying to unincorporated associations, and this demonstrates that there is room for contract law to encompass relations between citizens and organisations that contain strong voluntary elements but which are not primarily market relations. The possibility is in sight that the reform of the relationship between public services and users of them will result not so much in a contractualisation of the relationship which represents an assimilation to commercial contract, but a further broadening of contract law to reflect fully a broader conception of citizenship.

PLURALISM AND THE LIMITS OF CONTRACT

The picture which emerges from the above analysis is one of a contract law which has broadened beyond the mainly commercial orientation of the nineteenth-century law, and which is now the carrier of a plurality of norms and values. However, this normative pluralism is not very evident in the accounts of the law of contract provided in the standard texts. The main reason for this is the recurrent problem that the special rules, applying only to one kind of contract, get left out of the general accounts. The books on the general law reflect the cases and the (very few) statutes which are fit, on account of their general application, to be incorporated into a general work on contract law. The textbook accounts therefore reflect the narrowed base of the general common law of contract.

This process has been at work since the emergence of a general, abstract contract law in the nineteenth century. The central place accorded the general law of contract has meant that other streams in the wider law of contract have been seen as marginal: elements of good faith visible in such areas as agency, insurance, partnership and charterparties were not generalised to become part of the contract mainstream. Where the general rules were altered (usually by legislation) for particular situations, the new provisions were increasingly cast out from the scope of the general rules, with the result that the normative base of the general law has remained relatively narrow, in contrast to the increasing normative pluralism visible in the special rules.

This process of narrowing impedes innovation within the general rules, for these continue to reflect norms of commercial contract law, especially the more individualistic version which the general law has tended to embody. It may be that this process will continue and the general rules become increasingly distant from non commercial relations. But the problem with the narrowing of the base of the general rules is that legal change in the non commercial situations has become overreliant on legislation. The case by case incremental development of the law, so striking in tort and judicial review, has been constricted by the commercial grain in the general law of contract which is not hospitable to other norms.

In summary, the position that contract law finds itself in is therefore this. There is significant value pluralism to be found in the whole law of contract (comprising both general and special rules), to which the distinctive treatment of personal contracts has made a marked contribution. There is, however, an asymmetry between general and special rules, in that it is the special rules, frequently statutory, where pluralism has flourished most. And the very process of relying on legislation to remedy the inflexibility in the general law saps its ability to adapt in other situations. Is there any way out of this narrowing process, which would permit the general law of contract to evolve more effectively? In the rest of this book I argue that development of the general rules of contract is possible, and that there is no inherent reason why the pluralism evident in the wider law of contract should not be available within the rules of the general law.

One obstacle is the paucity of legal sources for deriving legal obligation within general contract law; we saw in Chapter 6 how the nineteenth-century law was virtually empty of any substantive grounds of obligation other than promise and agreement. One approach is for the courts to revitalise the process of producing general rules, but to do so by drawing on the exceptions to the mainstream. An example can be seen in the different idea of agreement embodied in some personal contracts which is at odds with the objective theory which permits parties to be bound by mere signature. In undue influence, lenders need in some circumstances to ensure the co-owner understood the contents of the legal charge and the attendant risks, and that they were encouraged to take independent advice about the proposed course of action. In relation to consumer credit, there are rules which require clear words in the contract and provide special rules for signing, and make cancellation a possibility. The Unfair Terms in Consumer Contracts Regulations 1994 impose a general plain language requirement. An agreed variation of an employment contract may not bind an employee if it does not have immediate effect (*Jones* v. *Associated Tunnelling Ltd* (1981)). It is arguable that these examples illustrate a different approach to ascertaining what and whether the parties have agreed. They do not apply generally, but then neither does the traditional approach: innovation in the law would be stimulated if the exceptions were organised into a competing principle which could be compared with the classical approach of cases like *L'Estrange* v. *Graucob* (1934).[13] Of course, synthesising principle from an amalgam of case law and statute raises special problems; these and the possibility of generalising from exceptions are explored in Chapter 11.

Another approach is for contract to borrow some of the concepts and principles from other legal subjects to fill the gap within contract itself. There is some evidence that the courts are drawing on the more flexible approaches in tort and judicial review to remedy the gap in contract. For example, one way of handling what I called the issue of fair treatment (the fairness of a term other than defining the main price/performance ratio) is to adopt the procedural approach to fairness to be found in administrative law. In its various manifestations, emphasis is placed not on the outcome of a decision, but the way it was reached. Thus natural justice regulates the way a disciplinary hearing is conducted by entitling the subject to know the charges, make representations, and be dealt with by a panel which is independent. Similarly, 'Wednesbury unreasonableness' is a ground for invalidating the decisions of a public body because of failure to take into account relevant considerations, or because irrelevant ones have been given weight. This approach has been used explicitly within contract law to deal with the expulsion of members of unincorporated associations such as unions and clubs and there are clear resemblances to the handling of the issue of unfair dismissal; the potential for contract of the public law principles employed in judicial review are explored in Chapter 9.

Other legal subjects are relevant to the gap in contract not just as sources of borrowed principles, but also as alternative legal routes. This is particularly true of the tort of negligence, which some commentators have argued has dealt with problems beyond an inflexible law of contract (Markesinis, 1987). This raises the issue of the scope of contract law, in particular what its limits are beyond the commercial paradigm at the heart of the general law. This issue is explored in Chapter 10.

9
Judicial Review and the Scope of Contract

CONTRACT AND JUDICIAL REVIEW

Of all the frontiers between contract and other legal subjects, that between contract and judicial review is the one which is least explored. When debate is conducted about the erosion of boundaries, it is tort, restitution, or property law that are usually inspected. In this chapter I argue that the connections between contract and judicial review are not only deep but illustrate how obligation can be imposed on the parties to a contract without even lip service being paid to their intent. And, more generally, the penetration of judicial review ideas into contract evidences exactly the kind of remaking of contract in a non commercial context that I raised in the last chapter.

How can this be when judicial review is not part of the law of obligations, or even part of private law? After all, judicial review is centrally concerned with the legality of the activities of public bodies, while contract law is principally concerned with the agreements of private individuals and bodies. Despite this, there is clear evidence that the legal principles used in judicial review decisions – known as public law principles – are applied by the courts in contract cases. But before exploring this, it is worth recalling the orthodox separation between contract and judicial review.

Contract creates an enforceable private obligation founded on agreement, while judicial review is concerned with the validity of the action of a public body whose legal power to act is typically derived from legislation. A good illustration of the differences is the way they handle the issue of abuse of discretionary power. In judicial review the purchase which the law obtains on the idea of discretion stems from the limited nature of public power: there must be law which provides the legal power for the public body or official to act in a particular way, and the growth of judicial review over the last thirty years has seen a shift from the courts being concerned primarily with whether a power exists at all to a wide scrutiny of the manner of its exercise. Thus, in addition to whether a public body is acting ultra vires in the traditional sense, the exercise of such power must comply with natural justice, not be irrational, and be proportionate. In the classical law of contract, on the other hand, no similar opportunity to review the exercise of discretionary power exists because the presumption is one of autonomy in that a natural person – save for children and the mentally ill – has the capacity in principle to enter any contract. And after a contract has been entered into, the question of the relationship between the parties is simply not conceived in terms of discretion or its control. In classical theory, the contract creates obligations and duties between the parties, which are to be discovered in either the express or the implied terms present at the making of the contract or in a conscious later act of modification. The parties are entitled to stand on their rights, and there are no general independent background norms of treatment or behaviour against which the exercise of a right is measured. There is no explicit control of the arbitrary or capricious use of power conferred by contract.

The idea I entertain below is that the law of contract can develop a theory of abuse of power: that judicial review principles about natural justice, irrationality and the unfair use of power in general may be extendable into the private sector or 'ordinary' market relations, carried where necessary within the contractual form. This would involve in one sense the reverse of the thrust conventionally ascribed to the contractualisation of the state: instead of transferring private sector goals, mechanisms and values into the public sector by contractualisation, there would be a reverse flow of public goals, mechanism and values into the private sector. Whether such a conjecture can amount to more than crass utopianism I deal with at some length below. But it is necessary first to say something of the procedural context.

Since 1977 there has been a special procedure for judicial review – an application for judicial review under Ord 53 of the Rules of the Supreme Court. Judicial review must therefore be pursued through a different procedure from an ordinary private law claim.[1] But before 1977 the procedural demarcation between the challenge of public and private power was much looser. It was common to challenge the exercise of power by a public body by seeking a remedy by way of declaration under Ord 15, which was the same procedure that was used for seeking declarations in private law, as for example in *Eastham* v. *Newcastle United* (1964). This state of affairs fostered the application of public law principles such as natural justice to contractual situations, notably in governing the relations between the members of an unincorporated association, and this application of public law principles has survived the procedural demarcation introduced by the 1977 reforms. In addition, there are some situations where the Ord 53 procedure can be used to apply for judicial review of a decision within a contractual relationship. The upshot is that public law principles may be applied to contracts either as part of the law of contract in an ordinary private law claim, or under an application for judicial review.

PRIVATE LAW JURISDICTION AND PUBLIC LAW PRINCIPLES

One of the most striking instances of innovation within contract doctrine has been the application of public law principles, most notably natural justice, to unincorporated associations, particularly trade unions, trade associations and clubs. An unincorporated association does not have independent legal personality and it was firmly established in *Lee* v. *Showmen's Guild of Great Britain* (1952) that an unincorporated association consists of a contract between its members on the terms of the association's rules, and that the contractual basis of the relationship can give rise to legal relations beyond the handling of association property. However, the flexible approach adopted by the courts in interpreting and supplementing the rules of unincorporated associations contrasts sharply with some of the restrained treatment applied to standard form contracts of the more usual kind. Thus, in *Lee's* case itself, where the plaintiff was expelled from membership of the Showmen's Guild after refusing to pay a fine imposed by the Guild under its rules for 'unfair competition', the Court of Appeal asserted its jurisdiction to determine whether the facts could reasonably justify such a finding. Further, Denning LJ emphasised not only that natural justice should be complied with in disciplining a member, but also made it clear that this requirement overrode any express provision in the contract:

> Although the jurisdiction of a domestic tribunal is based on contract ... the parties are not free to make what contract they like. There are important limitations imposed by public policy. (p 342)

The court would be particularly vigilant where membership of an association was (as is here) necessary to pursue a trade. In the process of pointing out that the court would ensure that an association applied the correct interpretation of its rules, Denning LJ made clear which way a court should lean:

> In theory their powers are based on contract. The man is supposed to have contracted to give them these great powers; but in practice he has no choice in the matter ... [Expulsion] is a serious encroachment on his right to earn a livelihood, and it is, I think, not to be permitted unless justified by a contract into which he has entered. (pp 343–4)

Following *Lee* there was a gradual development of the judicial review of the abuse of contractual power by unincorporated associations. The relationship between trade unions and their members was an especial focus of judicial concern, and in these cases the courts (with Lord Denning to the fore), shadowed – and in some cases initiated – the developments in the mainstream of judicial review of more obviously public power. The expulsion of members attracted the most judicial attention, and requiring strict compliance with some pretty robust criteria of natural justice was not uncommon.[2] These cases have been criticised by some commentators on labour law on the ground that the courts have shown insufficient appreciation of the context in which lay union officials operate, and have as a result entertained unrealistic expectations of what is possible in the conduct of union affairs (Wedderburn, 1987). This plausible argument does not, however, detract from the point that we see here an example of the courts being prepared to develop very significant incidents of a contractual relationship without being confined either by a literal interpretation of standard terms or the necessity of finding implied terms within the usual tests.[3]

The application of judicial review principles through the contractual form provides an important example of dramatic judicial development of contract doctrine, but it is one which has been excluded or consigned to footnotes in the traditional books. A major reason for this is the extreme difficulty which the classical rules encounter in analysing unincorporated associations as contracts. It is probably impossible to analyse the process of formation in terms of offer and acceptance, which is modelled on a bilateral not a multilateral relationship,[4] and it is especially implausible to treat content of the obligations as present at the times of formation, given the need to change rules, elect officers and so forth. The application of public law principles resembles the story of implied terms in law in many commercial contracts, in that grounds of obligation not derivable from agreement have been left aside from the general rules and so have not contributed to any renewal of the classical doctrine. But the innovations in the law of unincorporated associations differ from the terms implied by law in commercial contracts in one important respect. The touchstone for the latter is commercial usage and, although this can give judges wide scope to impose terms, such terms must be explained as being derived by a process of judicial notice of commercial usage. In contrast, the rules about natural justice are justified with more direct reference to why clubs or trade unions *should* be subject to such requirements. The result is reasoning which reveals without distortion the substantive reason for the obligations in question.

Where a person is a member of an unincorporated association the courts have a contractual 'peg' on which to hang control abuse of power. But even beyond contract, there is some scope for the control of abuse of power in private law, notably in relation to the granting of licences. It is settled that public bodies are subject to review when dealing with licences applications and renewals (*R* v. *Barnsley Metropolitan Borough Council, ex p Hook* (1976); Wade, 1988, p 428). But what about the position where a licence from the private body controlling the trade or sport is practically indispensable despite the fact that there is no legal requirement for it? This is the issue raised in the line of cases stemming from *Nagle* v. *Feilden* (1966) which have initiated some remarkable developments.

In *Nagle* the plaintiff had been refused a trainer's licence by the Jockey Club because she was a woman. She claimed a declaration that the refusal of her licence was capricious, unreasonable and contrary to public policy. The Court of Appeal had to decide whether the claim should be struck out as disclosing no reasonable cause of action and decided that it should not because the plaintiff had at least an arguable case despite there being no contract. Both Lord Denning and Salmon LJ emphasised the Jockey Club's effective monopoly in the running of racing and considered that there was sufficient basis to make the point arguable. There was, however, no doubt about their view of the general issue of whether it was acceptable for a body capriciously to deprive someone of their ability to earn a livelihood:

> The common law of England has for centuries recognised that a man has a right to work at his trade or profession without being unjustly excluded from it. He is not to be shut out from it at the whim of those having the governance of it. If they make a rule which enables them to reject his application arbitrarily or capriciously, not reasonably, the rule is bad. It is against public policy. The courts will not give effect to it. (Lord Denning, p 693)

Despite no further stage in the action ever being reported, the inchoate decision in *Nagle* has been influential, for example in the decision of Megarry VC in *McInnes* v. *Onslow Fane* (1978). The British Boxing Board of Control had repeatedly refused the plaintiff a manager's licence. The plaintiff sought a declaration that the Board had not complied with natural justice by denying him a hearing and refusing to give reasons for the decision. Although Megarry VC decided that in these circumstances natural justice did not require the elements claimed by the plaintiff, he thought that the Board were under a duty 'to reach an honest conclusion without bias and not in pursuance of any capricious policy' (p 221). An oral hearing and the giving of reasons could be required in other circumstances, for example where there had been an allegation of dishonesty. Megarry VC also expressed the view that such a requirement could apply to membership of an association where membership was equivalent to obtaining a licence.

These decisions are important not just because courts have created a free standing jurisdiction to review discretion beyond privity and consideration, but also because the criteria of review clearly go beyond natural justice: the reference to capricious reasons being unacceptable clearly indicates a concern that goes beyond procedural propriety. We see a substantive enquiry into whether reasons are good or bad, which has clear affinities with the general principle of irrationality identified by Lord Diplock in the *GCHQ* case (*Council of Civil Service Unions* v. *Minister for the Civil Service* (1985)).

These examples of the application of public law principles in private law actions demonstrate how contractual obligation can be given content by reasoning which acknowledges substantive arguments which are general in scope, and not reducible to promise or agreement. We now turn to examine how far the application for judicial review under Ord 53 can apply to contract.

CONTRACT AND THE JUDICIAL REVIEW PROCEDURE UNDER ORD 53: NON PUBLIC BODIES

There are two different sorts of contract which may be subject to the Ord 53 procedure: contracts with public bodies, typically local authorities, and certain contracts with non public bodies. We will consider the latter first.

Since the introduction of the Ord 53 procedure in 1977 there has been controversy over the extent to which this procedure could be used in relation to non public bodies. A further twist was added by the House of Lords in *O'Reilly* v. *Mackman* (1983) where it was held that, if a litigant wished to pursue a claim against a public body which called into question the validity of its action, they had to proceed by way of an application for judicial review under Ord 53 rather than through the usual writ action. This meant that where a particular action or decision was susceptible to judicial review, an application for judicial review was the only means of proceeding with a claim. It therefore became necessary for the courts to develop criteria to distinguish whether in any case a private or public law action should be brought. Until the 1980s judicial review of the decisions of public bodies was regarded as applying simply to the exercise of statutory powers. This was extended to cover prerogative power in the *GCHQ* case and in *R* v. *Panel on Takeovers and Mergers, ex p Datafin* (1987) a further step was taken in holding that the decisions of the Takeover Panel, a body exercising neither statutory nor prerogative power, might be susceptible to judicial review. The Takeover Panel was an unincorporated association, the members being representative associations such as the Confederation of British Industry and the Association of British Insurers. It exercised considerable de facto power in the regulation of takeovers and mergers but 'without any visible means of legal support' (Sir John Donaldson, at 824). The Court of Appeal held that the Panel's decisions were susceptible to judicial review because there was a public element arising from its role as an integral part of the governmental framework for regulating the City.

Datafin has been regarded by some as marking a shift to deciding the susceptibility to judicial review in terms of the function or nature of a power rather than its source. Holding that the decisions of an unincorporated association were susceptible to review therefore opened up a vista of possibilities stretching far beyond what had been thought reviewable before. With *Datafin* it became necessary to search for different criteria to draw the boundaries around reviewable power.

In *Datafin* itself Sir John Donaldson adopted a test based on the nature of the power, specifically whether there was a public element in the body's decision. This was satisfied because the Panel was performing a public duty in the regulation of takeovers and mergers. But this was qualified so that if the exercise of power was based on a contract – 'a consensual submission to the jurisdiction' – the decision would not be susceptible to the Ord 53 procedure.[5] Later cases have not, however, unambiguously followed the idea of using the contractual nature of jurisdiction to exclude the scope of an application under Ord 53. The diversity of judicial views on the point is well illustrated in three recent cases on whether decisions of the Jockey Club, the governing body of racing, are subject to review: *R v. Disciplinary Committee of the Jockey Club, ex p Massingberd-Mundy* (1993); *R v. Jockey Club, ex p RAM Racecourses* (1993); *R v. Disciplinary Committee of the Jockey Club, ex p Aga Khan* (1993).

The clearest challenge to the view that contract excludes the Ord 53 procedure came from Hoffman LJ in the Court of Appeal in the final case of the trio, *ex p Aga Khan*. Hoffman LJ adopted the test of whether or not the body exercised 'governmental' powers, holding that the Jockey Club did not. This was because it was not carrying out a Government function in the way that the Takeover Panel could be said to be doing,[6] and he found the so called 'but for' test – whether the government would establish a body with statutory powers but for the existence of the non statutory body – was not satisfied. But he was clear that if the governmental power did happen to have a contractual source it should be no bar to review.

If Hoffman LJ's governmental power test prevails it will undoubtedly be *more* restrictive of the range of bodies which are subject to review under the Ord 53 procedure than Sir John Donaldson's 'public element'. Although Hoffman LJ does not automatically exclude contractual powers, the notion of governmental power is much narrower than the public element test which is capable of covering, in the view of at least some judges, abuses of power beyond any specifically governmental context. An example is the much wider view of the scope of the Ord 53 procedure which was canvassed by Simon Brown J in the second

Jockey Club case, *ex p RAM Racecourses*. Although Simon Brown J regarded himself as effectively bound by the earlier Divisional Court decision (*ex p Massingberd-Mundy*), he indicated that he would otherwise have been inclined to hold at least some decisions of the Jockey Club amenable to review under Ord 53, in particular those concerning the granting of licences. In *ex p RAM Racecourses* the applicant was complaining that their legitimate expectation of being granted a licence to operate a new racecourse had been defeated. One of the arguments pressed by counsel for the Jockey Club was that it was possible for the applicant to pursue a remedy by way of declaration in private law even without being in a contractual relationship with the Jockey Club, as occurred in *Nagle* v. *Feilden*. Simon Brown J's response to this point was that today such claims would be better pursued in an application for judicial review:

> [those cases] had they arisen today and not some years ago, would have found a home in judicial review proceedings. As it was, consideration of public policy forced the courts to devise a new private law creature: a right in certain circumstances to declaratory judgments without any underlying cause of action ... [I] for my part would judge it preferable to develop these principles in future in a public law context than by further distorting private law principles. (p 247)

Thus Simon Brown J's remarks indicate a much broader scope of the judicial review procedure under the public element test than visualised by Hoffman LJ. He would not only construe public element as extending beyond the narrower 'governmental powers' test, but would also not regard the existence of a contract as a bar to the use of the Ord 53 procedure.

Nor is there unanimity of view among judges regarding the status of the private law supervisory jurisdiction. The fact that these developments occurred in cases where the action was for a declaration in the pre *O'Reilly* v. *Mackman* era meant that courts were not then concerned with the question of whether there was some public element in the role of the governing bodies sufficient to justify an application for judicial review under Ord 53. The modern need to probe the issue, especially after the decision in *Datafin*, has revealed a variety of judicial views about the status of the jurisdiction recognised in *Nagle* and *McInnes* in the more recent cases where the amenability of the bodies to judicial review under Ord 53 has been in issue. We have already seen how Simon Brown J in *ex p RAM Racecourses* thought that the jurisdiction in *Nagle* etc should now be exercised though the Ord 53 procedure. In the same case, however, Stuart-Smith LJ was clear that there had been a clear indication by the Jockey Club that the applicant would receive an allocation of races and they subsequently did not receive them, then a declaration could have been obtained by a writ action, on the basis that the Jockey Club were acting in restraint of trade, even without any contract existing. Similarly, Rose J in *R* v. *Football Association Ltd, ex p Football League Ltd* (1993) was in no doubt that the attempt to incorporate the jurisdiction in the *Nagle* line of cases into the Ord 53 was misguided: 'a requirement to comply with the requirements of natural justice does not of itself characterise a body as public or private'. And Hoffman LJ in *Aga Khan* not only disagreed with Simon Brown J about the consolidation of the private into the public law jurisdiction, but also doubted the survival of any jurisdiction outside of a contract: the decision in *Nagle* had an 'improvisatory air' about it.[7]

It is clear from the diversity of views in these cases that there is some blurring of the boundary between the public law procedure of judicial review, Ord 53 and ordinary private law actions. Lack of clarity in procedural demarcation is suggestive of an absence of a clarity in the reach of underlying principle; this can also be seen in the application of judicial review to contracts entered into by public bodies.

CONTRACT AND JUDICIAL REVIEW UNDER ORD 53: PUBLIC BODIES

The impact of judicial review on contracts entered by public bodies is a category which cuts across virtually all the usual heads of review and is not generally treated as a separate topic of administrative law. Nor do there appear to be any clear general rules or principles applying to all government contracts. The closest approach to a general rule or principle is the test that the courts frequently apply whether there is a sufficient 'public law element' in the circumstances to make a decision susceptible to judicial review: this has proved to be no clearer a test than in the non public body cases. The issues are well illustrated in the recent case of *R* v. *The Lord Chancellor, ex p Hibbit & Saunders* (1993). The Lord Chancellor's Department had decided to put court shorthand writing services out to tender, and the applicant firm, which had provided the service since 1907, was unsuccessful. Review was sought on the ground that the tendering process had been conducted unfairly because the announced rules were departed from. Both Rose LJ and Waller J were prepared to accept that the applicants had been treated unfairly by the Department, and that they had formed legitimate expectations which had not been satisfied. The outcome of the case therefore turned on whether the decision of the Department was susceptible to review at all. Rose LJ, although he was prepared to accept that the case was not beyond judicial review merely because it concerned a commercial function, held that 'it is not appropriate to equate tendering conditions attendant on a common law right to contract with a statement of policy or practice or policy decision in the spheres of Inland Revenue, immigration and the like, control of which is the especial province of the state ...' (p 12). Why this is not appropriate was not explained further. Waller J distinguished the issue of whether a tendering process had complied with the announced procedures, which did not have a public law element, from a policy decision setting the criteria for deciding between bids. Thus he thought that the exclusion of firms employing trade union members would clearly be reviewable, but not merely complying with announced procedures.

This case illustrates some of the considerations which are weighed when review is sought of the contracting decisions of public bodies. It is, however, difficult to discern much consistency in the cases in deciding whether a public law element is present. In the licence cases, where the refusal to renew some kind of market or trading licence is in issue, sometimes a public law element will be found and sometimes it will not be (Arrowsmith, 1990). Sometimes it is suggested that the statutory nature of a power is sufficient to make its exercise susceptible to review, while in some cases it is said that even that is beyond review if it concerns a private law function (*R* v. *IBA, ex p Rank* (1986)).

The search for the public law element has been a way in which the courts have negotiated the fundamental tension between two different approaches. One is that public bodies should be under an obligation in their contracting practice, beyond what is expected of private bodies, to observe norms of fairness and consistency which serve the public interest and which ensure fair treatment of individual contractors. The opposite view is that public bodies should be expected to enter the market under precisely the same rules as private bodies and therefore not be subject to any control by way of judicial review which is not part of the ordinary law of contract. The weight of argument for applying one or other of these approaches will clearly vary according to the context. It is partly the uncertainty which is endemic in the search for a public law element which has lead some commentators to argue that it should no longer be used as a way of filtering cases suitable for review. For example, Arrowsmith (1990) has argued that contracting powers should be seen, like other activities of government, as reviewable in principle, subject to being negated by specific policy factors in particular kinds of situation. Such an approach would force the courts to confront the question of when and why the exercise of contractual power should be subject to some control beyond what is found in the ordinary law of contract, and it would also bring into much sharper relief the central question of how far the arguments in favour of review in the public sector can also be applied to private contracting behaviour.

THE BLURRING OF PUBLIC AND PRIVATE

The procedural demarcation between public and private law has attracted much criticism, mainly on the ground that the issue of whether public law principles apply in any situation should be tackled head on as an issue of substance, and not distorted by being mediated through procedural criteria of dubious definition. In other words, the underlying reason why procedural demarcation is unsatisfactory is that it does not reflect any demarcation of *principle* between public and private law. A particularly good example of the difficulty in deriving a distinction between public and private – and one which cannot be seen as the product of the new procedural demarcation following *O'Reilly* v. *Mackman* (1983) – is provided by the legal regulation of the relationship between students and universities. It is now clear that the relationship between a student and a university or college requires the university or college authorities to comply, at the very least, with the principles of natural justice in any disciplinary proceedings. There has, however, been a degree of uncertainty about whether this obligation stems from a contract between the student and the university or whether it is imposed as a matter of public law.

The precise basis of the relationship appears to depend upon which of three kinds of institution is in question. The three possibilities are: institutions created by statute; institutions having a visitor; and institutions not falling into either category. In the first category are the UK universities created out of the former polytechnics in 1992. It was held in *R* v. *Manchester Metropolitan University, ex p Nolan* (1993) on an application for judicial review under Ord 53 that a statutory university was subject to review on the conventional grounds because it was 'a public institution discharging public functions' (per Sedley J). Thus the contractual relationship was not the source of the reviewability of the power, even though the student in question was on a course that was financed on an entirely fee paying basis.

The other two categories are not, it would appear, subject to judicial review under the Ord 53 procedure. To take the residual category first, this includes, in addition to those traditional universities established by royal charter but without a visitor, all wholly private colleges. Here, although the only basis for the relationship is a contract between student and university, the courts have been prepared in principle to regard natural justice as flowing from an implied term in the contract (*Herring* v. *Templeman* (1973)).[8] The position at institutions with a visitor – which includes many of the traditional universities as well as the colleges at Oxford and Cambridge – is that the visitor has exclusive jurisdiction in matters concerning what is known as the 'domestic law' of the institution, which includes the relationship between the institution and its students. The visitor is usually the Crown (typically advised by a senior judge) and is effectively a court which deals with disputes within its jurisdiction and from which there is no appeal. Recent cases have made clear that the visitor's jurisdiction extends to ordinary contractual matters and that it is only open to judicial review on the ground either that the visitor has exceeded his jurisdiction or has not complied with natural justice (*Thomas* v. *Bradford University* (1987); *Page* v. *Hull University Visitor* (1993)). There would therefore appear to be no appeal or review available if a visitor released an institution from the necessity to comply with the rules of natural justice, because judicial review is only available to compel the visitor to comply with natural justice in his proceedings. Nevertheless it seems that visitors will regard the contractual relationship between a student and institution with a visitor as the basis of the obligation to complying with natural justice; but whether the source of this requirement in institutions with a visitor is contractual in origin has been the subject of some judicial confusion (Wade, 1988, p 569, 648).

We see in the student cases the same picture observed in relation to unincorporated associations: a willingness on the part of the courts to be flexible and graft on to a contractual relationship norms usually associated with judicial review. It is striking, though, that the courts have been more surefooted in deciding that natural justice is required in the treatment of students in disciplinary proceedings than in clarifying its legal basis in the various situations. Uncertainty or inter-changeability of the legal basis suggests that it is the substance of the relationship between student and institution that matters rather than the legal form in which the disciplinary powers are cast.

It is clearly arguable that public law principles in addition to natural justice can be applied even where the relationship is wholly contractual in nature. In *ex p Nolan* an exam board's decision to fail the applicant was invalid because it had not taken into account relevant evidence about the applicant's circumstances. This could perhaps have been described as not complying with natural justice, but Sedley J regarded it as a separate ground of review, and in any case he found that all the usual grounds of review were potentially applicable. Although this case concerned a statutory university, it is hard to see any good reason why in principle students at Manchester Metropolitan University should receive more procedural safeguards than those at (for example) the University of Manchester.

The recognition of important limits on the exercise of contractual power has attracted little notice from commentators on contract, but the question has now been posed by writers on public law of how far the distinction between public and private law matters as far as the principles of review are concerned. The erosion of the distinction would pave the way for the wider application of judicial review criteria to contracts, potentially reaching into contract law far beyond the situations so far considered.

The orthodox explanations of judicial review and of contractual obligation cannot justify such a convergence. Although ultra vires can readily be used to cover the quashing of a decision which the public body simply had no power to make, it cannot explain the application of judicial review principles to a non public body. Equally, it is implausible to ground the application of the judicial review principles in the private law cases on the orthodox basis of promise or agreement. In none of the situations are we concerned with express terms, and, even in those situations where there is a contract in existence, the implied term rules have to be stretched a long way to accommodate the required outcome. In contract the implied intent of the parties fulfils exactly the same function as the implied intent of parliament in the case of judicial review: it provides an orthodox way of justifying the imposition of a duty which is determined quite independently of intent in both cases.[9]

Dawn Oliver (1987) has argued that because the private law supervisory jurisdiction has such clear affinities with judicial review proper – 'the boundaries between public and private law and their respective supervisory functions are breaking down' (p 556) – that both should be regarded as being based ultimately on an abuse of power theory under which the exercise of private power is subject to the principles of 'good administration':

> ... economic or contracting power, whether in public or private hands, may be used to restrict the freedom of action of individuals and organisations without their true consent; and it may be used against the public interest in various ways. There is a strong case that such power, whether in public or private hands, should be subjected to supervision and application of the principles of good administration. (Oliver, 1987, p 566)

Sir Gordon Borrie argued similarly (when he was Director General of Fair Trading) that private monopoly power should be subject to the supervisory jurisdiction of the court and, writing not long after the *Datafin* case, advocated a widening of the use of the Ord 53 procedure to achieve this end (Borrie, 1990).[10] The argument for an integrated approach to the control of abuse of power begins to provide some basis for the private law developments, but it leaves open the large question of *how much* private economic power should be open to review in this way. Oliver is not definite on the extent of private power which should be reviewable, but focuses mainly on private power wielded by the kind of bodies having domestic tribunals, principally the sports governing bodies or trade unions which have control over a person's ability to pursue an activity. Lord Denning argued eloquently for the control of domestic bodies in *Breen* v. *AEU* (1971). After spelling out the legal controls on abuse of discretion by a statutory body he continued:

> Does all this apply to a domestic body? I think it does, at any rate when it is a body set by one of the powerful associations which we see nowadays. Instances are readily to be found in the books, notably the Stock Exchange, the Jockey Club, the Football Association, and innumerable trade unions. All these delegate power to committees. These committees control the destinies of thousands. They have quite as much power as the statutory bodies of which I have been speaking. They can make or mar a man by their decisions. Not only by expelling him from membership, but also by refusing to admit him as a member; or it may be, by a refusal to grant a licence or to give their approval. Often their rules are framed to give them a discretion. They then claim that it is an unfettered discretion with which the courts have no right to interfere. They go too far. They claim too much ... Their rules are said to be a contract between the members and the union. So be it. If they are a contract, there is an implied term that the discretion should be exercised fairly. But the rules are in reality more than a contract. They are a legislative code laid down by the council of the union to be obeyed by the members. This code should be subject to control by the courts just as much as the code laid down by Parliament itself. If the rules set up a domestic body and give it a discretion, it is to be implied that body must exercise its discretion fairly. (p 1154)

On this view, the contractual basis of the exercise of discretion of an unincorporated association within its rules is seen almost as a technicality, which should not obscure its essential affinity with the exercise of discretion by a public body acting under statutory power.

However, the potential for an abuse of power theory in contract stretches beyond the context of domestic tribunals. In Chapter 8 I identified an aspect of fairness in contract law as fair treatment: this can be applied not just to the process of contract formation, but also to contract terms other than those fixing the main price:performance ratio. It is with issues of fair treatment that the public law principles are especially well equipped to deal. This stems from the emphasis on the way a decision is reached, which includes matters such as motive, factors taken into account, and opportunity for consultation with and representations by those affected. This emphasis is free of the sterile examination of the parties' intent about matters they never considered, and nor does it run into the thorny issue of the courts redefining the core of the contract which typically is agreed.

There is already a clear affinity between the public law scrutiny of the manner in which power is exercised and some rules on the treatment of one party by another. For example, the principles applied in unfair dismissal are in essence about distinguishing good and bad reasons for dismissing employees, clear echoes of judicial review being found where employees are given rights to consultation, warnings, or the dismissal is seen as capricious or arbitrary. There is clear scope for the more explicit application of these criteria to termination of contract, and even some authority for suggesting that at common law there can be scrutiny of the reason for bringing a periodic contract to an end by notice. In *Timeload Ltd* v. *British Telecommunications Ltd Plc* (1993) the plaintiffs ran Free Pages, a free phone service giving callers advice on choice of tradespeople. They had obtained the number 0800 192192 from BT, which was valuable because of its similarity to the well known number for directory enquiries. BT claimed this number had been obtained by wrongdoing and terminated the contract in accordance with its terms. P sought and obtained an interlocutory injunction preventing BT from cutting off the number. On appeal by BT Bingham LJ held there was a triable issue, and that it was arguable that there was an implied term not to terminate unreasonably: 'I can see strong grounds for the view that in the circumstance of this contract BT should not be permitted to exercise a potentially drastic power of termination without demonstrable reason or cause for doing so' (p 8).

This is not to suggest that public law principles are applicable to every contract. But an approach based on analysing abuse of power in terms of reasons for action has potential to provide content for obligation in a range of commercial as well as personal contracts, thereby offering a way of replenishing the sources of obligation in the general law of contract.

Overall, the examination of the contact between judicial review and contract is particularly valuable in opening up wider perspectives on how the legal relationship between parties to a contract may be conceived and structured. Whether the public law principles are applied as part of the private law, or to a contractual relationship under the Ord 53 procedure, they provide a striking contrast to the rules of the general law of contract. And, just as with boundary issues between contract and other parts of the law of obligations, contact with both the principles and procedure of judicial review puts the nature of contract into question: we now turn to reassess the province of contract.

10
The Province of Contract

If we highlight value pluralism in the law of contract, and for good measure advocate the public law principles of judicial review, can we sensibly describe what infusion is left as a law of *contract*? In this chapter I pursue the question of whether contract law is a useful category and what could or should be brought within in it.

The utility of categories can be judged against different measures, not all of which make the choice of categories a major matter. It is quite possible to regard the categorisation of obligations law or indeed law in general as no more than a matter of convenience in breaking down law into manageable parts, in which tradition, on grounds of familiarity, starts with an advantage (Hedley, 1985b). In any case, 'manageable' here usually means for the purposes of exposition in books and courses: the application of law in practice need not be confined by classification. But the stakes are higher when it is claimed that different categories reflect fundamentally different justifying principles. Thus the claim of Burrows (1983) and other restitution theorists that contract law is based on promise and restitution on unjust enrichment is not only a claim about a convenient division in the law of obligations, but also argues that such principles confine what obligations can properly be part of the subject matter of contract or restitution.

Below, I argue for understanding the province of contract in terms of consensual positive obligation. I do this not because it exposes any single fundamental underlying principle – it clearly does not – but because it widens the range of what can be understood as connected to, and hence capable of influencing, the orthodox conception of the law of contract. The first step is to probe further the boundaries between contract and tort, and contract and restitution.

THE CONTRACT/TORT BOUNDARY

Is there any principled way of drawing a distinction between liability in contract and tort? Commentators have found great difficulty in formulating principles which neatly explain exactly where the line is drawn in practice between the two.[1] The boundary is uneven and does not follow a straight line; it is more like a river whose seemingly haphazard course has been shaped by the peculiarities of local geology. But it is possible to search for some distinction of principle which is reflected, albeit imperfectly, in the law. Perhaps the best approximation is that favoured by Weir: '... tortfeasors are typically liable for making things worse, contractors for not making them better ...' (Weir, 1976, p 5).[2] On this view the plaintiff is thought of as having a base line position in terms of a bundle of interests such as bodily integrity and security of property and other wealth. Tort is concerned with interferences which make that state worse – negligent destruction of property, personal injury. Contract is concerned with failure to improve that state, principally by rendering services, transferring goods, or paying money. Tort duties are thus typically negative duties not to interfere with the plaintiff's activities – to leave well alone. Contract duties on the other hand are typically positive and involve an obligation to provide something specific to the plaintiff. From this it follows that the tort rules apply generally, in that everyone is under a similar duty not to interfere. But contract, being concerned with obligations to act, cannot apply generally, and there must be some trigger to create a special nexus between the parties which picks out the other party from the multitude as the one subject to an obligation to confer a benefit. Traditionally, that trigger is the exchange of promises forming an agreement. This general distinction can only be an approximation and not a description of the contract/tort boundary because there are situations that do not fit. In the present context the most interesting case of lack of fit is to be found in those claims in tort which, because they concern the failure to make someone better off, might have been expected to be found in contract. The development of recovery for negligently inflicted economic loss provides the leading example of such liability, and is in the process of tackling this issue that the recent exploration of the boundary between contract and tort has occurred.

By economic loss is meant financial loss to the plaintiff which is not accompanied by physical damage; the general rule in the tort of negligence is that such loss is not recoverable. Two general kinds of situation can be distinguished. The first is where the defendant negligently interferes with the business activities of the plaintiff, classically where the defendant cuts the power supply to a factory which then stands idle causing lost profits to the owners. After some uncertainty occasioned by the decision of the House of Lords in *Junior Books* v. *Veitchi* (1983), the rule in *Spartan Steel & Alloys* v. *Martin* (1973) that such loss is irrecoverable has been confirmed, and so is not now in any sense an exception to the general rule against recovery (*Candlewood Navigation Corpn Ltd* v. *Mitsui OSK Lines Ltd* (1986)).

The situation where tort can be seen to stray on to contract's territory is where there is some relationship between the parties and the claim is that the defendant has negligently failed to confer a benefit on the plaintiff. It is this category of case which has seen the greatest development, stemming from *Hedley Byrne & Co Ltd* v. *Heller & Partners Ltd* (1964). The novel feature of this case was the recognition by the House of Lords of liability in certain circumstances for economic loss caused by the negligent statements. The case has subsequently been applied to impose liability on those such as accountants, solicitors, surveyors and engineers whose negligent work has resulted in a plaintiff entering a further contract to their disadvantage.

At first it was the application of the *Hedley Byrne* principle to cases where there was no contract that seemed most striking. Lord Devlin in particular had stressed the closeness to contract, saying it would apply in relationships

> ... equivalent to contract, that is, where there is an assumption of responsibility in circumstances in which, but for the absence of consideration, there would be a contract ... I shall content myself with the proposition that wherever there is a relationship equivalent to contract there is a duty of care. (p 530)

Thus the duty has been used in one sense to circumvent consideration by creating an obligation to provide a service with reasonable care even though no contract exists.

It is also now finally settled that the *Hedley Byrne* principle can apply between parties to a contract (*Henderson* v. *Merrett Syndicates Ltd* (1994)), which means that the contractual relationship between the parties is given content in part by rules of tort law. And most recently, in a notably creative application of the principle, the House of Lords in *White* v. *Jones* (1995) has used it to circumvent the privity rule as well as the consideration rule. In this case the contract/tort boundary was debated very fully.

Following a family disagreement a man cut his daughters out of his will. There was a reconciliation and the father's solicitor was instructed to draw up a new will reinstating them. The solicitor did not attend to the matter promptly, with the result that the father died without changing the will. The daughters sued the solicitor for the value of the lost share of their father's estate. There was clearly no contract between the plaintiffs and defendant, and privity prevented any claim by the plaintiffs on the contract with the solicitor. Thus in contract those suffering the loss are without a remedy while the party to the contract (the father's estate) has not suffered the loss necessary to establish a claim. The case was therefore argued in the tort of negligence. In the earlier case of *Ross* v. *Caunters* (1980) (on similar facts except that the solicitor's negligence led to the will being invalid) Megarry VC had held that a duty was owed in negligence under the general principle in *Donoghue* v. *Stevenson* rather than under the rule in *Hedley Byrne*, in part because there was no element of direct communication between solicitor and plaintiffs characteristic of other cases where the *Hedley Byrne* principle had been applied.

Lord Goff recognised the strength of the conceptual problems in the plaintiffs' path: it was a claim for economic loss which was the value of a lost expectation; it involved an omission rather than an act and, as it depended on the contract with the father, any claim must be subject to any limiting terms in that contract, which a duty stemming from the tort of negligence could not be. All these pointed to recovery in contract or not at all.[3] Lord Goff acknowledged the attractiveness of the argument of some commentators, for example Markesinis (1987), that a remedy should be provided in such cases in contract:

> Attractive though this solution is, there is unfortunately a serious difficulty in its way. The doctrine of consideration still forms part of our law of contract, as does the doctrine of privity ... I myself do not consider that the present case provides a suitable occasion for reconsideration of doctrines so fundamental as these. (p 708)

The solution reached was to extend the principle in *Hedley Byrne*. Lord Goff recognised that there was not in reality an assumption of responsibility by the solicitor to the plaintiffs of the kind referred to by Lord Devlin, but said that in these circumstances a remedy should be found under the *Hedley Byrne* principle by holding that the assumption of responsibility by the solicitor towards his client should be held in law to extend to the intended beneficiary. This represents a refusal to apply any idea of privity to the liability arising from the assumption of responsibility under the *Hedley Byrne* principle and is a way of, in effect, enabling a third party to enforce a contract for their benefit in tort.

The recovery of economic loss within some relationships has generally been limited to situations where there has been reliance in the sense that negligent advice has resulted in the plaintiff entering a contract which turns out to be disadvantageous: this is where the *Hedley Byrne* principle has typically been applied. *White* v. *Jones* (1995), however, represents a step beyond this because there was clearly no reliance of this kind. This is even more clearly the case in *Spring* v. *Guardian Assurance plc* (1994). As in *White* v. *Jones*, there was no element of the plaintiff acting to his detriment on negligent advice: he had been dismissed by the defendants from his occupation as a life insurance salesman and, because of the rules applied by Lautro, the regulatory body, needed a reference to obtain employment in the insurance industry. The plaintiff claimed that the defendants had been negligent in providing an untrue and damning reference, and succeeded before the House of Lords in establishing a duty of care. Lord Goff dealt with the fact that the loss was only economic by holding that the *Hedley Byrne* principle applied because there had been a voluntary assumption of responsibility, while the majority (Lord Woolf, Lord Slynn and Lord Lowry) derived the duty of care using the general tests for the existence of a duty of care laid down in *Caparo* v. *Dickman* (1990). It is now clear that the *Hedley Byrne* principle has created a liability in tort for negligently failing to confer a benefit, a kind of claim typically seen as the province of contract. This can take the form of adding obligations where there is an existing contract between the parties; by making certain contracts benefiting third parties effectively enforceable by them, or by creating obligation where there is no contract in sight. Doctrinal limits of contract stemming from the rules on consideration, privity or implied terms melt away; the potential reach of the *Hedley Byrne* principle, especially when cast in Lord Goff's preferred form of the voluntary assumption of responsibility, is immense.

The use of tort to remedy rigidities in contract has been applauded, but the explicit recognition of such a role for tort in a case such as *White* v. *Jones* threatens the integrity of the existing limiting doctrines of contract. The closer to contract that the territory occupied by *Hedley Byrne* seems to be, the more thought will be given to whether such development could not take place within contract. This kind of backwash effect on contract is already visible in *Spring*. In that case an alternative line of argument had been that there was an implied term in the contract obliging the defendant to use reasonable care in providing a reference. The House of Lords avoided the unattractive conclusion of holding that the implied term argument produced a result different from the tort argument by holding that the same duty to take reasonable care was owed on each ground. The result is that the approach to the implied term is pulled in a more flexible direction by the existence of the alternative argument in tort; it is not difficult to envisage this flexibility affecting cases where no tort argument is advanced.

The reason why tort has been able to relieve some rigidities within contract is that contract and tort vary in the flexibility with which they can handle the liability issue in novel situations. In tort, there is a flexible approach to claims of new duties of care, even after the mauling meted out to the idea expressed in *Anns* v. *Merton* (1978) of a prima facie duty (*Murphy* v. *Brentwood* (1991)). The tests of reasonable foreseeability, proximity, and whether a duty is just and reasonable may not be terribly coherent, but they do permit incremental development in response to the merits of a situation. Such flexibility has not existed within contract: consideration, privity and the rules on implied terms have provided a cage which severely hampers innovation. But it is not by any means self evident that there is any good reason for such sharply different approaches to innovation. The idea that obligation in contract always flows from agreement has long been too compromised to justify any general resistance to explicit innovation. And it is arbitrary to say that innovation is appropriate for obligations not to interfere, but not in relation to obligations to make parties better off. The reality is that tort, in the form of the *Hedley Byrne* principle, has provided the means to release contract from the cage. Future cases may well push further on: it was presumably no accident that Lord Goff described *White* v. *Jones* as an unsuitable case for the reconsideration of fundamental doctrines, rather than ruling out such reconsideration completely.[4]

CONTRACT AND RESTITUTION

Unlike the separation between contract and tort, which was part of the emerging of the classical law, the recognition of a distinction between contract and restitution is recent. We noted in Chapter 5 the way in which the absorption of restitutionary claims into contract during the nineteenth century obscured the fact that obligations such as the repayment of money under mistake of fact, or payment of a reasonable sum for goods or services, are not sensibly derivable from the agreement of the parties. Over the last thirty years Goff and Jones, followed by Birks, Beatson and Burrows, have forged a sophisticated analysis which attempts to establish the coherence of restitution as a subject, distinct from contract, and defined by a concern with unjust enrichment; recent judicial pronouncements appear to have blessed this academic labour (*Lipkin Gorman* v. *Karpnale* (1992); *Woolwich Building Society* v. *Inland Revenue Commissioners* (1993)).

In the context of my argument that there is potential to transcend the narrowed conception of contractual responsibility which classical contract introduced, the emergence of restitution is of especial interest. Restitution is in one sense a model of such change: legal principles which were suffocated by classical contract are rejuvenated by being removed from the distortions of the implied contract theory and allowed to proclaim their true basis in unjust enrichment. But although restitution provides an instance of obligations found within the law of contract being released from a forced affiliation with agreement, in another sense it inhibits any further broadening of contract. For some restitution theorists the casting out of their subject from contract is a purification which enhances the coherence and intellectual strength of what is left behind.[5] Hence Burrows' argument that the threefold division of the law of obligations between contract, tort and restitution reflects different principles of liability (Burrows, 1983; above p 25).

It is, however, questionable whether Burrows's justification of the threefold division is based on principles of liability at all. This is because the principles he cites have little or no normative content. He sees tort as based on the principle of compensation for wrongful harm, but there is no definition of what *counts* as wrongful harm: it says nothing about any principle of justice against which the infliction of harm may be regarded as wrongful. Burrows might reply that it is only a general principle and its content must necessarily reside in the detail of the law, in this case tort law. That would be a fair observation, but does not meet the present point. It is possible to regard tort as a category on the basis that most of its component torts share a common *function* (the compensation of wrongful harm), but it does not follow from this that there is a common underlying principle of justice which defines what counts as wrongful. Thus, although existing tort law is dominated by the fault principle, it exists alongside others, for example strict liability or risk based liability (Cane, 1987). It is therefore inaccurate to say that the rules of tort law can in some sense be *justified* by the principle of compensation for wrongful harm, because it is only in these rules that the conception of wrongful harm is given any content or meaning. 'Compensation for wrongful harm' is simply a description of what tort law does, rather than a normative justification for why it does it.

A similar point can be made about the lack of content of the restitution principle of 'unjust enrichment', in that the principle says nothing about when enrichment is unjust. Goff and Jones (1986), in the pioneering English work on restitution, refer to unjust enrichment as an 'abstract principle of justice'. Birks (1985), the author of the second major English work, argues that unjust enrichment is a generic conception in that it describes in a general way the sort of situation which the law of restitution concerns:

... whatever adjective was chosen to qualify 'enrichment' its role was only to identify in a general way those factors which according to the cases themselves, called for an enrichment to be undone. No enrichment can be regarded as unjust, disapproved, or reversible unless it happens in circumstances in which the law provides for restitution. (p 17)

Again, 'reversal of unjust enrichment' defines what the law of restitution does rather than why it does it.

Burrows's principle of the fulfilment of expectations engendered by promises is somewhat different. This does have normative content, albeit very thin, given the very wide meaning he ascribes to promise (see above p 29). This means he is mixing normative and descriptive categories, and it is arguable that the categories are, for that reason, non comparable; certainly, there is no reason to suppose that they are mutually exclusive.

The distinction drawn by Weir between positive and negative obligation provides an interesting comparison. Weir's treatment of tort is virtually the same as Burrows's: wrongful harm and making people worse off are the same essential idea. It is arguable that Burrows's scheme would be more consistent if we insert Weir's other functional category – obligations to make people better off – in the place of promise. Replacing the thin normative principle of promise with the functional category of positive obligation has two important implications.

The first implication is that, if restitution is seen as based on unjust enrichment, it does not fit a system of classification which distinguishes between whether someone is made worse off (tort) or not made better off (contract). This distinction focuses on the nature of the plaintiff's loss, while unjust enrichment focuses on the defendant's gain. They are different ways of focusing on matters of enforceability and remedies, and it is frequently the case that one situation will display both features: in an action for money paid for goods never received, or for a reasonable sum for work done, the defendant's gain *is* the plaintiff's loss.

In this way it is arguable that contract and restitution do not occupy mutually exclusive territory, but quite simply overlap. This is not to deny the functional coherence and utility of treating restitution as a body of law concerned with reversing enrichment, but it does question whether the situations handled by restitution should *only* be considered within that category. Applying instead the rough contract/tort distinction in terms of positive and negative obligation, it is arguable that those parts of restitution originating in contract might equally well belong there. If contract law is understood only as grounded on promise, then clearly the case for treating what was called implied contract (such as the obligation to pay a reasonable sum for goods) separately from contract is strong. But if we construe contract as about the creation of positive obligation based on a variety of principles (including the remedying of unjust enrichment) then there is no need to cast out quasi contract to maintain conceptual purity. It is possible to draw a distinction between two kinds of restitutionary claim involving loss by the plaintiff, one of which resembles the enforcement of positive obligation. The distinction is between those claims which restore the status quo, and so avoid an exchange, and those which in some sense complete an exchange. In the former category – no exchange – are recovery of money paid under mistake of fact and under a total failure of consideration or ineffective contract. In all these instances the aim is to return the parties to their prior position, and the affinity is with tort rather than contract. In the other category – completed exchange – are the claim of a reasonable sum for services rendered (*quantum meruit*) or goods received (*quantum valebat*), and the claim for a sum for services provided in necessitous circumstances. The relevant difference between these kinds of claim is that only in the completed exchange cases does the remedy result in an altogether new position being adopted by the parties, and so the obligation to pay a reasonable sum for goods or services is an obligation to make the recipient better off than if the exchange had never happened at all.

It is perhaps odd that the most strenuous argument for the traditional scope of contract has come from commentators whose primary concern is not contract at all, but establishing the coherence of restitution as a subject. But it is not necessary to cling to contract as being *only* about promise in order to defend the functional coherence of restitution. In a world where the overlap of categories was an offence against the laws of taxonomy, we would have to think very hard before plumping for one classification at the expense of others. But legal classification is not like that: cross cutting and overlapping categories are not only inevitable, but positively beneficial in fostering flexibility and cross fertilisation.

The second implication of adopting the positive/negative distinction is that it identifies space for the imposition of positive obligation beyond promise and agreement. It is a weakness in the work of restitution theorists that their perception of the artificiality in classical contract law tends to be most acute in those parts of it claimed by restitution. It is as though the existence of *some* agreement, about price or selection of goods, is enough to obscure the artificiality in regarding promissory liability as arising in situations where parties are bound by obligation they have not consented to. Examples are implied terms, rules about the quantification of damages, standard form conditions of which parties are ignorant, and after the Unfair Contract Terms Act, where obligations are simply imposed irrespective of consent.[6] It is possible to use the idea of positive obligation to carve out a distinctive function for contract.

THE PROVINCE OF CONTRACT RECONSIDERED

It is a fundamental claim of this book that it is not satisfactory to understand either the content or boundaries of contract doctrine as being grounded on a single principle, or indeed a small number of principles. The province of contract I contend for is not based on any shared value or principle as the defining basis of contractual liability, but on a functional category.

One kind of functional classification is context or fact based, grouping all the law relating to an activity – consumer law, labour law, family law are familiar examples. This is the kind of fragmentation which I suggested in Chapter 4 follows from a primary focus on the reality of contracting practice. But following the contextual route means we lose any *general* focus on the grounds for imposing obligation on citizens. The law of contract as traditionally understood, despite the many problems, does maintain such a focus, albeit one which is empty of much explicit substantive normative content. So what kind of functional definition are we left with? One possibility might be to use the simple idea of a market transaction to define the province of contract. This would be unduly narrow because, as we saw in Chapter 8, contracts exist outside of such transactions. Another possibility would be to use the wider category of legally recognised contracts, but this would be wholly self referential, as it contains no independent criterion.

The functional category which seems to encompass virtually all of the situations regarded as contracts is that adumbrated by Weir in his general distinction between contract and tort: consensual positive obligation. Denoting the province of contract as being about positive obligation does not indicate any single principle for imposing such obligation. The category is empty of normative content, as is the tort category of wrongful harm. Nor am I suggesting that the idea of positive obligation can be used to produce yet another grand theory of a neat and principled division in the law of obligations: the hubris necessary for such an enterprise can hardly survive an encounter with the facts. We have seen that contract law contains a diverse body of rules, based on a plurality of reasons for imposing obligation. Identifying the province of contract in this way is intended to offer a frame that does not (like promise and agreement) attempt to define the boundaries of the subject using principles which have seen their usefulness outstripped in explaining obligation within it. The failure to establish any satisfactory alternative to promise or agreement as the basis of contract entails that there is no principled way of defining the boundaries of contractual obligation.

It may be objected that the idea of positive obligation is so wide that it could include the whole of the law of trusts and company law. This is partly true, but it is not a problem. In the first place, I exclude relationships which have no consensual element at all, whether in the formation or content. For the rest, they do come within the category of positive obligation arising out of consensually entered relationships. But I am not claiming that contract law should *exhaust* the category of consensual positive obligation. My aim in identifying contract with positive obligation is to allocate to it some responsibility for innovation in the residue of situations which fall outside established bodies of law such as trust or company law.

The importance of identifying the province of contract with positive obligation is thus modest and lies in the way it draws attention to a field of liability which is otherwise marginalised or completely overlooked. Promise and agreement do not exhaust the reasons or circumstances for creating positive obligations, whether it be within a contract or outside one. This is already well illustrated by the examples drawn from tort and restitution in this chapter and from judicial review in Chapter 9. In tort, not only does the *Hedley Byrne* principle impose positive obligations where there is reasonable reliance, but cases such as *Spring* v. *Guardian Assurance* and *White* v. *Jones* impose positive obligation even where no reliance is present. And the application of public law principles to contractual relations, whether in private law or under Ord 53, imposes additional positive obligations about how one party may treat another.

All these are examples of positive obligation which have struggled for recognition because they do not fit well within the 'marked slots' of the classical law of contract. Although tort, judicial review and now restitution have provided the legal basis on which such liabilities can be built, their dispersal tends to stifle the recognition that they share an important feature: they are positive obligations which are not grounded on promise or agreement.

Dispersal renders innovation in positive obligation more difficult. Within judicial review and tort the enforcement of positive obligations leads a precarious, marginalised existence. Restitution confines its scope by requiring claims to be relatable to unjust enrichment, thereby ignoring claims for example for fair treatment, where there is no enrichment, and by eschewing any concern with what appears to be the enforcement of a contract. Placing non agreement based positive obligations within contract not only aligns them with the bulk of other such obligations, but also connects them with those parts of the law of contract not claimed by other subjects which are not derivable from agreement. I am therefore arguing for a conception of the law of contract which is explicit in its recognition that promise or agreement police neither its content nor boundaries, in the hope that innovation will be possible within such a frame. In the final chapter I explore some of the forms such innovation could take.

11
The Potential of Contract

Over the last thirty years, judicial review and tort (especially negligence) have rapidly expanded their boundaries through judicial innovation. Restitution has finally seen firm judicial recognition as a free standing part of the law of obligations. In contract, the main changes have been legislative reform limited to particular types of contract, and this process has seen the scope of the general rules continue to shrink. Is it feasible or desirable for the common law of contract to be touched by the dynamic judicial law making which has characterised those other areas? It hardly needs to be said that there are many reasons why such change in contract seems unlikely. But, as legal change is partly dependent on a belief that change is possible, I will explore the potential within the present doctrine for judicial change to take place. It may seem in some of the suggestions below that I am jumping a long way beyond what seems feasible, treating, so to speak, straws as in a wind when they are about to settle back to earth. Yet, it is also worth recalling that doctrinal change is sometimes like the collapse of the Soviet Union, foreseen by no one, but afterwards regarded as inevitable.

The notion that law can have potential may seem strange; within the black letter tradition rules have meaning rather than potential: they either apply or they don't. But to speak of potential is really no more than to generalise from the activity of lawyers in particular cases, when they assess the chances of success of novel legal argument. The potential of any body of general rules for development in particular directions is affected by a range of factors, not least the willingness of judges, especially in the appellate courts, to innovate. Moreover, a necessary condition for innovation in any area is raw case material of a type which permits novel legal issues to be raised. The opportunities for dramatic innovation may be few and far between if chances of success in novel actions are rated low by lawyers, but once a novel decision has been reached it can stimulate further litigation which will provide the opportunity for the elaboration and entrenchment of a novel principle: the development of the principle in *Hedley Byrne* illustrates this well.[1]

The prospects for innovation are not simply a matter of judicial attitude. Important too are the content and structure of the doctrine into which an innovation must be stitched. Although no doctrine may be safe in the hands of an extreme iconoclast, in practice doctrine varies in its susceptibility to innovatory change. Some doctrines or principles are regarded as so deeply ingrained in the law that judicial modification of them, although technically possible by the House of Lords, seems remote (see *White* v. *Jones* (1995), above p 139). Yet even apparently settled principles can be opened up unexpectedly, notably the redefinition of consideration in *Williams* v. *Roffey* (1991).

One avenue of change is legislation, although this is not a product of any potential for judicial change. In fact, it may be that the prospects of law reform are greatest where the judge made law has become becalmed or rigid and therefore least likely to adapt. It is the potential for judicial innovation in the ordinary law of contract with which I am concerned in this chapter, and I aim to show that there is important potential for change within the existing resources of contract law.

Engaging with the potential of contract means asking many questions. They include: is there any limit on the kinds of relationship which are analysable as a contract? does there have to be an exchange, or can activities as far from the classical paradigm as the free use of public health and education services be understood as contractual? are there any limits on the kinds of obligation that can be imposed within contract? Responding to these questions involves probing the limits of the rules in particular situations, and the scope within the law for transcending these limits. I will tackle these issues in three stages. First, I will look at the scope for change in relation to three general doctrinal issues: the implication of terms, the threshold of contract formation, and the remedy of declaration. The first two raise questions about the content and existence of contractual obligation which are fundamental to prospects for change, while the third offers a means circumventing the doctrine of privity. Secondly, I examine the potential for change in two types of relationship: consumer contracts, where the prospect of a general reworking of contract law being ushered in by the Unfair Terms in Consumer Contracts Regulations 1994 will be considered, and the relationship between the provider of a free public service and its users, where I will entertain the possibility of conceiving of such relationships as at least in part contractual. Finally, I address a number of general questions about the process of doctrinal development, especially the role of legislation and the Law Commission.

IMPLIED TERMS AND THE CONTENT OF POSITIVE OBLIGATIONS

Most of the evidence for the emerging divergence between personal and commercial contract law is drawn from outside the general law. The general law has not proved as adaptable, partly because of the persistence in the general law of ideas and values which are most appropriate in commercial contracts, foremost among which is the enduring conception that the obligations of the parties are to be derived ultimately from the agreement they have made. We saw in Chapter 6 the resultant weakness in the law's ability to establish obligation in the absence of agreement. Although the courts have been able to use the absence of real agreement as the basis of new reasons to deprive a contract of binding force (notably economic duress), they have been inhibited from developing an equivalent strand of case law which provides the basis for creating rather than removing obligation. The doctrine on implied terms contains the story of this failure to develop a basis for positive obligation which is outside the agreement of the parties. Yet, the picture here tells both of the bias of classical law *and* the potential for that bias to be overridden.

The origin of the problem was identified in Chapter 6: the dominance of agreement ideas in the classical law in the nineteenth century left the courts without the means adequately to handle situations where there was in fact no agreement. The problem was twofold: on the one hand the obstacles placed in the way of importing terms by way of implication, and on the other the easy incorporation of one sided standard terms which had not been agreed.

The classical law has never found a satisfactory explanation of implied terms – how it is that the parties come to be bound by terms they have not agreed. The simple fact is that the courts have supplemented rudimentary agreement by imposing obligation, although homage is paid to the governing classical principles. Referring to these obligations as *implied* terms contributes to the appearance that they were present, albeit embryonically, in the original agreement. And the emphasis on agreement ensures that implied terms continue to be regarded as exceptions in need of special justification. Thus the process of implying terms in law from the nature of the transaction has never produced any generalisable grounds for discovering contractual obligation, and the codification and consequent petrification of important bodies of these terms, most famously in the Sale of Goods Act 1893, isolated them from any prospect of being woven into a body of more general principle.

It is in the test for terms other than those stemming from the nature of the transaction – usually called terms implied in fact – where obligation has been most restricted. Although the two leading traditional tests – the officious bystander test and business efficacy test – are hardly determinate, they have been used by the courts restrictively. Lord Denning regarded these tests as artificial and attempted to clear the ground in the 1970s. In a number of cases he departed from orthodoxy by claiming terms could be implied where it was reasonable to do so.[2] He cited the support of Lord Wright, who said of implied terms that: '[t]he court is in this sense making a contract for the parties – though it is almost blasphemy to say so' (Wright, 1939, p 259).

This was one of Lord Denning's less successful initiatives. It was effectively extinguished by the House of Lords in *Liverpool City Council* v. *Irwin* (1977) in which Lord Wilberforce dubbed the reasonableness test for implication as extending 'a long, and undesirable, way beyond sound authority'. Lord Wilberforce applied the test of necessity: 'In my opinion such obligation should be read into the contract as the nature of the contract itself implicitly requires, no more no less; a test in other words of necessity.'

The consequences of this drawing back are visible in a case such as *Reid* v. *Rush & Tompkins* (1990). The plaintiff was an employee of the defendant working in Ethiopia on a construction project. He was badly injured a road accident (while on his employer's business) for which the defendants were in no way responsible and for the consequences of which he did not get compensation because those that were responsible were not insured. The plaintiff originally claimed compensation from the employer on the basis of an implied term in the contract of employment, either requiring the employer to provide insurance cover for accidental injury, or requiring the employer to inform the employee that insurance cover was essential given the conditions which prevailed in Ethiopia. These submissions were not only not accepted by the court but were conceded as *unarguable* before the Court of Appeal by counsel for the plaintiff on the basis of the test of necessity for the implication of terms laid down in *Liverpool City Council* v. *Irwin*. Ralph Gibson LJ recognised the policy arguments supporting the plaintiff's contentions, but thought that there was no way the courts could embody this policy in the law without the assistance of the legislature (p 234). The general approach of the Court of Appeal is caught well by Davies and Freedland (1984) in their comment on the tests of implication in the context of employment contracts:

> ... even though they in fact give courts quite wide discretion in deciding whether to imply terms or not, [they] tend to present themselves psychologically as fairly unyielding obstacles to the process of implication. (p 308)

The stunting of the development of a mature jurisprudence of implied terms has helped to make the framework of general contract law inhospitable towards arguments which contend for positive obligations between the parties other than those that can be plausibly grounded in the idea of agreement. The classical approach to standard terms is in striking contrast. The rule in *L'Estrange* v. *Graucob* (1934) that parties are bound by the terms of a document they have signed meant that one sided standard forms were routinely incorporated into contracts, however oppressive the terms. Thus the paradoxical result was reached that reasonable terms might not be incorporated by implication, while unreasonable ones could be incorporated by bare signature.

This does not mean that the law is incapable of expressing obligation other than based on agreement; rather that the grain of the general law exerts a closure on outcomes and makes some much easier to reach than others. We have already encountered in the shape of natural justice an important instance where the rules on implied terms have permitted wholesale imposition of obligations which are difficult to reconcile with the usual tests for the implication of terms. Two recent decisions of the House of Lords also suggest that the approach to implied terms may be loosening. In *Scally* v. *Southern Health and Social Services Board* (1991) the House of Lords held that there was an implied term in the contract under which doctors were employed that required the employer to inform them of a change in the rules about pension contributions. Emphasis was placed on the fact that the contract had been negotiated by a representative body and that it was unrealistic to expect the doctors to know of the change unless it was drawn to their attention. The term was regarded as implied by law by virtue of the nature of the transaction, but was a remarkable development because there was previously a clear trend to regard terms implied in law as attaching to broad categories of contract, for example employment as a whole. Lord Bridge, however, advocated defining the category of relationship much more narrowly. This may, by making it even more difficult to distinguish the term implied in law in a narrow subset of situations from a term implied in fact, contribute to the erosion of the distinction itself.[3]

This approach was followed and extended in *Spring* v. *Guardian Assurance plc* (1994). The plaintiff was unable to obtain employment selling life assurance policies because of the bad reference supplied by the defendant, the plaintiff's former employer: the plaintiff claimed this was untrue and had been supplied negligently. The House of Lords held that there was an implied term in the contract with the former employer to use reasonable care in the provision of the reference. Lord Woolf followed the approach of Lord Bridge in *Scally*, which he regarded as extending the established protection of an employee's physical wellbeing to include protection of the employee's economic wellbeing. Although Lord Woolf refers to this as a necessary implication, this seems little more than paying lip service to the authorities: it is much less restrictive than the approach in *Reid*. Given that it was the employee's economic wellbeing that was in issue in *Reid*, it seems doubtful that the court in *Spring* would have regarded the contention of an implied term to advise on the need for insurance as unarguable.

There are therefore clear signs of a more flexible approach to the implication of terms. But it remains puzzling why the tests of officious bystander, business efficacy, and necessity should have been used restrictively when they are so vague. Paradoxically, it may be precisely their vagueness which is the reason for the restrictive approach. The root of the problem is the way the tests appear to translate the issue of imposed obligation into a question of fact – what the parties would have told the officious bystander, what is required for business efficacy, what is necessary. The reality, as Lord Wright acknowledged, is that few cases surrender to such empirical enquiry. The result is that judges are armed with tests that do not work, and their response in the face of the realisation that they can frequently be used to justify any term or no term is extreme caution: they are thus very sparing in implying obligation. The alternative approach would be for the courts to conduct the discussion of what obligation is to be imposed in a more open way which acknowledges the nature of the operation, much as proposed by Lord Denning. The decision in *Spring*, where the implied term analysis and the more flexible duty concept in negligence produced the same result, suggests that this may be happening. Thus equipped, the stage is set for the courts to develop implied terms incrementally, and to do so in a way that reflects the substantive reasons – as instanced by Lord Woolf's reference to economic wellbeing in *Spring* – rather than bury them under unworkable tests. This would bring the approach to novel implied terms into line with the approach to novel duty situations in the tort of negligence: it is not obvious why the tests for the implication of terms should be more restrictive than the tests for the existence of a duty of care.

THE THRESHOLD OF CONTRACT

The flexibility in doctrine identified so far has related to the content of obligation in an existing contract. Traditionally, there is much less room for manoeuvre about whether a contract exists in the first place, and the rules relating to the formation of contract are therefore especially important in policing what is arguable as a contractual obligation. What scope is there for pushing back the threshold of contract formation?

Courts have been prepared on occasion to clothe the early stages of negotiation with some contractual force. Especially notable is *Blackpool and Fylde Aero Club* v. *Blackpool BC* (1990). The Council invited tenders from selected parties to run pleasure trips from the Council's airfield. Tenders had to be submitted in the prescribed form by the deadline of noon on a certain day. The plaintiff club (which already held the concession) put the tender into the Council's letter box at 11 in the morning on the stated day but it was overlooked. The tender was therefore ruled out, but it proved to have been the highest and therefore likely to have been the one accepted. The orthodox position on tenders is that the body inviting tenders is not bound to accept any tender at all, but the Court of Appeal held that there was a contract imposing an obligation to *consider* tenders which conformed with the conditions of the invitation. Bingham LJ regarded the invitation to tender as the offer, and submission of a timely and conforming tender as the acceptance.   .

The decision in this case is analogous to the approach in cases where the court has held that a unilateral offer may not be revoked where an offeree has begun performance. The leading example is *Errington* v. *Errington* (1952), where a man bought a house for his son and daughter in law to live in. He paid one third of the price himself and borrowed the rest on a mortgage, saying that he would convey the house to the couple if they paid all the mortgage instalments. The Court of Appeal held that the father's offer could not be revoked as long as the couple were actually paying the instalments. The similarity with the *Blackpool* case lies in the recognition of enforceable ground rules about the process of entering into the main transaction, and in both cases the court reached this result despite a strong orthodox argument that no offer had been accepted.

The courts have also probed the threshold of contract in relation to the membership of unincorporated associations. In cases of expulsion or other disciplinary proceedings the courts have had the contractual peg provided by membership on which to hang the control abuse of power. But even in situations short of contract there are instances of the court controlling discretion. The courts have not developed any general right to join, and *Faramus* v. *Film Artistes' Association* (1964) is regarded as deciding that an association is entitled at common law to deny membership under its rules to whomever it wishes. Nevertheless, there are dicta in *Edwards* v. *SOGAT* (1971) suggesting limits on exclusion where there is a closed shop. (Lord Denning based this on the notion of a right to work, Megaw LJ more narrowly on the restraint of trade doctrine; the defendants had conceded membership, however.) In *Nagle* v. *Feilden* Salmon LJ thought it arguable that membership of an association could not be refused unreasonably where it was necessary for the pursuit of a trade or profession. Where an association's rules specify eligibility criteria which a person satisfies, there may be an effective right to join. In *Woodford* v. *Smith* (1970) Megarry J held that the officers of a ratepayers' association had no power to refuse an application for membership where the applicants were in agreement with the objectives of the association. The rules are a kind of standing offer which no officer has any power to revoke. On this basis a right to join can arise, at least where the rules do not give officers discretion in accepting membership applications.

But although the traditional concepts can be stretched to fit, some commentators have regarded the finding of a contract in such situations as artificial. Arrowsmith, for example, has argued that the recognition of an obligation to comply with announced rules is better based on a reliance or estoppel theory, and that the finding of a contract in the *Blackpool* case is 'fictitious' (Arrowsmith, 1994). She drew a parallel between *Blackpool* and *R* v. *The Lord Chancellor, ex p Hibbit and Saunders* (1993), where the failure of a public body to comply with announced tender procedures was held not to be susceptible to judicial review because of the absence of the necessary public element (see above p 130), arguing that the failure of both public and private bodies to comply with announced procedures could be handled as a matter of private law using the concept of reliance. Although reliance may well be an important part of the explanation here, it is problematic to describe the finding of a contract in such circumstances as fictitious.

To speak of the contract as fictitious presupposes that there is some test, outside the flexible boundaries of contract doctrine, of whether a contract *really* exists. We could, for example, stipulate that a contract must have some factual essence – perhaps a market exchange – or claim that the existing doctrine should be construed in a narrow way so as to place the imposition of ground rules beyond the scope of contract law. But Bingham LJ in *Blackpool* did not see the outcome as legally dubious – 'I am pleased that what seems to me the right legal answer also accords with merits as I see them' (at 31) – and it is not clear what pressing ground there is for restricting the scope of contract law to some factual or legal essence of contract. I argued in Chapter 8 that the broadening of the kinds of relation recognised as contractual was a desirable development and one which has ushered in a more plural-istic conception of the subject matter of contract law. The removal of the ground rules of contracting in an attempt to purify the content of contract law 'proper' is not only unnecessary but potentially restric-tive of the obligations which may be imposed.

The explanation of the enforcement of announced ground rules around the making of a contract as based on an independent ground of reliance which is outside of contract could be restrictive because reliance does not exhaust the reasons for imposing such obligations. For example, it is arguable after the decision in *Blackpool* that an employer could be bound by rules announced as applying to the selection of a person for a job. The classical rule giving parties the right to take arbitrary decisions over whether they contract with any individual or not is already circumscribed by the law on discrimination on grounds of sex or race. It is now plausible to argue that the common statements in job advertisements stating that the employer is 'committed to implementing its equal opportunities policy' or 'positive about disabled people' could form the basis of a contractual obligation owed to applicants actually to implement those policies in the appoint-ments process. Although the advertisement is obviously not an offer of a job, it may be capable of being construed as an offer to deal with applications in a certain way, which is accepted by the submission of an application form. Reliance is clearly present here, but reliance on its own does not capture the strength which the case for obligation derives from the argument against arbitrary discrimination.

The issue in the discrimination example above has a clear affinity with the *Nagle* v. *Feilden* line of cases (see above p 126) where some judges at least were prepared, in a private law action, to restrain the use of arbitrary power even in the absence of a contract. It is the dimension of the arbitrary exercise of power – private as well as public – which the explanation of obligation in terms of reliance can obscure. In *Blackpool* itself the court can be seen as responding to the exercise of arbitrary power in abandoning rules which it has been indicated will apply to a group or the public at large. A competitive process, which is initiated by an advertisement for tenders or for a job which states the principles on which the selection will be conducted, has affinities with the situation where competitors in a sport can be said to enter a contractual relationship with the governing body (or with each other) for mutual compliance with rules (*Law* v. *National Greyhound Racing Club* (1983)). In such situations the exercise of the contractual power of the governing bodies is subject to many of the principles of public law (Beloff, 1988).

So, although reliance is part of the explanation for liability in such cases, it is not the whole story: the strand of concern with the exercise of arbitrary power is also present. Where two or more arguments for obligation converge it seems preferable to deal with them under the pluralistic umbrella of contract than to handle the issue on the basis that reliance is the only possible ground. One motive for Arrowsmith's argument for seeing the obligation in cases like *Blackpool* or *ex p Hibbit and Saunders* as deriving from reliance is to establish a basis for the control of tendering procedures where the court will not entertain an application for judicial review under Ord 53. This is an attractive goal, but it is debatable whether it is necessary or desirable to forego public law principles in favour of resting the argument on reliance. Given that there are already areas of contract where the public law principles controlling arbitrary power are utilise it may well be better for these to be made part of the explicit basis of any obligation to comply with the announced ground rules, clothed in the form of a contract regulating the contracting process.

THE DEVELOPMENT OF CONSUMER CONTRACT LAW

One legacy of the doctrinal failure of the general common law of contract to cope with exclusion clauses is that most of consumer contract law is legislative in origin: the rules relating to consumer contracts appear as a series of exceptions to the general doctrines. Even where those doctrines do apply to consumers, it is in a sense misleading to speak of these doctrines as being part of consumer law, in that little of it has been generated in the handling of consumer cases. The result is that no body of principle articulating and responding to the distinctiveness of consumer issues has been developed in the case law. Legislation, such as the Consumer Credit Act 1974 and the Unfair Contract Terms Act 1977, has made important modifications to the doctrine, but such provisions have been inert as sources for the wider development of principle. Moreover, legislative provision for consumers relating to credit or exclusion clauses makes it even less likely that the general law can adapt to deal with other consumer issues. Since the 1977 Act there has been very little development of the common law rules on exclusion clauses, or indeed on all kinds of terms in consumer contracts. Now, if the 1977 Act really did deal with all the conceivable problems with such clauses in all situations, then perhaps it would not matter that the resources of the common law have withered. As this seems unlikely – witness the wider scope of the Unfair Terms in Consumer Contracts Regulations (1994), considered below – the result of specific legislation in this instance has been to cauterise emerging principle in the common law.

One of the obstacles in the way of the general law developing a greater sensitivity to consumer issues is its tendency to operate with a commercial model of contract, which places agreement at the centre of the relationship and which is insensitive to the distinguishing features of personal contract law discussed in Chapter 8. Seen through these spectacles, the most noticeable thing about consumer contracts is what marks them off from the ordinary commercial contract. Thus inequality of bargaining power was an important idea in the courts' campaign against exclusion clauses, and was used in an attempt to explain the limits of the ordinary contract rules. But this is to see consumer contracts in terms of the absence of factors which are taken to be present in the 'normal' case. It can offer a reason for disapplying the rules of classical contract, and so explain why a consumer is not bound by a term or contract: it provides a means of expressing what the relationship is not, but is less good at expressing what its basis actually is. If we were to start from scratch and choose the most appropriate language in which to express the private law obligations arising in the consumer/supplier relationship, it seems doubtful that we would reach for the language of classical contract and speak in terms of what had been *agreed* by the parties. Almost invariably, the issues which give rise to complaint, such as the quality and fitness of goods and services, are handled by either standard terms or by statutory implied terms, neither of which has in any meaningful sense been agreed by the parties. Instead of seeing the relationship as presumptively a consensual one, in which messy reality has to be supplemented by obligations which are not agreed, it makes more sense to reverse the presumption. In other words, the consensual part of the relationship – typically the choice of goods or services at a set price – is dwarfed by the obligations which are imposed by virtue of the nature of the transaction.

One consequence of the lack of general principles of consumer contract is that innovation is blocked. Legislation moves the law forward in narrowly defined increments, but leaves the residue of situations subject to the general rules of contract. For example, insurance contracts, which were excluded from the scope of the Unfair Contract Terms Act 1977, have been the object of extraordinary abuse in some fields, notably the high pressure sale of endowment policies to house buyers for whom they are frequently wholly inappropriate. Yet there has been no judicial innovation to counter the abuse, which has now been tackled by regulatory means under the Financial Services Act 1986.

Even more remarkable is the position in relation to the enforceability of manufacturer's guarantees. The orthodox analysis is that such guarantees run into the problem that there is no privity of contract between manufacturer and consumer, and the only way a guarantee can be enforceable is if some consideration can be found for the manufacturer's promise contained in the guarantee; this appears to depend on whether the goods were bought with knowledge of the guarantee.[4] The policy argument that such guarantees should be enforceable (and probably transferable too) seems overwhelming, yet the issue has never received judicial elaboration.

The appearance of the Unfair Terms in Consumer Contracts Regulations 1994, implementing the European Union Directive, creates the conditions for a more principled development of consumer contract law. The regulations apply to terms other than those defining the 'core' terms of price and performance, and provide that where such terms in a consumer contract have not been individually negotiated they will be invalid if unfair. An unfair term is defined as one which 'contrary to the requirements of good faith causes a significant imbalance in the parties' rights and obligations under the contract to the detriment of the consumer' (reg 4(1)). For common lawyers, the arresting thing about this provision is its extreme vagueness. Good faith is not an elaborated concept in English contract law, and the method of calibrating significant imbalance is far from clear. Schedule 3 contains an indicative list of seventeen kinds of terms that may be unfair, but it is likely that there will be other terms which will need litigation to clarify their validity. This will provide the courts with an opportunity to fill out the meaning of the concepts of good faith and significant imbalance, thus fashioning a more explicit body of principle about the norms to be applied in consumer contracts.

It is not a foregone conclusion that this will happen, however: much will depend upon the style of decision-making which the courts adopt. The important issue is the degree to which the meaning of unfairness under the regulations is subject to judicial elaboration in case law. Although a standard can be a mere legislative peg on which to hang judicial law-making, sometimes the legislative formulation is kept relatively clean of precedent, with few cases being seen as having value as precedents. An example of the latter approach is the treatment of the reasonableness test under the Unfair Contract Terms Act 1977. The decision of the House of Lords in *Mitchell (George) (Chesterhall) Ltd v. Finney Lock Seeds* (1983) has constricted judicial development of the meaning of reasonableness by limiting the role of appellate courts to deciding whether a first instance decision is obviously wrong. This, together with the fact that many cases are disposed of at county court level, has meant that surprisingly few cases on reasonableness have been reported. In contrast is the elaboration of the idea of unfair dismissal under the Employment Protection (Consolidation) Act 1978, which has seen the emergence of a sophisticated body of case law elucidating the issue of whether a dismissal is unfair.

It is therefore difficult to foresee the extent of judicial elaboration of the idea of unfairness under the regulations. Litigation of consumer cases to a level where they can become precedents remains rare. One factor responsible for the judicial elaboration of the concept of unfair dismissal is that the decisions of the Employment Appeal Tribunal, to which parties can appeal from the decisions of the relatively informal industrial tribunal, are routinely reported. The jump to the Court of Appeal from the county court is much bigger for consumer litigants, even more so if the case is started under the small claims procedure in the county court.

The tendency for consumer litigation to remain below the precedent 'horizon' may be countered by the possibility of the Director General of Fair Trading exercising his power under reg 8 to apply for an injunction to restrain the continued use of terms thought to be unfair. Such actions will clearly provide potential for the superior courts to develop a case law which elaborates the meaning of unfairness. The exciting possibility therefore opens up that English law will elaborate a principle of good faith in consumer contracts. The content of the principle of good faith remains contested: as Collins points out, it could be narrowly construed and seen as essentially about unfairness in the negotiating process, or it could draw on the fuller conception in German law (the basis of the EU Directive) which includes the issue of substantive fairness (Collins, 1994). Either way, the legal machinery is now in place for a judicial engagement with such issues which may see the evolution of norms to be applied to consumer contracts, relatively free of the constriction of the commercial grain of the

general law. There is perhaps irony in the fact that a notion of substantive justice which (Gordley claimed) left a hole in contract doctrine
when it was lost during the reception of Civilian principles of contract
into the common law 200 years ago, may now be finding its way in
through the good offices of the European Union (see above p 67).

One instance where there is potential for a principled recognition
of consumer interests to spill over and exert influence beyond the strict
scope of the regulations is the way the consumer interest is recognised
in the rules about damages. We have already noted judicial recognition of the special nature of losses in personal contract law with the
emergence of damages for disappointment, which are not available in
commercial contracts. But there is some considerable way still to go,
as is well illustrated by the effect on the liability of surveyors of the
recent Court of Appeal decision in *Watts* v. *Morrow* (1990). This was
condemned by the Consumers' Association for undercompensating
consumers who buy houses on the strength of a surveyor's report
which turns out to have been negligent. The plaintiffs had bought a
second home in Dorset, with paddock and fishing rights, to provide
relaxation at weekends away from their stressful, highly paid jobs in
the City. The defendant surveyor they hired to inspect the property negligently missed serious defects and, for eight months while repairs were
being carried out, their use of the house was severely hampered. The
plaintiffs claimed about £34,000 as the cost of the repairs of the defects
missed by the defendant surveyor, but were awarded only £15,000, the
amount by which the house was worth less than the purchase price.

The Court of Appeal arrived at the difference of value rather than
the cost of repair as the correct measure by applying the expectation
principle – putting the plaintiffs in the position they would have
been in if the contract had been performed. Thus the court asked
what the plaintiffs would have done if the surveyor had taken reasonable
care and revealed the defects. They would either have renegotiated and
bought at a lower price or not have bought this house at all. If they
would have renegotiated and repaired, then the difference in value is
clearly the correct measure – the only difference between the actual and
contractual position is that they have paid £15,000 more. It was
accepted, however, that the plaintiffs would not have bought this
house as they did not want one requiring a lot of work. The court
applied the difference in value measure here too, on the basis that the
plaintiffs would instead either have kept the purchase money, or
bought another house for the same figure, which would be presumed
to be worth its price. Either way, they were only £15,000 worse off than
they would have been if the surveyor had performed the contract.
Giving the plaintiff the cost of repairs, it was said, would be to put them
in a position they would not have been in even if the contract had been
performed.[5]

The court also refused damages for the mental distress and disappointment resulting from the house not being available, limiting damages to the mental distress consequent on the physical inconvenience associated with the breach. This was explained on the basis the contract was not one for the provision of peace of mind and freedom from distress; this was 'an impossible view of the ordinary surveyor's contract' according to Ralph Gibson LJ (at 1442).

The problem with the general law of contract which this reveals is a tendency to conceive of consumer losses as though they are commercial ones. The particular flaw in the reasoning is that it assumes that the difference between the actual position of the plaintiffs and the contractual position can be satisfactorily understood in pecuniary terms. If the surveyor had not been negligent the plaintiffs would have bought, settled in and become attached to a house that was – as far as reasonable care by a surveyor could make it – trouble free. The reality is that this opportunity has gone for good and they have ended up in house that needs major and disruptive repairs. They are faced with the choice between the arduous business of finding another house, or repairing the one they have got: they cannot in any real sense regain the contractual position by an award of damages based on the difference in value of their assets. Damages here are not the cost of a replacement performance, but compensation for a lost opportunity which is not wholly pecuniary, and repairing may be a reasonable step in the mitigation (but not avoidance) of such a loss when set alongside the cost and disruption of selling up. On this view, the approach of Judge Bowsher at first instance in addressing whether in all the circumstances it was reasonable for the plaintiffs to stay and repair seems to reflect the real nature of the losses in this kind of case more accurately. The court's approach seems wholly right in relation to property acquired for commercial purposes, but insensitive to the different nature of the consumer interest. (Macdonald, 1992)

The distinctiveness of the consumer relationship with a surveyor was recognised in *Smith* v. *Eric Bush* (1990) where, in the context of the reasonableness of a disclaimer of liability Lord Griffiths accepted that it was justified to treat consumers differently. Now that the Unfair Terms Directive is implemented, there is the potential for the emergence of *general* principles about the nature of consumer contracts which will counteract the tendency of cases such as *Watts*.

THE USE OF PUBLIC SERVICES: A CONTRACTUAL RELATIONSHIP IN THE MAKING?

The most obvious means of challenging the legality of a decision of a public body is judicial review. In addition, an action in tort, either in negligence or for breach of statutory duty, is possible in some situations, most obviously in relation to medical negligence by employees of the National Health Service. But is it possible to conceive of the relationship between the user and provider of a free public service as a contract?

Traditionally, the use of a service provided by a public authority has not been seen as contractual. The case law is most plentiful where services such as gas are paid for by the user; it was settled in the eighteenth century that the postal service was not supplied contractually (*Whitfield* v. *Lord Le Despencer* (1778)) and this approach was applied to the supply of gas, electricity and water by public authorities acting under statutory powers. Privatisation of these utilities has introduced the possibility of supply by special agreement, although it does not seem entirely clear whether the ordinary household user has a contract with the utility company: the position across all utilities may not be uniform (Harden, 1992).

The case law is extremely scanty when it comes to the free provision of services, although one might expect a contract to be even more difficult to establish where there is no payment. Absence of any payment is not, however, fatal to finding a contract. Although it may seem far-fetched to see the relationship between a parent or pupil and state school as a contract, this is precisely the way that the similar relationship between universities and their students is conceptualised.

We saw in Chapter 9 that, while the susceptibility of a university to judicial review under Ord 53 depended on its being a creation of statute, it is now thought that the principles of natural justice are implied as terms in the contracts between universities and their students where the university is not a statutory body, as is the case with the 'old' universities which are incorporated by royal charter. And, despite this distinction for the purposes of judicial review, it seems that in both types of university a range of issues between a university and a student are commonly thought to stem from a contract; these include the process of obtaining a place and the treatment of students in deciding progression from one year to the next (*Herring* v. *Templeman*). It is not difficult to construe the relationship as contractual where the student is paying fees, as with many postgraduates and overseas undergraduates. But how can there be a contract when the student pays no tuition fee? Academic commentators, although divided on the appropriate jurisdiction of the university visitor, agree that the relationship with students is contractual (Wade,1969; Bridge, 1970; Samuels, 1973).

The process of making such a contract has received little discussion in case law; a recent instance is *Moran* v. *University of Salford* (1993), where the view was expressed that a contract with offer, acceptance and consideration could be established. In *Moran* the plaintiff had applied for a place on the physiotherapy degree at University College Salford.[6] He was made an unconditional offer which he accepted, but it turned out that the offer had been a clerical error. The college refused to admit the plaintiff and he sought an interlocutory injunction compelling them to do so. On appeal, all the members of the court thought that offer and acceptance were clearly present. Consideration for the college's promise could be found in the plaintiff's suffering detriment by withdrawing from the clearing system, through which he would otherwise have sought a place (per Glidewell and Evans LJJ).[7] Although relief was refused on other grounds, the decision on the contract point is especially notable in the light of the circumstances: this was a case of a clerical error resulting in a moderately qualified candidate being offered a place on a very oversubscribed course, and it was a decision that there was a strong arguable case, not just of a contract to educate, but a contract to enrol: in fact, it was accepted on all sides that enrolment would bring a contract into being. Where enrolment actually takes place, it would seem that there are a number of ways of finding consideration: it could lie in the counter promise to abide by the institution's regulations, or conceivably in the benefit to the institution where its public funding depends on the numbers enrolled.[8]

Evans LJ referred to the following statement in the PCAS handbook, the guide used until 1993 entry by applicants to the former polytechnics when completing their forms:

> Should you become a student at a polytechnic, college, or one of the new universities established under the 1992 Further and Higher Education Act, it will be a term of your contract with that institution that it will take all reasonable steps to provide the educational services described in its prospectus ...

A similar statement now appears in the handbook produced by UCAS, the successor admissions service to PCAS and UCCA, which since 1994 entry has handled undergraduate applications to all UK universities.

Once the platform of a contract is established, it has potential to be used as the basis to assert a number of claims. This extends beyond natural justice in disciplinary matters, and could include such things as conduct of the examination and assessment process, substandard teaching, departures from announced provision of accommodation or other facilities, the withholding of degree results or degrees from debtors, and non compliance with the terms of its students' charter. It would be possible in mounting such arguments to rely on legislation; for example, on the assumption that a university would be treated as dealing in the course of a business for purposes of the Unfair Contract Terms Act 1977, it is possible to challenge the withholding of degrees in the face of debts under s 3(2)(b)(i). This provides that a party contracting on standard terms (for example, a university) cannot 'claim to be entitled to render a contractual performance substantially different from that which is reasonably expected' unless the term in question is reasonable. By withholding a degree a university is withholding a major part of its performance under the contract, and any term purporting to entitle an institution to do this in the case of minor debts could well be unreasonable. Similar arguments could also be mounted under the Unfair Terms in Consumer Contracts Regulations 1994 for, although the original EU Directive did not expressly refer to services not paid for, the terms of the regulations do not appear to exclude them; at the least, they would apply unproblematically to fee paying students.

In this way it is possible to use a contractual analysis to prise open a set of issues that might otherwise remain beyond the reach of the law. To what extent is this kind of analysis transferable to schools and other free public services? There are two legal hurdles to surmount if a contract is to be established: that a contract in such a situation is not ruled out by public law, and that a contract has come into existence under the ordinary law of contract.

One obstacle is the different legal status of state schools compared with universities, which reflects the different history of the emergence of free provision. The development of free school education was a gradual process which saw both the foundation of new schools and the taking over by public authorities of some existing schools offering a mix of free and paid for education, as with many grammar schools. After the Education Act 1944 these were funded and managed through an essentially unified system run by local authorities, but wholly private schools (fee paying, confusingly also called public schools) were left outside this structure and remained in the private sector. In the case of the universities, the move towards state financing which accompanied free provision included all universities, so that there was no private sector left behind. However, universities retained their separate identity as chartered corporations, and continued to receive some fee paying students, while most state schools found their identity submerged within that of the local authorities and took no fee paying pupils. The public/private divide, which has become blurred in the universities, has therefore traditionally been more intact in relation to schools.[9]

Does the statutory basis of state schools make a contract unarguable? The significance of the existence of a statutory power or duty for a private law claim has received more judicial elaboration in tort than in contract. In tort, there are two ways in which the existence of such a power or duty can relate to a claim. The action for breach of statutory duty arises where there is a class of people for whose protection a duty has been imposed, as in the classic instance of the claim for damages following an industrial injury occasioned by breach of a safety regulation; this is unlikely to apply to legislation in the areas of education and social services (*E* v. *Dorset County Council* (1995) per Lord Browne Wilkinson). The well established common law duty to take care in the exercise of at least some species of statutory power has a larger scope, and most recently in the *Dorset* case the House of Lords held that there was an arguable case that a duty of care may be owed by a local authority when providing psychological advice in the exercise of its powers under the Education Act 1981 in relation to a pupil with dyslexia.

In relation to contract, there do not appear to be any inherent obstacles to the recognition of a contract of use. *Moran*, which concerned a statutory university, suggests that a basis of statutory powers and duties does not prevent institutions entering contracts with students. As a matter of principle, the competence of a statutory body to enter a contract would depend in part on whether it had, expressly or impliedly, been granted that power by statute: the fact we are not contemplating a contract to *sell* the service in question removes the most powerful objection to such an argument.

Even if there is no absolute bar in public law to the existence of a contract relating to the free provision of a public service, this leaves the second hurdle: could the relationship with a user qualify within the ordinary law of contract? Apart from the university cases, there does not appear to be any reported case where an action has been brought for breach of contract, but the issue did arise indirectly in a case of judicial review, *R* v. *The Governors of Haberdashers' Aske's Hatcham College Trust, ex p Tyrell* (1994). The applicant sought judicial review of the school's refusal to admit him, claiming that the announced admissions criteria had not been adhered to. It was argued on behalf of the school that its status as a City Technology College (it was not administered within the statutory powers applying to other maintained schools but under an agreement with the Secretary of State) meant that it was not susceptible to judicial review. In order to avoid depriving pupils and parents of any remedy, counsel for the school argued that the relationship was contractual. Dyson J held that the school was in the same position as any other publicly funded school and therefore susceptible to judicial review; he gave the contract argument short shrift:

> In my judgment, the relationship between parents and CTCs is no more founded in contract than that between parents and maintained schools. It has never been suggested that there is a contractual relationship between parents and maintained schools. In my view there is no such relationship, since even if there is consideration, there is no intention to enter into contractual relationship on either side (p 34).

It is interesting that the claim of contract founders on intention to create legal relations: does this mean that there are no other difficulties within the ordinary law of contract? We will briefly survey the possible obstacles.

The main reason why the contractualisation of the organisation of public services, as with the internal market in the National Health Service or the creation of Next Steps agencies, does not result in enforceable contracts is that the organisations do not have separate legal personality and therefore lack the capacity to enter a contract (Harden, 1992, p 46). This does not apply to the relationship with users, however: the individual user (or their parent) clearly has capacity, and there will be some type of corporate body responsible for service provision.

Of the elements of formation, offer and acceptance would appear to give the least difficulty. Things might have been different when pupils were allocated to schools only using a catchment area rule, but now that parents may have at least a theoretical choice between schools, there is a process of application forms followed by allocation of a place which is not that different from the procedure used for universities. Also, people typically have some choice over which general practitioner they become a patient of. In fact wherever the user has some degree of choice about the provider, it may be possible to find a sufficient consensual element on which to base offer and acceptance.

Consideration also could be present, by analogy with arguments voiced in *Moran* above: parents could act to their detriment by relying on the promise of a place in various ways, including no longer seeking a place at other schools, and taking such preparatory steps as purchasing a school uniform. And where the provider's income depends on a formula linked to numbers, as with schools and general practitioners, it is also arguable that consideration will lie in the benefit received by the provider. There is at least *something* which could be construed as consideration for, for example, the promise of a place or undertakings about the nature of educational provision in the school prospectus.

The doctrine of privity will pose a problem if there is a contract between a school and the parents of a pupil: it will mean that the pupil will have no action. This was recognised in *R* v. *Fernhill Manor School, ex p Brown* (1992). The applicant was expelled from a fee paying school without being given any opportunity to respond to the allegations made against her. Brooke J accepted that there had been a clear breach of natural justice, but held that private schools are not susceptible to judicial review because the required public element was absent. The relationship was entirely contractual, and although the school was bound by contract to comply with natural justice (in addition to terms contained in the school prospectus) privity meant that only the parent, not the pupil, was entitled to a remedy. Privity will bite hardest where the claim is for damages for loss suffered by the pupil, but where the remedy sought is a declaration of rights then the fact it is the parent who brings the action would not appear to matter.[10]

This leaves the element of intention to create legal relations. First elaborated in the context of a domestic agreement (*Balfour* v. *Balfour* (1919)), it is another doctrine which seeks to translate into an empirical question – what did the parties intend? – what is in essence an issue of policy. Although the question will sometimes be capable of meaningful answer, parties do not typically address their mind to the issue of whether their relationship should give rise to legal enforceability. And in the context of public services, where judicial review may be available, it is stretching things to suppose that users or providers habitually distinguish between enforceability in private and public law. In reality, the doctrine is a control device – '[t]he legal relations doctrine gave the judges *carte blanche* to impose or refuse contractual liability in unfamiliar contexts' (Hedley, 1985a, p 403). If this is the only barrier to establishing a contract, it is one that the judges, at least in a case of first impression, are able to chose whether to put in their own way.

But even if it is at least arguable that the technical legal requirements of a contract in relation to the provision of a public service could be overcome, why on earth *should* the user relationship be conceived as a contract? One reason stems from changes in the substance of the relationship, away from the provision on an entirely take it or leave it basis towards one where the decisions of individual users and providers play more of a role in shaping the service than previously. This picture is clearest in relation to schools. Changes have included: permitting parents some degree of choice of school, which has been achieved by a policy of open enrolment, coupled with formula funding, so that schools can recruit and receive funding up to their physical capacity; devolution of greater management responsibility to school level, under both the local management initiative in LEAs and under the grant maintained system; the greater involvement of parents as members of the Governing Body; the requirement for the provision of more information in terms of exam results, prospectuses, an annual report to a meeting of parents, and the preparation of action plans following Ofsted inspections. All of these introduce a greater degree of voluntariness into the school/parent relationship, which make it more appropriate to be conceived as a contract.

This point is reinforced by the increasing use of free standing organisations to 'deliver' public services under contract with commissioning or purchasing authorities. The most well known example is the internal market introduced into the National Health Service, whereby health authorities or fund holding general practitioners purchase health care from providers such as hospitals. There are clearly problems in regarding the purchaser/provider relationship as a contract in law (Vincent-Jones, 1994) but the separation of the provider from departments of state may make it more arguable that the provider/user relationship is at least part contractual. This is, after all, the position that the universities have long been in, as autonomous institutions providing a public service with funds supplied for that purpose by the state.

The other reason for conceiving of the relationship in terms of contract is that a private law action has advantages compared with the application for judicial review. As well as certain procedural drawbacks of the Ord 53 procedure,[11] there is the important fact that some of the possible claims may be beyond the reach of judicial review. For example, competition between schools has led to schools promoting themselves to parents through glossy prospectuses, and the issue can arise of whether the factual statements are wholly accurate, or whether the promise or undertakings are fulfilled. This is the standard fare of contract law, but in judicial review it would turn on whether any decision of the school or LEA could be brought within one of the accepted grounds of review and (which is rather doubtful) whether the doctrine of legitimate expectation could apply. Also, it seems that it is much more difficult within judicial review to entertain the possibility that duties may be placed on parents, which is perfectly possible within a contractual analysis. And it does not follow that because some aspect of the relationship is contractual that judicial review is completely ousted, as the *Nolan* case demonstrates.

One approach for the courts to adopt is to draw a sharp line between public and private sectors, so that private is the exclusive preserve of contract and other private law and public the exclusive preserve of judicial review. But we saw in Chapter 9 the degree of penetration of public law principles into private law and contract in particular, and the reach of the tort duty of care into public law is well established. Positing that free public services could be conceived of as contracts is not, therefore, a massive step and is in line with the blurring of the public/private divide which the Conservative Government's reforms of the state have ushered in.

None of this is intended to suggest that the user's relationship with a public service should be narrowly conceived as a commercial contract: as I argued in Chapter 8, the recognition of this sort of relation as contractual contains the possibility of developing a conception of contractual obligation which draws much more widely, and which recognises and is responsive to voluntary relationships which are not market relations, but which are not wholly bureaucratic ones either. In essence, I am arguing that the idea of contract need not collapse when the element of monetary payment is withdrawn.

Nor am I suggesting that the legal analysis presented above *describes* any settled legal position. I contend only that it is *arguable* that the voluntary non market relations concerned with public services are analysable as contracts: my point is to establish the potential of contract, thereby conveying that what prevents such argument succeeding is nothing which is internal to the law of contract itself.

CONTRACT, PUBLIC INTEREST LITIGATION, AND THE DECLARATION

It seems rare for contract law to be the basis of public interest litigation, that is a legal action in which an individual or group seeks to further not just their own interest but that of an affected group, or the public at large. This is increasingly common in tort, where group actions are pursued in respect of drug side effects and environmental harms, and in judicial review where pressure groups such as Greenpeace have now been held to have a sufficient interest to apply to the court under Ord 53 (*R v. Inspectorate of Pollution, ex p Greenpeace Ltd (No 2)* (1994)). The only instance where contract law is used in this way is probably in relation to discrimination in employment, where employees, usually assisted by trade unions, have pursued cases which have resulted in significant improvements in employment protection.

What scope is there for public interest actions in contract outside employment? Consumers are the obvious category who may suffer a 'group' harm, and this is recognised in the provision in the Unfair Terms in Consumer Contracts Regulations 1994 for actions by the Director General to test the legality of standard terms. This role for the Director is the UK's means of implementing Article 7 of the Directive which requires Member States to provide that preventative action can be taken by 'persons or organisations, having a legitimate interest under national law for protecting consumers'. The UK's exclusion of non governmental bodies from the right to initiate preventative action was controversial, and it is debatable whether the UK's means of implementing the Directive would survive challenge in the European Court. However, despite the narrow implementation of the Directive, there is scope for public interest actions in contract to make use of the remedy of declaration to reach a similar result.

A declaration is a remedy which is available in public and private law, although it is accorded scant treatment in the contract books. The litigant simply asks the court to declare the law in relation to a particular set of facts. Although the declaration is in one sense a toothless remedy – no one is ordered to do or refrain from doing anything – it has nevertheless proved remarkably effective, presumably because the organisations, whether public or private, typically subject to a declaration usually wish to avoid having their actions branded as unlawful.

One of the most remarkable uses of the declaration in contract has been in restraint of trade cases. The courts have, since the eighteenth century, held contract terms restraining a person's freedom to trade void if they are unreasonable. This seemed, however, to have an important drawback as a control on monopoly power: it could only be used to invalidate a contract term if a party to the contract was also a party to the action before the court. As most participants in cartels were perfectly happy for them to continue, the doctrine was unable to assist a third party whose interest was affected by agreements in restraint of trade. A novel way around the third party problem was followed by Wilberforce J in *Eastham* v. *Newcastle United Football Club Ltd* (1964). The plaintiff was a professional footballer with Newcastle United who had been refused a transfer to another club. Under the transfer system run by the Football League with the Football Association he was unable to play for any other club until Newcastle chose to release him. The problem facing the plaintiff was that the transfer system which he wanted to challenge as being in unreasonable restraint of trade was effectively contained in the contract between the Football League and the Football Association. It had been settled by the House of Lords in *Mogul Steamship Co* v. *McGregor, Gow & Co* (1892) that no tort was committed when members of a cartel deliberately injured a competitor. Wilberforce J, however, held that the court had power to grant a declaration that the term in the contract between the Association and the League was in unreasonable restraint of trade even though the plaintiff had neither an action for damages nor an injunction in contract or tort against either party.[12]

The question of whether a declaration can be obtained without an otherwise enforceable private right in private law has never been entirely resolved. Although *Eastham* was applied in similar circumstances in *Grieg* v. *Insole* (1978) (the case about the 'Packer Affair' in international cricket), remarks by the House of Lords in *Gouriet* v. *Union of Post Office Workers* (1978) have resulted in the courts in some cases requiring the actual or potential infringement of some private right before granting a declaration: see *International Commercial Bank plc* v. *Meadows Indemnity Ltd and the Insurance Corporation of Ireland* (1989).[13]

The potential of the declaration lies in the way it enables a litigant to hold up for legal scrutiny a contract which affects their interest, although they are not a party to it. What are the prospects for the declaration to be used in more widely in private law? The reasoning behind relaxation of the locus standi rule for judicial review to allow pressure groups to apply under Ord 53 provides an instructive comparison.

The reasons included a recognition that a common interest group could have a legitimate interest in the issue at stake, and also that they could bring expertise to bear beyond the scope of the individual litigant, as well as being 'good for' any award of legal costs. Exactly the same arguments could be used to support, for example, the Consumers' Association or a trade union being able to apply for a declaration of the validity of a standard form contract introduced by a supplier or employer. The orthodox objection is that this is private not public law, and the validity of a contract is no business of persons who are not parties to it, still less if they are not even affected by it. But the existence of a public interest in terms on which goods and services are traded has long been acknowledged in the form of regulation of the conditions of trade, and there are strong arguments for permitting representative actions to test the legality of practices which affect large classes of people who are infrequently in a position to litigate themselves. This much has perhaps been recognised in the Unfair Terms in Consumer Contracts Regulations in the provision in Reg 8 for the Director General of Fair Trading to challenge standard terms as unfair under the regulations. But the courts *could* achieve a similar result – and arguably one required by the Directive on which the regulations were based – by enabling interest groups to seek a declaration of the validity of a standard form. The declaration sought by an interest group could make a valuable contribution to the development of personal contract law; it will require persistent litigants and bold judges to achieve it.

POTENTIAL OF CONTRACT AND THE PROCESSES OF LEGAL CHANGE

The identification of the potential for judicial innovation in contract by prising open existing doctrine is a necessary but not sufficient condition for such change to take place. The other requirement – assuming a flow of suitable raw material from litigation – is judicial participation. The issue here is not about judicial conservatism, in the sense of a general unwillingness to contemplate change: tort, judicial review as well as areas more distant from contract have seen plenty of judicial activism in recent years. The issue is more about judges' perception of what it is legitimate for them to do in relation to the division of responsibility between the executive and the legislature. Although an extended exploration of the issue is beyond the scope of this book, there are two aspects of it which are particularly related to contract: the relation between common law and legislation, and the effect of the creation of the Law Commission in 1965.

Much of the law relating to personal contracts, especially consumer, employment and private tenancy contracts, is to be found in legislation. Is it possible for principles underlying such legislation to influence the rest of the law? Just because we can mould a descriptive generalisation which includes legislation and some case law, it does not mean that it is a plausible legal argument to argue that the generalisation is a legal principle which has persuasive weight. On the contrary, the opposite is traditionally thought to be the case. The orthodox view is that the common law is a kind of background or default body of law which applies to every situation unless it is altered by legislation. The scope of any alteration is a matter of statutory interpretation, concerned only with whether the legislative provision on its true construction applies to the case in hand. But although this view is dominant, it is not the only possible view, nor the only one reflected in the law.

Another approach is to see a legislative provision not just as the source of a binding rule, but also as a manifestation of the principle underlying the rule. This is to see legislation in a similar way to case law, as an instance from which it is possible to produce a generalisation which can apply beyond the instance itself. On this view, it is possible to reason by analogy from legislation, not just by interpretation. The standard objection to such an approach is that, since validity of legislative change in the common law is based on the intention of parliament, it must equally be presumed that parliament intended no change in situations not expressly provided for. Certainly, there are plenty of examples in the law of contract where detailed legislative changes have left the general principles intact, and I have argued above that it has been precisely this process which has narrowed the base of the general law. Authoritative academic opinion has, however, recognised some such influence of statutes beyond their stated scope (Cross, 1977; Atiyah, 1985). We have already encountered an instance of statutory influence on the common law in the House of Lords' decision in *Photo Productions*, where Lord Wilberforce said that the passing of the Unfair Contract Terms Act 1977 meant that freedom of contract could be left to operate more freely in situations untouched by the Act. Here, a statute was being treated as a reason to alter the line of direction of the common law, albeit to one which is divergent from rather than in tune with the principles of the statute. Treitel (1995, p 437) considers it arguable that a contract discriminating on the ground of religion would now be struck down as contrary to public policy despite this type of discrimination having been omitted from legislation dealing with discrimination on grounds sex or race. Using a statute as the basis of reasoning by analogy is not orthodoxy, but neither is it inconceivable.

In the case of contract, such a development could gradually raise the lock gates separating the various kinds of special rules cast in statutory form from the general law, and permit some intermingling of principle which would provide a basis for the renewal of the law in non commercial situations.

One originator of some of the statutory change in contract is the Law Commission, and its role as a standing law reform body also has wider implications for the prospect of judicial innovation in general contract law. The Law Commission, created in 1965, was the brainchild of the new Lord Chancellor, Lord Gardiner, who took office in the Labour Government elected in 1964. The Commission was charged with keeping all the law under review, in pursuit of systematic development and reform, with codification as an important mechanism of modernisation and simplification. Contract law was at the centre of the plans, and the first programme included the proposal for the codification of the law of contract. This has never been achieved, but its legacy has been a steady stream of reports on aspects of contract, most notably the reports on exclusion clauses, although some others have been permanently shelved (Zellick, 1988).

The relative lack of major judicial activism in contract since the 1960s may be partly explained by the ambitious programme set out for reform of contract by a different route. A kind of 'planning blight' may have afflicted judicial innovation in areas where the Law Commission had published a working paper, and there may have been be a more general impact on judge's perceptions of the scope of legitimate innovation. This is part of a wider issue about the division between the courts and the Law Commission of responsibility for development of the common law. It seems that there was a failure at the conception of the Law Commission to think through fully the role of the Commission compared with that of the courts, government departments, and legislature, and this may account in part for the rather grander plans which shaped the ambitious vision of the founders not being realised, although there has been much detailed work of immense value and importance.

It may be that the wider vision of the Law Commission was very much a child of its time, not just in the optimistic confidence in rational planning on which it drew, but also in the more conservative judicial approach to change in the common law which made such a reform initiative seem necessary. It is ironic that another of Lord Gardiner's initiatives was the Practice Statement of 1966 which declared that the House of Lords would no longer be bound by its own decisions. Arguably, this change eventually made the Law Commission less necessary as an agent of reform, for it played a large role in fostering a gradual expansion of judicial willingness to innovate and restate the law, with effects which are clearer in many areas of the law than they are in contract.

Does it matter if the Law Commission's role has resulted in the attenuation of judicial development in contract? After all, surely the development of the law through a deliberative and consultative procedure is preferable to judicial law-making constrained by the random processes of litigation? A counter argument lies in the role of experimentation which judge led change in the common law permits. Law Commission proposals are either implemented with the final authority of legislation or kept out of circulation as a legal source altogether. Judicial change is more incremental and can vary in terms of both its authority and bindingness. Because innovations can be adapted and extended, reversed or overruled with relative ease, the risk of getting it wrong does not automatically stultify any innovation other than the most obvious. The Law Commission, on the other hand, is rightly more cautious in proposing reform to be cast in the form of legislation. It is intriguing to reflect on the judicial elaboration of administrative law over the last thirty years (probably the most celebrated example of judge made law this century) and what its fate might have been if the Government had acceded to the request from the Law Commission in 1969 for it to make a full enquiry into administrative law.

CONTRACT AND THE STATE: THREE TYPES OF RELATIONSHIP

The role of the Law Commission and the relation between common law and statute raise fundamental questions about where responsibilities for legal change lie. My argument about diversity and pluralism in contract law tangles with these questions, for it provides a role for vigorous judicial innovation. Some of the issues can be clarified by exploring different views about types of relationship between contract law and the state. By way of conclusion, I will sketch three ideal typical models of this relationship: the liberal, the social democratic, and the pluralist. Each is defined in terms of two dimensions – the importance of consensually assumed obligation, and the implied view of the role of general principles of private law.

In the liberal model, contracts entered into in the market are the only source of positive obligation outside the family. The state is the 'night-watchman' state, responsible for the security of person and property, defence and other necessary public goods which the market is incapable of providing, but it is not involved in welfare. The state does not itself contract on any large scale, and where it does so it is treated as an ordinary contracting party. It does not otherwise regulate the terms of exchange. The private law of contract and tort (and restitution if recognised) therefore provides a virtually complete account of *all* personal (as opposed to proprietary) obligations. The content is not determined by political or legislative act (except for codification) and is the product of incremental judicial development. The UK has never actually reached this position but perhaps came closest in the third quarter of the nineteenth century.

In the social democratic model, the state has added wide ranging welfare and economic management functions. The creation of public services – education, health, pensions – imposes obligations and provides benefits outside the market system. The state also reaches into market relations and regulates by legislation the conditions of exchange, including the obligations of buyers and sellers in consumer and employment contracts. The result is that contract is only one way of creating positive obligation, and tort only one way of remedying misfortune. But a sharp line remains between the market sector and state based taxation and redistribution, and this is reflected in the demarcation between the general principles of private law and the special rules for employees, tenants, and consumers; the provision of public services remains beyond private law completely.

The separate existence of the market and state systems poses problems for legal commentators seeking coherence and rationality: this can be found by persisting with the liberal model of obligations law and effectively ignoring the social democratic sources of obligation which compete for the same territory. Only by construing obligations law as excluding the various emanations of the state can elegant theories fitting classification on to foundational principles be rendered remotely plausible. The separation also inhibits development of obligations law by the judges, who may avoid innovation by leaving the job to the legislature. The 1960s and 1970s were the zenith of this conception in the UK.[14]

The pluralist model is a possibility arising out of the decline of the social democratic model. The sharp line between market and state is blurred, especially the separation between a private sector run by the market, consisting of self-interested individuals and organisations, and a state sector run as a planned economy. Thus the provision of public services edges towards a more contractual or market based system, but the idea of contract here may diverge from the real market, in particular in the absence of payment by the user. Also important is the recognition of the role of voluntary but non profit-making organisations: these include not just the traditional types of cooperatives, but also housing associations, charities, and other organisations which may be involved in the 'delivery' of public services.

Independent of any public service delivery are the wide range of common interest groups focussed on sports, leisure pursuits, together with pressure groups, and amenity groups. A focus on the importance of associations which are neither merely market driven corporations nor state organs is shared by some commentators of both right and left. Although some right wing libertarian thinkers advocate a return to what is effectively a liberal model (De Jasay, 1991), there are conservative thinkers who see voluntary associations as playing an important integrative role which, by fostering the identification and allegiance of individuals within groups, counteract the corrosive effects on human relations of an untrammelled market order (Willetts, 1994). From the left it has been argued that the flourishing of associations can produce an associative democracy which avoids the bureaucratisation of big government characteristic of social democracy (Hirst, 1994).

This blurring of the distinction between the private and state sectors creates the conditions for a more integrated approach to the law of obligations. A sharp demarcation between the law of the market sector and the public sector can no longer be justified as reflecting deep differences in reality. The seepage of the norms of judicial review into the handling of unincorporated associations noted in the last chapter is an illustration of such blurring. Such innovation was possible in part because of the obvious distance of such situations from the commercial sale. The commercial model has prevailed more easily in situations closer to the commercial paradigm, for example consumer and other personal types of contract. But with recognition of a spread of different kinds of situations beyond the commercial paradigm it comes to seem incongruous that the general default principles of the law of contract should be dominated by the commercial sector, and there is a need for law which can reflect the plurality of consensual relationships.

I do not claim that the pluralist model is a simple description of where we have arrived. But given some of the reforms of the state during and since the 1980s and the wide and differently based interest in the role of associations, it is a plausible trajectory. I have attempted to show in this book that neither the history nor the modern shape of contract law make the narrowing which has taken place inevitable. The law is becoming increasingly characterised by pluralism, and there is the potential in the law for the courts to play a role in the renewal of the general law of contract to allow such pluralism to be reflected more widely.

Notes

CHAPTER 1

1 The main American contributions I have in mind are: Unger, 1983; Macaulay, 1963; Horwitz, 1974; Gilmore, 1974; Macneil, 1978; Posner, 1992; and Dalton, 1985. In the UK, the most prominent non traditional scholar has been Atiyah (1979; 1986). Beale and Dugdale (1975) followed up Macaulay's work on the study of contracting practice, and Simpson (1975a; 1979) engaged in an important debate with Horwitz about the emergence of nineteenth-century contract law; see p 52.

2 Earlier, the important work of Atiyah (1979; 1986) was followed by Collins's *Law of Contract* (1993, first edition 1986), and Adams and Brownsword's *Understanding Contract* (1994, first edition 1987). Beale, Bishop and Furmston's cases and materials book (1990, first edition 1985) also broadened the range of material significantly. See also the work of Vincent-Jones (1989; 1994), Campbell (1990) and Campbell and Harris (1993).

3 A reasonableness test was applied to certain carriers' exclusions as far back as the Railway and Canal Traffic Act 1854 (see p 60) and the Transport Act 1962 prevented any exclusion by carriers of the duty of care owed to passengers. Notable support for fundamental breach came from Grunfeld (1961), Guest (1961), Wedderburn (1957) and Atiyah (1957); the leading scholarly work on the development of the doctrine (Coote, 1964) was not enthusiastic. Sales (1953) published an impressive critique of standard form contracts and proposed a legislative solution involving prior approval of terms by a 'Contracts Commission'.

4 An example of the barrier to innovation they pose is the tendency to assume in discussions of contractualisation of state functions that the law of contract is incapable of significant change (Freedland, 1994, p 100).

CHAPTER 2

1 It has been said that the threat of a lawful act may be illegitimate, the usual example of which is blackmail, where the threatened act

may be lawful, for example the publication of non defamatory information (see Lord Scarman in *The Universe Sentinel* (1983)). However, it was held in the Court of Appeal in *CTN Cash and Carry Ltd* v. *Gallaher Ltd* (1994) that it would be rare for the threat of a lawful act to amount to duress in the context of arm's length commercial dealings.

2   Versions of the exploitation theory have been advanced by Birks (1985, p 184); Burrows (1993, p 182).

3   The problem of confinement was well recognised in some of the early leading American cases which restricted the scope of the duress doctrine. See for example *Goebel* v. *Linn* (1882) where an ice seller's insistence on doubling the agreed price in the knowledge that the purchasing brewer would lose all their beer production without it was held not to amount to duress. For further analysis of the confinement problem see Kelman (1987, p 22).

CHAPTER 3

1   The main sources are Atiyah (1979) and the collection of essays on contract, especially 'Contract, Promises and the Law of Obligations', Atiyah (1986).

2   This model follows the well known one of Fuller and Perdue (1936) except that he uses the expression 'status quo interest' instead of Fuller and Perdue's 'reliance interest': his purpose is to include that part of the law of obligations which protects the status quo interest – tort – in addition to the reliance on a contract (Burrows, 1983, p 218).

3   Burrows does refer to Fuller and Purdue's discussion of this kind of reliance, but appears to think it marginal because it would only arise in a perfect market. Even granted the impracticality of the perfect market, this seems to be an unsatisfactory justification for ignoring 'lost opportunity' reliance. Such a loss will arise whenever the plaintiff has, by relying on a contract with the defendant, lost the opportunity of making a profit on a similar contract elsewhere. It is true that it is part of the abstraction of the perfect market that such similar opportunities would be available. But it does not follow from this that such similar opportunities are *only* available in a perfect market. It is normal for similarity of price and other terms to coexist with all manner of market imperfections, perhaps most notably total cartelisation. And, even if the absence of a perfect market were to mean that the value of the opportunity lost in reliance on the contract was not as great as the gain expected under that contract, there would still be *some* loss which would justify compensation on a reliance theory yet not fall within Burrows's status quo interest.

4   The confusion which can occur when these senses of reliance are
    not separated is illustrated by a case well known to students,
    Anglia TV v. *Reed* (1972). Anglia TV planned to make a film and
    contracted with the actor Robert Reed to take the leading part. Reed
    soon withdrew, and Anglia, having decided not to go ahead with
    the film, claimed damages for lost expenditure. The contentious
    element was the £2,750 spent *before* they entered the contract with
    Reed. The Court of Appeal awarded this, on the basis that it was
    not too remote: it was within Reed's reasonable contemplation
    when entering the contract that such precontractual expendi-
    ture would be wasted as a result of a breach by him. The judgments
    themselves do not speak in terms of reliance or expectation, using
    the simpler contrast between lost expenditure and lost profit.
    However, some commentators have analysed this case as protecting
    the plaintiff's reliance rather than expectation interest (Downes,
    1993, p 330; Burrows, 1994, p 249, but see also p 255). The
    problem here lies in the tendency to treat awarding damages for
    lost expenditure as equivalent to protecting the reliance interest.
    These categories are not coextensive. In *Anglia*, the expenditure
    was before the contract with Reed, and therefore cannot be
    described as being made in reliance on that contract: precontractual
    expenditure is not recoverable under a measure of damages rule
    that aims to put the plaintiff in the position he was in immedi-
    ately before entering the contract. However, if we construe reliance
    as a criterion of liability, then it is possible to explain the award
    of damages. The reliance which triggers liability is the post con-
    tractual conduct of Anglia TV in continuing work on the film and
    (in particular) not taking further steps to secure the services of
    another actor for the leading role; the result was the lost oppor-
    tunity to complete the film. These acts of reliance could be the basis
    for the usual kind of damages, which is lost profit. In *Anglia* itself,
    it was not possible, because of uncertainty, to prove the loss of any
    opportunity to make profit. In the absence of such proof, recovery
    of the precontractual expenditure can be plausibly seen as the best
    the court can do to compensate the plaintiff for the opportunity
    of gain which has been lost in reliance on the contract with the
    defendant. This approach can account for the rule that expendi-
    ture is not recoverable if the defendant can show the plaintiff would
    not have recouped it if there had been no breach, and does not
    need to invoke any switch in justifying principles to do so (*CCC
    Films (London) Ltd* v. *Impact Quadrant Films Ltd* (1987)).
5   The point here follows the general argument of Sagoff (1988) in
    relation to the environment. It is of course possible to translate
    questions of ethics back into efficiency, distribution or rights, but

my claim is that it is distorting to do so. See also the similar argument of Titmuss (1970) in relation to the donation of blood.

CHAPTER 4

1   The seminal article, in which the research discussed in the text is reported, is Macaulay (1963). See also Macaulay (1977) and (1985).
2   We cannot treat the doctrine on intention to create legal relations as containing empirical claims. The general principle is that the requisite intention for enforceability will, in the absence of contrary evidence such as an explicit 'gentlemen's agreement' be presumed in a commercial contract. But this does not mean that commercial 'contractors' actually have such an intent unless they express the contrary. A central point revealed by the empirical work is that many business people operate with no regard to the law of contract, including its doctrine on intention to create legal relations.
3   Macneil's work is complex as well as voluminous. Macneil (1978) is directly concerned with the ideas discussed in the text. Campbell (1990) provides a valuable overview.
4   Even where there appears to be a greater use of contract law, in sectors such as construction, it is not the general rules that appear to be of significance: the industry has in effect provided its own law and means of enforcement which has little connection with the general rules. A plausible generalisation is that contract law is used most in precisely those situations where the general rules have been superseded by detailed provision in standard forms. The corollary, of course, is that the general rules on their own, unsupplemented by detailed standard forms, are used very little.
5   See especially the contributions in Daintith and Teubner (1986), and Williamson (1979).
6   Macneil distinguished between classical, which is promise based, and the neoclassical, which is reliance based. This distinction makes most sense in the context of American law, where reliance has been recognised as playing a larger role than in English law (Macneil, 1978).

CHAPTER 5

1   The classic account of the rise of assumpsit at the expense of debt and covenant is Simpson (1975b). See also Simpson (1991), Baker (1990), Milsom (1981), Baker and Milsom (1986), Hamburger (1989), and Teeven (1990).
2   It is worth pausing to reflect how it is that scholars, working from a relatively confined body of primary material in the reports,

are able to diverge so sharply in their description of what actually happened. The problem is not just that we are unable at this distance to resolve our historical telescopes clearly enough to see the detail of the law. The state of the law loosely associated with contract was not such as to enable determinate statements to be made about many aspects of it simply because the law was not yet organised in the systematic and rational way it came to be during the nineteenth century. There were no treatises on contract until Powell's *Essay Upon the Law of Contracts and Agreements* in 1790; the four volumes of Blackstone's *Commentaries* (published 1765–69) gave only forty pages to contract, treating it principally as a means for the transfer of interests in land. There are therefore problems in applying the modern conception of substantive law which is systematised and discoverable. There was not a total absence of substantive law in relation to what became seen as contracts, but a scattered, uncoordinated, and emphatically non general law which had different lines of cases applying to different situations.

3 This assessment is consistent with the more recent work of Oldham (1992) on the manuscripts of Lord Mansfield. Lord Mansfield (1705–93, Lord Chief Justice 1756–88) exerted considerable influence on commercial law, although some of his views on contract were later seen as heretical. Oldham suggests that the notebook evidence indicates that there was concern with substantive fairness in comments to juries and (drawing on unpublished work) also that the implied warranty of quality may have been more common than generally supposed.

4 Simpson points out that holding the return promise as consideration was unavoidable if the bet was to be enforced. This is true, but even here there is a sense in which the agreement was not entirely executory in that the contest had taken place. What would have been the position if one party attempted to cancel the bet before the contest took place?

5 Oldham (1992) claims that the evidence of Lord Mansfield's notebooks indicates that the contract litigation around the middle of the eighteenth century was normally about the enforcement of partly performed rather than wholly executory contracts.

6 This shared view has been questioned by Hamburger (1989) who argues that the origin of what he calls the consensus theory is traceable to indigenous English sources (rather than Civilian ones) in the middle ages.

7 To appreciate fully how far the logic of the contractual approach was taken, it needs to be recalled that in *Thompson* (1930) the Court of Appeal did not only decide that the limitation clause buried in

the companies' timetable was incorporated by notice, but also that no reasonable jury could find otherwise.

CHAPTER 6

1   There are two passages above all others which have done earnest duty in conveying in striking phrases the importance of contract and especially freedom of contract.

the movement of the progressive societies hitherto has been a movement from *Status to Contract*.

If there is one thing more than another that public policy requires it is that men of full age and competent understanding shall have the utmost liberty of contracting ...

The first is from Sir Henry Maine's *Ancient Law*, first published in 1851 (Maine, 1920, p 174), and the second from the judgment of Sir George Jessel in *Printing and Numerical Registering Company* v. *Sampson* (1875, p 475).

2   This link has also been questioned from another angle by Hamburger (1989). He argued that Civilian influence has been overstated and that the consensus basis of nineteenth-century law was discoverable in the earlier common law, thereby discounting the link to liberal philosophy. In one sense he goes further than Simpson (see Chapter 5) by claiming that the consensus basis of the classical law was nothing terribly new in the nineteenth century.

3   Atiyah (1979), p 374; see also Cornish and Clark (1989), p 69 for a discussion of judges and ideology.

4   *Household Fire* v. *Grant* (1879, at 239); see also *British and American Telegraph* v. *Colson* (1871). Similarly, his view that equity's protection of the borrower who fettered the redemption of a mortgage was that it would be better if equity had held people to their bargains (*Salt* v. *Marquess of Northampton* (1892)) and he refused to countenance the majority interpretation of the Bills of Exchange Act 1882 to the effect that a person could be liable to a bank for a forged promissory note on his account (*Bank of England* v. *Vagliano Brothers* (1891)).

5   Another example of indeterminacy is his well known dissent in *Parker* v. *South Eastern Railway* (1877). Bramwell's preferred test for whether written terms on (or referred to by) a ticket were incorporated into a contract by notice turned on whether the terms were usual. If they were, then they should be incorporated without notice, and if not then attention had to be drawn to them. The

majority, in the judgment of Mellish LJ, held that the issue turned on whether a reasonable party would have expected to find terms on the ticket, and the content of the terms was not relevant. It seems difficult to classify either outcome as uniquely required by a will theory.

6 Other major developments suggesting the practical importance of the enforceability of contract were the codification of the law of sale in the Sale of Goods Act 1893 and of the law relating to negotiable instruments in the Bills of Exchange Act 1882. The casting of the law on negotiable instruments into statutory form helped to insulate it from the potentially unhelpful doctrine of privity, and the Bills of Lading Act 1855 (which provided that the consignee or subsequent endorsee of a bill of lading was to be treated effectively as party to the contract formed between the shipper of the goods and the carrier) similarly avoided the established practice in relation to international sales from being unpicked by arguments based on privity.

7 Another way of meeting the same need was use of standardised terms which were becoming established in certain sectors by the end of the nineteenth century, for example the Joint Contracts Tribunal referred to on p 39.

8 In the case of the sale of horses it seems that buyers and sellers did habitually think in terms of whether the animal was warranted to be sound or not (Atiyah, 1979, p 466).

CHAPTER 7

1 The distinction drawn here between different kinds of infringement of freedom of contract is in essence that drawn by TH Green in 1881 in his famous lecture *Liberal Legislation and Freedom of Contract* (Nettleship, 1888).

2 For example, Coote, in the leading scholarly work on exclusion clauses, regards the imposition of liability in the teeth of validly incorporated exclusion clauses as a reversion to status (Coote, 1964, p 114; Adams & Brownsword (1994, p 187)).

3 Tackling such questions as these bristles with methodological difficulty. First, there is the issue of what precisely is included in the group of phenomena against which the generalisation is to be tested. The ideals of justice are themselves drawn in terms of a market order as a whole, not just the legal component of it, but they are applied to all the law of market transactions, which includes not just parts of private law in addition to contract but also massive bodies of regulation (p 8). Secondly, there is the problem of how one decides whether a general description, when applied to the identified phenomena, tends to capture the

dominant tendency of the phenomena taken overall. Although recognising any dominant tendency implicitly relies on some notional process of totting up conforming and non conforming instances, the problems of individuating instances and then ascribing appropriate weights are serious, and possibly intractable. Thirdly, there is an inevitable degree of indeterminacy in the application of such general criteria, much as we saw in relation to promise and reliance and benefit rationales in Chapter 3. This accommodates the stretching of fit favoured by the proponent of a generalisation as much as the narrowing of its scope by the doubter. Troublesome though these problems are, they do not undermine the viability of any attempt at generalisation, but call for care in the process of evaluation.

4   See *Scrutton on Charterparties and Bills of Lading* (Mocatta, Mustill and Boyd, 1984), pp 79–80.

5   Collins does discuss some of these examples on pp 197–8 under the heading of abuse of trust, but this is in the course of his analysis of the transformed law.

6   There was particular scope in international sales because of argument about the place of acceptance; see for example *Van den Huck* v. *Martens* (1920), and generally Sassoon and Meren (1984).

7   Although I have not dealt with Adams and Brownsword's analysis of contract law in the terms market-individualism and consumer-welfarism in the text, much the same argument about the failure fully to reveal diversity applies. Although they are not making a claim of transformation, there are real problems in regarding the two types as usefully coherent wholes.

One problem is that the market and individualistic aspects can be in tension, for accommodation of commercial practice may sit very uncomfortably with individualism. Trade offs are frequently necessary, usually in the interests of commercial convenience. Some examples: parties may have to be bound by acceptances they have never received for the sake of certainty (*Household Fire* v. *Grant* (1879)), be bound by exclusion terms they have never agreed to (*The Eurymedon* (1975)) or bound by implied terms they have not agreed because they are necessary (*Liverpool City Council* v. *Irwin* (1977)), or simply because the term is one implied because of customary usage. Nor is it always the case that the accommodation of commercial practice requires duties in relation to fraud and duress etc to be kept to a minimum, as the examples of good faith already noted suggest.

It is in fact arguable that many of the aspects of consumer-welfarism could be seen as accommodating commercial practice or promoting transactional security (Wightman, 1989).

CHAPTER 8

1   Wilhelmsson (1993, p 22) persuasively identifies the increased tendency of modern contract to take into account personal characteristics of the parties, although he does not draw a general distinction between contract law where personal characteristics matter and where the idea of legal subject remains strong.

2   See 'Pecuniary Restitution on Breach of Contract', Law Commission 1983, especially the note of dissent by Brian Davenport QC advocating the preservation of the rule in precisely these circumstances.

3   The literature referred to by Lord Mustill was an article by Harris, Ogus and Phillips (1979) which argued that the award of damages for mental distress or disappointment which were larger than the contract price could be explained by reference to the economic concept of consumer surplus. This is a concept which is used to value the net utility which a consumer gets when buying a good or service, and is notionally measured as the difference between what the consumer actually pays and what they would pay if they had to.

4   The requirement of manifest disadvantage does not apply where the undue influence is actually proved rather than presumed from a relation of confidence (*CIBC Mortgages* v. *Pitt* (1994)).

5   An example where the boot has been on the other foot is the obligation of a party entering a contract of insurance to disclose factors affecting the risk; the resulting asymmetry is especially striking in consumer cases. Thus an insurance company may take the benefit of a right to withhold payment under a policy because of a wholly innocent omission to disclose a factor affecting the risk, while a consumer will be bound by technical and onerous terms which restrict claims and which the company has no obligation to explain. The privileged position which insurance companies have enjoyed may be coming to a close, however: although they successfully lobbied to be excluded from the scope of the Unfair Contract Terms Act 1977, consumer insurance contracts are subject to the Unfair Terms in Consumer Contracts Regulations 1994.

6   Perhaps the most extreme case is *Pascoe* v. *Turner* (1979) where the man on moving out promised the woman that the house would be entirely hers. The Court of Appeal held that his acquiescence in the expenditure by her of about £230 on the house was sufficient to raise an estoppel which required him to transfer to her the ownership of the whole.

7   One effect of employers' need to demonstrate that there has been no unlawful discrimination in appointments has been the adoption of much more systematic procedures of selection, with specified criteria against which candidates are measured. This can make discrimination on any ground more visible and therefore in all probability less likely.

8   This generalisation derives from a fairly detailed position, which is as follows. Where the wife claims a relationship of confidence with the bank, then in order to raise the presumption of undue influence she must show that the transaction was manifestly disadvantageous to her and that there was indeed such a relationship on the facts of the case (*National Westminster Bank* v. *Morgan* (1985)). The presumption will be rebutted by showing that the wife was advised to obtain independent advice. Many of the recent cases have concerned the issue of the bank's responsibility for the husband's wrongdoing. In *Barclays Bank* v. *O'Brien* (1994) the House of Lords provided that the bank will be liable for the husband's wrongdoing where the wife is acting as surety and the bank knows they are cohabitees, unless the bank ensures the wife is told at a meeting without her husband of the amount of the liability and the risks involved and recommended to take independent advice. Where the wife or cohabitee is not acting as surety but receives a joint advance, then the bank will be liable for misconduct by the husband where on the facts the bank had actual or constructive notice of it (*CIBC Mortgages* v. *Pitt* (1993)).

9   The use of law as a mechanism for pursuing policy goals of the modern state is a feature noted by many commentators. See especially 'Beyond Bourgeois Individualism: The Contemporary Crisis in Law and Legal Ideology' (Kamenka and Tay, 1975); Unger, *Law in Modern Society* (Unger, 1976). The manifestation of instrumentalism in the traditional doctrine of private law has been seen as undermining the integrity of the classical doctrines, and Hayek has responded with a forceful critique of the corruption of private law by social legislation (Hayek, 1973).

10   Brownsword excludes consumer protection from his weaker version of welfarism (minimal) because consumers can be rich (p 40); he is undecided whether it is part of the stronger version (maximal) (p 44). Wilhelmsson (1994) does not doubt it should be counted within welfarism. Another problem with his analysis lies in the attempt to analyse the law on commercial contracts in terms of welfarist ideas. Paradoxically, the type of welfarism which fits best is the most extreme form, which is characterised as being about cooperation. Although the extent of cooperation he describes is unusual in commercial law, it does fit with the kind of relational commercial contract law discussed by Macneil.

11 To a degree the extent of the problem turns on the motive which is attributed to the use of the state mechanisms. On one socialist view, the welfare state is the outcome of class struggle between workers and capitalists. It is a vehicle of redistribution from rich to poor and so state mechanisms are a necessary (even if not sufficient) counter to the inherent injustice produced by a capitalist market order. On the other hand, a centrist or 'middle way' conception of the welfare state (George and Wilding, 1994) places more emphasis on the idea that welfare provision is based on insurance, and Beveridge himself saw it as vital that unemployment benefit was funded by contributions from those in employment, payment of which was a qualifying condition for the receipt of benefit. Although compulsory insurance is a much shorter step from a voluntary market transaction than wholesale redistribution from rich to poor, even a centrist view argues for the provision of health and education on essentially redistributive criteria: free at the point of use and funded out of general taxation. And the universalist principle that benefits should be payable without means test to all including the rich – as with the old age pension and child benefit – similarly reinforces the idea of the welfare state as providing strong modification of a pure market allocation of resources.

12 Irritation caused to the public by the switch to calling railway passengers 'customers' in public announcements is presumably justified on the basis that it gradually changes the way railway workers conceive of themselves and the function of the railway.

13 The method of synthesising counter principles from exceptions to mainstream principles is explored by Unger (1983).

CHAPTER 9

1 The main differences are: an application for judicial review (AJR) must normally be made within three months of the decision in question, while in contract the usual limitation period of six years applies; leave is necessary for AJR, but not for a writ action; many contract claims qualify for action in the county court, but all AJRs are made to the Divisional Court of the Queen's Bench Division.

2 See *Leary* v. *NUVB* (1971) where Megarry J found the procedural defects at the original branch meeting when the plaintiff had been expelled rendered the expulsion invalid despite the fact that the issue went though five subsequent stages, culminating in a two day hearing by the union's appeals council.

3 In fact the most general view now seems to be that natural justice is not the product of an implied term but simply imposed by law.

Davies and Freedland (1984, p 594) also point out the contrast between the tight jurisprudence of implied terms in the context of the contract of employment and the lax approach to the contract on which the trade union membership obligations are based. Note also the contrast between the willingness to review the trade union contract and the unwillingness at common law to review dismissal.

4   In discussing *The Satanita* (1895), where the issue arose of whether participants in a yacht race were bound by its rules, Treitel stated, '[t]he competitors, no doubt reached agreement, but they did not do so by a process which can be analysed into offer and acceptance' (1995, p 46). The analysis is even more complicated where there are newcomers to an existing relationship, as is typically the case with societies and clubs.

5   This seemed to confirm the position established in *Law* v. *National Greyhound Racing Club* (1983) where the Court of Appeal held the decisions of the club which acted as an effective national governing body of greyhound racing were not susceptible to review under the Ord 53 procedure: the club's jurisdiction was based on the contract between it and participants in the sport, the terms of which were contained in the club's rules.

6   As also were the Advertising Standards Authority in *R* v. *Advertising Standard Authority Ltd, ex p The Insurance Service plc* (1989) and the Investment Management Regulatory Organisation in *Bank of Scotland* v. *IMRO* (1989).

7   Hoffman LJ doubted whether an injunction would be available after a decision of the House of Lords in *Siskina* v. *Distos Cia Naviera SA* (1979); the jurisdiction was also doubted by Browne Wilkinson VC in *Cowley* v. *Heatley* (1986).

8   It should be said, however, that in the cases recognising the applicability of natural justice in principle there has frequently been some further reason why the student has not succeeded. The most notorious example is *Ward* v. *Bradford Corporation* (1972).

9   Although Lord Denning appears to say in *Breen* v. *AEU* (1971) that an implied term is the origin of the controls on discretion, he has also traced it to public policy. In *Lee* the requirement to comply with natural justice in the expulsion of members derived from public policy. Basing a rule on public policy does not, of course, tell us anything about any reason or justification for it, only that it cannot be brought under the umbrella of the intentions of the parties. Nevertheless, natural justice is an unusual manifestation of public policy, which is otherwise only used as a reason for holding an express term creating an obligation as invalid in some way because it is contrary to public policy, as is well illustrated by the restraint of trade doctrine. In the case of natural justice,

however, we see public policy being used to *impose* an obligation, and this is something that in other situations is done (if at all) by using the technique of the implied term.

10 This has not occurred, however, and the more restrictive trend in the most recent cases has led critics of *O'Reilly* v. *Mackman* (1983) to argue that the procedural separation between public and private law inhibits the development of an integrated approach to review which emphasises the function and nature of a body rather than the source of its powers. See Fredman and Morris (1994); Tanney (1993).

CHAPTER 10

1 There are important practical effects which turn on whether the action is in contract or tort: for example, limitation periods are computed differently, and the remoteness of damage rules are more restrictive in contract than tort.

2 For similar distinctions see Markesinis and Deakin (1994, p 9), and Rogers (1994, p 6).

3 The argument was also advanced on behalf of the defendant that contract and tort occupy mutually exclusive domains and that to allow such a claim in tort for work not carried out properly would infringe the exclusive 'zone' of contract. This argument was regarded as untenable as a result of the decision in *Henderson* v. *Merrett* (1994) which clearly accepted the coexistence of tortious and contractual liability (p 721).

4 Commentators who have argued that the liability for the negligent performance of promises should be permitted in contract rather than tort include Markesinis (1987) and Burrows (1994).

5 Although I focus here on Burrows's arguments, Birks puts a similar (but I think less sweeping) case; see especially Birks (1983).

6 There are also many situations within contract, but not included within restitution, where a promissory theory is artificial, and where it is plausible to see unjust enrichment as an underlying principle. An example is the restriction (both common law and statutory) on exclusion clauses, for the effect is to prevent suppliers retaining full payment after supplying defective goods or services. The reach of unjust enrichment is such that it can also be plausibly seen as underlying much of tort. One rationale of both the fault principle and much strict liability is in terms of risk theory. One version of this holds that liability should be placed on those who benefit from the creation of risk. Thus it is possible to say that a firm which generates profit by exposing workers to the risk of injury is unjustly enriched at the worker's expense when injury occurs.

CHAPTER 11

1   There seems to be have been little investigation of how cases in
    which ground breaking judicial innovations have been made
    ever got to court. In some the innovatory argument runs alongside
    a more conventional one, but there remains a residue of cases
    where it is tempting to hypothesise that innovation in the
    common law was a result of a stubborn litigant acting on ques-
    tionable legal advice about the prospects of success.

2   In *Liverpool City Council* v. *Irwin* (1975) he went through a list of
    implied term cases and then said:

> If one reads a discussion in those cases, one will see that in none
> of them did the court ask: what did the parties intend? If asked,
> each party would have said that he never gave it a thought; or
> the one would have intended something different from the
> other. Nor did the court ask: is it necessary to give business
> efficacy to the transaction? If asked, the answer would have been:
> 'It is reasonable, but it is not necessary.' The judgments in all
> those cases show that the courts implied a term according to
> whether or not in all the circumstances it was reasonable to do
> so. Very often it was conceded that there was some implied term.
> The only question was: What was the extent of it? Such as, was
> it an absolute warranty of fitness, or only a promise to use
> reasonable care? That cannot be solved by enquiring what they
> both intended, or into what was necessary. But only into what
> was reasonable. (p 664)

3   The introduction of an implied obligation to explain the meaning
    of complex terms not actually negotiated by the parties is of
    course pregnant with possibility. Lord Bridge observed:

> The problem is a novel one which could not arise in the classic
> contractual situation in which all the contractual terms, having
> been agreed between the parties, must, ex hypothesi, have
> been known to both parties. But in the modern world it is
> increasingly common for individuals to enter contracts, par-
> ticularly contracts of employment, on complex terms which have
> been settled in the course of negotiation between representative
> bodies or organisations and many details of which the individual
> employee cannot be expected to know unless they are drawn
> to his attention. (p 779)

Many of the standard forms which have given the courts such problems in consumer cases clearly fall within this: a fortiori, given the infrequency of any negotiation by representative bodies on behalf of consumers. Could an implied obligation to explain have performed the job of fundamental breach more effectively?

4 Incredibly, there is no actual consumer case which pins this down. The nearest is about the purchase of paint for a pier (*Shanklin Pier* v. *Detel Products* (1951)); on the basis of this it is said that the guarantee will be enforceable as a collateral contract if the buyer bought with knowledge and because of the guarantee. See Lowe and Woodroffe (1991, p 60).

5 According to Ralph Gibson LJ, awarding damages based on the cost of the repairs would be to treat the defendant as having warranted the condition of the house, when it was perfectly clear he had not as he was only obliged to use reasonable care. However, the fact that a warranty would have provided a basis for such an award does logically entail that it is the only possible basis.

6 The name of the institution seems to have been erroneously recorded in the title of the transcript of this case. It is in fact University College Salford, not the University of Salford. This matters because University College Salford is the creation of statute, while the University of Salford is one of the 'old' universities, constituted by royal charter. See p 132 above for the significance of this difference.

7 Evans, LJ thought that, if a request from the college to withdraw from clearing was necessary for consideration to be present, that this could be implied. Although not made explicit, the issue here is at the edge of what will be recognised as consideration in a unilateral contract.

8 The possibility of consideration moving from a promisee where his action brings about the benefit, although he does not directly provide it in the form of payment, was recognised in *Williams* v. *Roffey* (1991). This would be less arguable where the institution was oversubscribed and could always fill any vacant place.

9 I am using the term state school to include all the various types of maintained and voluntary aided schools which receive the bulk of their funding from public sources and which do not charge fees. The Governing Body of a grant maintained school constitutes charitable corporations which own or rent the buildings and are parties to contracts of employment and supply. Maintained schools run by Local Education Authorities do not have separate legal personality.

10 There is an argument, strongest where fees are paid, that the principle in *Jackson* v. *Horizon Holidays* (1975) could apply to permit a claim by a party to a contract for loss suffered by the party

on whose behalf they were contracting; see p 101 above for discussion of the special susceptibility of personal contracts to this kind of loss. And it is also arguable that the usual privity rules would not prevent an affected third party obtaining a declaration (*Eastham* v. *Newcastle United Football Club* (1964)) or even an interlocutory injunction (*Newport Association Football Club Ltd* v. *Football Association of Wales Ltd* (1995)).

11   The application must be made normally within three months of the decision which is impugned; leave is required from the court to make the application; the application cannot be made in the local county court.

12   The words of Wilberforce J are worth quoting:

> Is it open to an employee to bring an action for a declaration that the contracts between the employers are in restraint of trade? To my mind it would seem unjust if this were not so. The employees are just as much affected, indeed aimed at by the employers' agreement as the employers themselves. Their liberty of action in seeking employment is threatened just as much as the liberty of the employers to give them employment, and their liberty to seek employment is considered by the law an important public interest. Is the defence of that interest to be left exclusively in the hands of the employers themselves, who have set up the ring against the employee who have (as here) shown every intention of maintaining it as long as they can, left to the chance that one day there may be a blackleg amongst the employers who may challenge it? In my judgment to grant a remedy by way of declaration to the persons whose interests are vitally affected would be well within the spirit and intent of the rule as to declaratory judgments. (p 442)

13   The restriction is criticised in the leading work on declarations, Woolf and Woolf (1993, p 211).

14   The tendency towards separate spheres for public and private law led some commentators to identify a tension between them, proceeding to crisis (Kamenka and Tay, 1975).

Bibliography

Adams, J N (1983) 'The Carrier in Legal History', in E W Ives and A H Manchester (eds) *Law, Litigants and the Legal Profession*. London: Royal Historical Society.

Adams, J N and Brownsword, R (1987) 'The Ideologies of Contract', 7 *Legal Studies* 205.

Adams, J N and Brownsword, R (1994) *Understanding Contract*. London: Fontana.

Andrews, G (1991) *Citizenship*. London: Lawrence and Wishart.

Anson, W (1879) *Principles of the English Law of Contract and of Agency in its Relation to Contract*. Oxford: Clarendon Press.

Arrowsmith, S (1990) 'Judicial Review of the Contracting Powers of Public Authorities', 106 *Law Quarterly Review* 277.

Arrowsmith, S (1994) 'Protecting the Interests of Bidders for Public Contracts: the Role of the Common Law', 53 *Cambridge Law Journal* 104.

Arthurs, H W (1985) *Without the Law*. Toronto: University of Toronto Press.

Atiyah, P S (1957) *Sale of Goods*. London: Pitman.

Atiyah, P S (1979) *The Rise and Fall of Freedom of Contract*. Oxford: Clarendon Press.

Atiyah, P S (1985) 'Common Law and Statute Law', 48 *Modern Law Review* 1.

Atiyah, P S (1986) *Essays on Contract*. Oxford: Clarendon Press.

Atiyah, P S (1989) *An Introduction to the Law of Contract*. Oxford: Clarendon Press.

Baker, J H (1990) *An Introduction to English Legal History*. London: Butterworths.

Baker, J H and Milsom, S F C (1986) *Sources of English Legal History: Private Law to 1750*. London: Butterworths.

Barron, A and Scott, C (1992) 'The Citizen's Charter Programme', 56 *Modern Law Review* 526.

Bartrip, P W J and Burman, S B (1983) *The Wounded Soldiers of Industry*. Oxford: Clarendon Press.

Barton, J L (1987) 'The Enforcement of Hard Bargains', 103 *Law Quarterly Review* 118.

Beale, H G and Dugdale, T (1975) 'Contracts Between Businessmen: Planning and the Use of Contractual Remedies', 2 *British Journal of Law and Society* 45.

Beale, H G, Bishop, W D and Furmston, M P (1990) *Contract Cases and Materials*. London: Butterworths.

Beloff, M (1988) 'Boundaries of Judicial Review', in J Jowell and D Oliver (eds) *New Directions in Judicial Review*. London: Stevens and Sons.

Birks, P B H (1983) 'Restitution and the Freedom of Contract', *Current Legal Problems* 141.

Birks, P B H (1985) *Introduction to the Law of Restitution*. Oxford: Clarendon Press.

Blackstone, W [1765–69]/(1979) *Commentaries on the Laws of England*. Oxford: Chicago: University of Chicago Press.

Borrie, G (1990) 'The Regulation of Public and Private Power', *Public Law* 552.

Bridge, J (1970) 'Keeping Peace in the Universities', 86 *Law Quarterly Review* 531.

Brownsword, R (1994) 'The Philosophy of Welfarism and its Emergence in the Modern English Law of Contract', in R Brownsword, G Howells and T Wilhelmsson (eds) *Welfarism in Contract Law*. Aldershot: Dartmouth.

Brownsword, R, Howells, G and Wilhelmsson, T (eds) *Welfarism in Contract Law*. Aldershot: Dartmouth.

Burrows, A S (1983) 'Contract, Tort and Restitution: A Satisfactory Division or Not?', 99 *Law Quarterly Review* 216.

Burrows, A S (1993) *The Law of Restitution*. London: Butterworths.

Burrows, A S (1994) *Remedies for Torts and Breach of Contract*. London: Butterworths.

Campbell, D (1990) 'The Social Theory of Relational Contract: Macneil as the Modern Proudhon', 18 *International Journal of the Sociology of Law* 75.

Campbell, D and Harris, D (1993) 'Flexibility in Long-term Contractual Relationships', 20 *Journal of Law and Society* 166.

Cane, P (1987) 'Justice and Justifications for Tort Liability', 2 *Oxford Journal of Legal Studies* 30.

Charny, D (1990) 'Nonlegal Sanctions in Commercial Relationships', 104 *Harvard Law Review* 373.

Cheshire, G C, Fifoot, C H S and Furmston, M P (1991) *Law of Contract*. London: Butterworths.

Citizen's Charter Programme (1991) Cm 1599. London: HMSO.

Collins, H (1992) *Justice in Dismissal: The Law of Termination of Employment*. Oxford: Clarendon Press.

Collins, H (1993a) *The Law of Contract*. London: Butterworths.

Collins, H (1993b) 'The Transformation Thesis and the Ascription of Contractual Responsibility', in T Wilhelmsson (ed) *Perspectives of Critical Contract Law*. Aldershot: Dartmouth.

Collins, H (1994) 'Good Faith In European Contract Law', 14 *Oxford Journal of Legal Studies* 229.

Coote, B (1964) *Exception Clauses*. London: Sweet and Maxwell.

Cornish, W R and Clark, G de N (1989) *Law and Society in England, 1750–1950*. London: Sweet and Maxwell.

Cross, R (1977) *Precedent in English Law*. Oxford: Clarendon Press.

Daintith, T and Teubner, G (eds) (1986) *Contract and Organisation: Legal Analysis in the Light of Economic and Social Theory*. Berlin/New York: Walter de Gruyter.

Dalton, C (1985) 'An Essay in the Deconstruction of Contract Doctrine', 94 *Yale Law Journal* 997.

Danzig, R (1975) 'Hadley v Baxendale: a Study in the Industrialization of Law', 4 *Journal of Legal Studies* 249.

Davies, P and Freedland, M (1984) *Labour Law: Text and Materials*. London: Weidenfeld and Nicolson.

De Jasay, A (1991) *Choice, Contract, Consent: A Restatement of Liberalism*. London: Institute of Economic Affairs.

Downes, T A (1995) *Textbook on Contract*. London: Blackstone Press.

Dworkin, R (1986a) 'Is Wealth a Value?', in *A Matter of Principle*. Oxford: Clarendon Press.

Dworkin, R (1986b) 'Why Efficiency?', in *A Matter of Principle*. Oxford: Clarendon Press.

Dwyer, J L (1977) 'Immoral Contracts', 93 *Law Quarterly Review* 386.

Fairfield, C (1898) *Some Account of Baron Bramwell*. London: Macmillan.

Feinman, J (1983) 'Critical Approaches to Contract', *UCLA* 829.

Ferguson, R B (1977) 'Legal Ideology and Commercial Interest: The Social Origins of the Commercial Law Codes', 4 *British Journal of Law and Society* 17.

Ferguson, R B (1984) 'Commercial Expectations and the Guarantee of the Law: Sales Transactions in Mid 19th Century England', in G R Rubin and D S Sugarman (eds) *Law in Economy and Society*. Abingdon: Professional Books.

Fletcher, E G M (1932) *The Carrier's Liability*. Cambridge: Cambridge University Press.

Flood, J and Caiger, A (1993) 'Lawyers and Arbitration: the Juridification of Construction Disputes', 56 *Modern Law Review* 412.

Fox, A (1974) *Beyond Contract: Work, Power and Industrial Relations*. London: Faber and Faber.

Fredman, S and Morris, G (1994) 'The Costs of Exclusivity: Public and Private Re-Examined', *Public Law* 69.

Freedland, M (1994) 'Government by Contract and Public Law', *Public Law*, 86.

Fried, C (1981) *Contract as Promise*. Cambridge, Mass: Harvard University Press.

Friedman, L M (1967) *Contract Law in America: a Social and Economic Case Study*. Madison, Wisconsin: University of Wisconsin Press.

Friedmann, W (1972) *Law in a Changing Society*. Harmondsworth: Penguin.

Frug, M J (1985) 'Re-reading Contracts: a Feminist Analysis of a Contracts Casebook', 34 *American University Law Review* 1065.

Fuller, L and Perdue, W (1936) 'The Reliance Interest in Contract Damages', 46 *Yale Law Journal* 52.

Gabel, P and Feinman, J (1990) 'Contract Law as Ideology', in D Kairys (ed) *The Politics of Law*. New York: Pantheon Books.

George, V and Wilding, P (1994) *Welfare and Ideology*. London: Harvester Wheatsheaf.

Gilmore, G (1974) *The Death of Contract*. Columbus, Ohio: Ohio State University Press.

Goetz, C J and Scott, R E (1977) 'Liquidated Damages, Penalties, and the Just Compensation Principle: Some Notes on an Enforcement Model and a Theory of Efficient Breach', 77 *Columbia Law Review* 554.

Goff, R and Jones, G (1986) *The Law of Restitution*. London: Sweet and Maxwell.

Gordley, J (1991) *The Philosophical Origins of Modern Contract Doctrine*. Oxford: Clarendon Press.

Gordon, R W (1985) 'Macaulay, Macneil, and the Discovery of Solidarity and Power in Contract Law', *Wisconsin Law Review* 565.

Grunfeld, C (1961) 'Reform in the Law of Contract', 24 *Modern Law Review* 62.

Guest, A G (1961) 'Fundamental Breach of Contract', 77 *Law Quarterly Review* 98.

Hamburger, P A (1989) 'The Development of the Nineteenth-century Consensus Theory of Contract', 7 *Law and History Review* 241.

Harden, I (1992) *The Contracting State*. Milton Keynes: Open University Press.

Harris, D, Ogus, A I and Phillips, J (1979) 'Contract Remedies and the Consumer Surplus', 95 *Law Quarterly Review* 581.

von Hayek, F A (1973) *Law Legislation and Liberty*, vol 1 *Rules and Order*. London: Routledge and Kegan Paul.

Hedley, S (1985a) 'Keeping Contract in its Place: Balfour v Balfour and the Enforceability of Informal Agreements', vol 5, *OJLS* 391.

Hedley, S (1985b) 'Unjust Enrichment as the Basis of Restitution' 5 *Legal Studies* 56.

Hirst, P (1994) *Associative Democracy*. Oxford: Polity Press.

Horwitz, M (1974) 'The Historical Foundations of Modern Contract Law', 87 *Harvard Law Review* 917.

Ireland, P (1983) 'The Triumph of the Company Legal Form' in J Adams (ed) *Essays for Clive Schmittoff.* Abingdon: Professional Books.

Kahn-Freund, O (1965) *Law of Carriage by Inland Transport.* London: Sweet and Maxwell.

Kamenka, E and Tay, A (1975) 'Beyond Bourgeois Individualism: the Contemporary Crisis in Law and Legal Ideology', in E. Kamenka and R S Neale (eds) (1975) *Feudalism, Capitalism and Beyond.* London: Edward Arnold.

Kelman, M (1987) *A Guide to Critical Legal Studies.* Cambridge, Mass: Harvard University Press.

Kennedy, D (1976) 'Form and Substance in Private Law: Adjudication', 89 *Harvard Law Review* 1685

Kennedy, D (1982) 'Distributive and Paternalist Motives in Contract and Tort Law with Special Reference to Compulsory Terms and Unequal Bargaining Power', 41 *Maryland Law Review* 563.

Kennedy, D and Michelman, F (1980) 'Are Contract and Property Efficient?', 8 *Hofstra Law Review* 711.

Kingdom, E (1988) 'Cohabitation Contracts – a Socialist–Feminist Issue', 15 *Journal of Law and Society* 77.

Kronman, A and Posner, R (1979) *The Economics of Contract Law.* Boston: Little Brown.

Law Commission (1983) *Pecuniary Restitution on Breach of Contract.* London: HMSO.

Lowe, R and Woodroffe, G (1991) *Consumer Law and Practice.* London: Sweet and Maxwell.

Macaulay, S (1963) 'Non-contractual Relations in Business', 28 *American Sociological Review* 55.

Macaulay, S (1977) 'Elegant Models, Empirical Pictures, and the Complexities of Contract', 11 *Law and Society Review* 507.

Macaulay, S (1985) 'An Empirical View of Contract', *Wisconsin Law Review* 561.

MacDonald, E (1992) 'Negligent Valuations and Lost Opportunities'. *New Law Journal* 632.

Macneil, I R (1978) 'Contracts Adjustments of Long-term Economic Relations Under Classical, Neoclassical, and Relational Contract Law', 72 *Northwestern University Law Review* 854.

Macneil, I R (1980) *The New Social Contract.* New Haven: Yale University Press.

Macneil, I R (1981) 'Economic Analysis of Contractual Relations: Its Shortfalls and the Need for a "Rich Classificatory Apparatus"', 75 *Northwestern University Law Review* 1018.

Macneil, I R (1982) 'Efficient Breach of Contract: Circles in the Sky', 68 *Virginia Law Review* 947.

Maine, H S [1851]/(1920) *Ancient Law.* London: John Murray.

Malcolmson, R W (1981) *Life and Labour in England 1700–1780*. London: Hutchinson.

Markesinis, B S (1987) 'An Expanding Tort Law – the Price of a Rigid Contract Law', 103 *Law Quarterly Review* 354.

Markesinis, B S and Deakin, S F (1994) *Tort Law*. Oxford: Clarendon Press.

Milsom, S F C (1981) *Historical Foundations of the Common Law*. London: Butterworths.

Mocatta, A, Mustill, M and Boyd, S (1984) Scrutton on Charterparties and Bills of Lading. London: Sweet and Maxwell.

Murdoch, J and Hughes, W (1990) *Construction Contracts*. London: E and F N Spon.

Nettleship, R L (ed) (1888) *Works of T H Green*. London: Longmans.

Oldham, J (1992) *Mansfield Manuscripts*, vol 1. Chapel Hill: University of North Carolina Press.

Oliver, D (1987) 'Is Ultra Vires the Basis of Judicial Review?', *Public Law* 543.

Posner, R (1992) *The Economic Analysis of Law*. Boston: Little Brown and Co.

Powell, J (1790) *An Essay Upon the Law of Contracts and Agreements*. Dublin.

Reiss, E (1934) *The Rights and Duties of Englishwomen: a Study in Law and Public Opinion*. Cambridge: Sherratt and Hughes.

Rizzo, M J (1980) 'The Mirage of Efficiency', 8 *Hofstra Law Review* 641.

Rogers, W (1994) *Winfield and Jolowicz on Tort*. London: Sweet and Maxwell.

Rubin, G R (1984) 'Law, Poverty and Imprisonment for Debt', in G R Rubin and D Sugarman (eds) *Law, Economy and Society*. Abingdon: Professional Books.

Sagoff, M (1988) *The Economy of the Earth*. Cambridge: Cambridge University Press.

Sales, H B (1953) 'Standard Form Contracts', 16 *Modern Law Review* 318.

Samuels, A (1973) 'The Student and the Law', 12 *Journal of the Society of Public Teachers of Law* 252.

Sassoon, D M and Meren, H O (1984) *CIF and FOB Contracts*. London: Stevens.

Simpson, A W B (1975a) 'Innovation in Nineteenth Century Contract Law', *Law Quarterly Review* 247.

Simpson, A W B (1975b) *A History of the Common Law of Contract: The Rise of the Action of Assumpit*. Oxford: Clarendon.

Simpson, A W B (1979) 'The Horwitz Thesis and the History of Contracts', 46 *University of Chicago Law Review* 533.

Simpson, A W B (1981) 'The Rise and Fall of the Legal Treatise: Legal Principles and the Forms of Legal Literature', 48 *University of Chicago Law Review* 632.

Simpson, A W B (1991) 'Introduction to the Law of Contract', in G C Cheshire, C H S Fifoot and M P Furmston *Law of Contract*. London: Butterworths.

Stetson, D (1982) *A Women's Issue*. London: Greenwood Press.

Sugarman, D and Rubin, G (1984) 'Towards a New History of Law and Material Society in England 1750–1914', in G R Rubin and D Sugarman (eds) *Law, Economy and Society*. Abingdon: Professional Books.

Tanney, A (1993) 'Procedural Exclusivity in Administrative Law', *Public Law* 51.

Teeven, K M (1990) *A History of the Anglo-American Law of Contract*. New York: Greenwood Press.

Thomson, A (1991) 'The Law of Contract', in I Grigg Spall and P Ireland (eds) *The Critical Lawyer's Handbook*. London: Pluto Press.

Titmuss, R M (1970) *The Gift Relationship: from Human Blood to Social Policy*. London: Allen and Unwin.

Trakman, L E (1983) *The Law Merchant: the Evolution of Commercial Law*. Littleton, Colorado: Fred B Rothman and Co.

Trebilcock, M J (1980) 'An Economic Approach to the Doctrine of Unconscionability', in B J Reiter and J Swan (eds) *Studies in Contract Law*. Toronto: Butterworths.

Trebilcock, M J (1993) *The Limits of Freedom of Contract*. Cambridge, Mass: Harvard University Press.

Treitel, G H (1995) *The Law of Contract*. London: Sweet and Maxwell/Stevens and Sons.

Unger, R M (1976) *Law in Modern Society*. New York: Free Press.

Unger, R M (1983) 'The Critical Legal Studies Movement', 96 *Harvard Law Journal* 563.

Veeder, V V (1994) 'Mr Justice Lawrance: "the true begetter" of the Commercial Court', 110 *Law Quarterly Review* 292.

Veljanovski, C G (1982) *The New Law and Economics*. Oxford: Centre for Social Legal Studies.

Vincent-Jones, P (1989) 'Contract and Business Transactions: A Socio-Legal Analysis', 16 *Journal of Law and Society* 166.

Vincent-Jones, P (1994) 'The Limits of Public Order in Public Sector Transacting', 14 *Legal Studies* 364.

Wade, H W R (1969) 'Judicial Control of the Universities', 85 *Law Quarterly Review* 468.

Wade, H W R (1988) *Administrative Law*. London: Butterworths.

Weber, M (1954) *Law and Economy in Society*. New York: Simon and Schuster.

Wedderburn, K W (1957) 16 *Cambridge Law Journal*.

Wedderburn, Lord (1987) *The Worker and the Law*. London: Penguin.

Weir, T (1976) 'Complex Liabilities' in vol xi *International Encyclopaedia of Comparative Law*. The Hague: Morton.

Wheeler, S and Shaw, J (1994) *Contract Law*. Oxford: Clarendon Press.

Wightman, J (1989) 'Reviving Contract', 52 *Modern Law Review* 115.

Wilhelmsson, T (1993) 'Questions for a Critical Contract Law', in T Wilhelmsson (ed) *Perspectives of Critical Contract Law*. Aldershot: Dartmouth.

Wilhelmsson, T (ed) (1993) *Perspectives of Critical Contract Law*. Aldershot: Dartmouth.

Wilhelmsson, T (1994) 'The Philosophy of Welfarism and its Emergence in the Modern Scandinavian Contract Law', in R Brownsword, G Howells and T Wilhelmsson (eds) *Welfarism in Contract Law*. Aldershot: Dartmouth.

Williamson, O (1979) 'Transaction Cost Economics: the Governance of Contractual Relations', 22 *Journal of Law and Economics* 233.

Willetts, D (1994) *Civic Conservatism*. London: The Social Market Foundation.

Woolf, Lord and Zamir, I (1993) *The Declaratory Judgment*. London: Sweet and Maxwell.

Wright, Lord (1939) *Legal Essays and Addresses*. Cambridge: Cambridge University Press.

Zellick, G (ed) (1988) *The Law Commission and Law Reform*. London: Sweet and Maxwell.

Index